D1235442

TAKE THE NEXT EXIT

TAKE THE NEXT EXIT

New Views of the Iowa Landscape

Edited by
Robert F. Sayre

Iowa State University Press / Ames

Robert F. Sayre is a former English professor at the University of Iowa, where he taught courses in literature and landscape and in American autobiography. His *Take This Exit: Rediscovering the Iowa Landscape* (Iowa State University Press, 1989) was called by J.B. Jackson, "the book about rural America that we have been waiting for" and "the best guide to Iowa since the great WPA guide of 1938." He has also written many travel articles for daily newspapers as well as scholarly books such as *Thoreau and the American Indians* and is editor and contributor to *Recovering the Prairie* (1999).

Iowa State University Press
2121 South State Avenue, Ames, Iowa 50014

Orders: 1-800-862-6657   Fax: 1-515-292-3348
Office: 1-515-292-0140   Web site: www.isupress.edu

♾ Printed on acid-free paper in the United States of America

First edition, 2000

Library of Congress Cataloging-in-Publication Data

Take the next exit : new views of the Iowa landscape / edited by
Robert F. Sayre.—1st ed.
    p. cm.
  Sequel to: Take this exit.
  Includes index.
  ISBN 0-8138-2030-8 (acid-free paper)
    1. Iowa—Guidebooks. 2. Landscape—Iowa. 3. Prairies—Iowa.
  4. Cities and towns—Iowa—Guidebooks. I. Sayre, Robert F.

  F619.3.T34 2000
  917.7704′34—dc21   00-040995

The last digit is the print number: 9 8 7 6 5 4 3 2 1

Contents

Part III. Nature's Places

Part IV. Tourism, Commerce, and the Landscape

Acknowledgments

Anyone who thinks that the Iowa landscape is plain and simple should talk to the people who have studied it carefully. There are local historians all over the state, as well as local museums, conservationists and authorities on natural history who have collected and examined this prairie landscape, past and present, in all kinds of interesting ways. There are also authorities on the many businesses, churches, schools, and civic organizations. All these authorities whom I've met or called and asked for help have been exceedingly generous with their time and advice, and I want to say thank you. The other contributors and I could not have written this book without you.

I also want to say a special thanks to people whom I've called on several times or talked to at length: Jim Cory of the Iowa Retail Hardware Association; Bart Yotty, and J. C. Herbert; Susan Heathcote and Teresa Opheim of the Iowa Environmental Council; Dr. Ronald Harms, Don Winkler, and Donald A. Beneke of Pocahontas County; Jean Prior, Deb Quade, and Jim Giglierano of the Geological Survey Bureau; Louie Falleson and Laurie Carlson of Humboldt County; Vivian Campbell at Historic Central School, Lake City; Dave R. Holstad and Michael P. Mahn of the Iowa Department of Natural Resources; Betty Brotherton, town historian of Wall Lake; George R. Hallberg and Wayne Peterson, who answered some of my early questions about hydrology; Mary Bennet of the State Historical Society; and Merle Davis of the University of Iowa Law Library. I also want to thank, Gabe Wasserman, my former research assistant, and my friends Gayle Hollander and Connie Mutel.

Mira Engler's "Drive-Thru History: Theme Towns in Iowa" first appeared in a slightly different form in the magazine *Landscape,* vol. 32, no. 1, pp. 8-18, 1993. The publisher has granted permission to reprint it.

Finally I want to thank my fellow hikers, canoers, and bicyclers—John and Susan Loomis and Hutha Sayre. Neither rain nor snow, heat of summer, frosts of October, winds of March, nor cows in the night have kept us from our gunkholing; and no research and recreation was ever so much fun.

TAKE THE NEXT EXIT

ϡ 1 ϟ

Introduction:
Seeing and Reading Iowa

Robert F. Sayre

Back in 1986, in the midst of the so-called "farm crisis" of the 1980s, when many promoters of the state were saying that Iowa should develop a tourist industry, I thought that Iowa first needed a new guidebook. It should not be just a hotel guide or guide to scenic attractions; these already existed. It should be a guide to the more commonplace, dominant landscape—or vernacular landscape—that was nevertheless little appreciated and understood. It should not just tell people what to see but how to look.

The result was *Take This Exit: Rediscovering the Iowa Landscape*, which was published by Iowa State University Press in 1989. It has had a good effect, I think, in sensitizing people to the special qualities of the Iowa landscape. People say things like, "I really liked that essay on barns. I know now how to identify their age, their use, and how they have changed." A number of people say they have read a different essay each week and then have gone out to look at examples of its subject. A person from Wisconsin even wrote me that he no longer drives across Iowa at night, as he and many Badgers used to do! He drives in the daytime, carrying *Take This Exit* and taking a different route each time.

So here is a sequel, *Take the Next Exit*, intended to further promote intelligent tourism. Coincidentally, we are now in another so-called "farm crisis." Corn and soybean prices have been very low. Hog prices have been lower than the cost of production. The number of farms in Iowa, which was 109,000 in 1988, was down to 90,792 in 1997, and is predicted to fall further. (In 1930, as I noted in *Take This Exit*, it was 215,361.) With every loss of a farm, comes a loss in farm population, a loss for small-town businesses, and a loss in the vitality of rural life. At the same time, while state population remains roughly constant, Iowa's cities and larger towns grow, with more parking lots, shopping malls, and suburban streets. The whole appearance of the state is changing.

The usual explanations for these changes are declines in farm exports; the increasing size of farms and farm equipment (some-times called increasing farm productivity); and the ever-increasing mobility of the farm and rural population, thanks to more cars and better roads. But a more fundamental explanation, I believe, is the increase in available investment capital. This capital, coming from both farmers and non-farmers, underlies the purchases of the larger machinery, the building of bigger animal confinement operations, the merging of farms, and the development of biotech-nology to increase yields. It also pays for the construction of the malls and highways and suburbs. What we see, in Iowa, as else-where in America, is the landscape of capitalism.

But whatever our explanations are for these vast changes in the landscape of Iowa and many other parts of America, we are also confronted with another pressing question, What is the rela-tion of such changes to tourism? Tourists aren't directly responsi-ble for the decline of rural Iowa. But they are increasingly sought by the towns and even the farms that have been marginalized by these changes. People convert old Main Street stores to antique shops and open their houses as bed-and-breakfast inns. Indeed, whole towns, as Mira Engler shows in Chapter Thirteen, redesign themselves as "theme towns" in order to attract more tourists, not just along the Interstate highways but throughout the state. So tourism does have its own impact on the landscape. But is it for good or bad? Do such places become better places to visit, and/or to live? Can tourists themselves have a positive effect, becoming "eco-tourists" not to the rain forests of the Amazon, but to the farms, prairies, and small towns of Iowa?

The reader might like to jump ahead to Mira Engler's "Drive-Thru History: Theme Towns in Iowa" because it confronts these questions directly. "Small-town Iowa," she says, "is catering to tourists," and doing this more energetically each year. Ethnic traditions, pioneer history, small-town culture, and country charm are being commercially packaged and sold to visitors. Fairs and festivals are one means of accomplishing this. Restored buildings and even imported buildings like the Danish Windmill in Elk Horn are another. Bed-and-breakfasts, craft and antique shops, local museums, and homes of famous sons and daughters are further means to attract visitors and get them to spend money.

But do we want this? A lot of it, according to one's taste, is kitsch, funky provincialism, and a waste of time, rather than instructive and charming. It may also offend as many people as it pleases. The residents of a once rather ordinary Iowa town, with its mixture of religious and ethnic groups are not all made happy when the town suddenly becomes advertised and redesigned as, let's say, a Czech village. Even the members of the group that becomes publicized may complain. Who wants to put on wooden shoes and funny hats just to please some rubes from out of town? Worse yet, a heritage that is simplified and sold inevitably becomes cheapened.

On the other hand, there can be pleasure and self-discovery as well as money in such play-acting. It may bring a town together and provide novelty. This, I think, is one of the things revealed in Hanno Hardt's very sensitive photographs in Chapter Four. The people playing their roles in the various fairs and festivals he loves to go to know each other in their daily roles as well. They thus communicate with their eyes, their silent expressions, and the stances and movements of their bodies. A participant becomes momentarily two people—the person in the mask or costume and the person behind it. Likewise, we could say, does the town. It renews itself, takes on a sort of stage-life it did not have before. A woman living in the spacious upper floors of an old downtown store in Albia—a building restored to a Gay Nineties look, with her rooms made into a penthouse—is said to have told a reporter that she loves this new look, that it has made Albia as attractive as Disneyworld! The irony is that the old-time main-street look in Disneyworld was initially an imitation of nineteenth-century midwestern towns like Albia. It took the imitation to revive the reality. And now the reality is in a sense an imitation. But the joy of living there may be greater. A similar bit of cosmopolitan small-town luxury has been added to an old downtown building in Fort Madison, which also might be called a "theme town," because it has a recreation of the original frontier fort and groups who come into town to re-enact frontier battles. But the building now has a deck in back that overlooks the Mississippi and gives

Fig. 1.1. *The Deck to the Third Floor Apartment* in the James Block Building in downtown Fort Madison, added by Bryan and Leslie Humphrey when they remodeled the building in 1987. They used the ground floor for Bryan Humphrey's law office; the deck has a view of the Mississippi, a view that opened when an adjacent building was torn down. The playhouse in the corner imitates a blockhouse from the New Fort in the riverfront park. (Photograph by Robert F. Sayre.)

the occupants a balcony seat for observing the goings-on in the park along the river (Fig. 1.1).

The best way to accommodate tourists, many of us would say, including Mira Engler, is with things that also enhance the life of the citizens, of everyone. Several years ago, when Mason City was looking for a "theme," or an aspect of its history to develop and promote, it faced a choice. On one hand was its unique status as the only small town in the country with so many interesting examples of Prairie School architecture; a former bank-hotel designed by Frank Lloyd Wright, the Stockman house (1906), which Wright designed as "A Fireproof House for $5,000"; and the Rock Glen neighborhood of houses designed by Wright's students. Most of these houses are still in mint condition. The Stockman house was being moved to a new location. And the City National Bank and Hotel Building (1908–10), though disfigured by modifications, was of special historic interest because of its influence on European architects. Restoration would have been expensive, but could have made it a major civic attraction. On the other hand, Mason City was the hometown of Meredith Wilson, composer of *The Music Man*. The house where he grew up was still standing near the downtown, and he was revered all over Iowa. (He also composed the University of Iowa fight song.) Which to promote?

Mason City chose Meredith Wilson, and although I do not know the details of the decision, a good argument for the choice is that the Meredith Wilson "theme" does more for Mason City residents. In the last few years his house has been restored (Fig. 1.2), and now a museum-auditorium building is nearly finished behind it. The auditorium will be used for concerts, plays, and recitals. The city has become the site of an annual band festival in May. Many more high school students and their parents, in Mason City and elsewhere, are interested in school bands than in architecture. On the other hand, finding a new use for the Wright bank-hotel might have been difficult—would the city have been left with a Wright Elephant? Also, not many owners of the homes in Rock Glen would want hundreds of visitors coming through. There is a possible danger that in the blare of "Seventy-Six Trombones," Mason City will become stereotyped as "River City," and its prairie houses and other facets of its history and culture, like its Greek food, will be overlooked. But for the time being, I would say, the band concerts and auditorium will do more for the people of Mason City than a restored Wright building and an architectural tour would have. Tourism that does not benefit the local citizenry—and benefit more than just their wallets and bank accounts—is exploitation.[1]

Good travelers would also rather see the authentic customs of a place than ones that have been invented or re-invented just for show. Therefore we open here with delightful studies of four aspects of traditional Iowa culture—porches, cafés, local fairs and festivals, and baseball—that are interesting to travelers but are not *just* for travelers.

Fig. 1.2. *Music Man Meredith Wilson's House,* Mason City, has been restored, and a museum–auditorium has been built behind it. (Photograph by Robert F. Sayre.)

A PLACE OF CUSTOMS

The restoration of the porches in towns like Mt. Vernon, as noted by Richard Thomas in Chapter Three, is an excellent example of something of interest to visitors but of primary benefit to residents. As Mt. Vernon's unofficial town historian and a long-time leader of the movement to restore porches, not only in Mt. Vernon but around the state and nation, Dick Thomas could tell a hundred stories. He can also relate porches to feminism, changing concepts of the family, speeds of travel, and, of course, the Iowa weather. But he knows that underlying all this, the deepest reasons why people around Iowa and the rest of the Midwest are restoring their porches are that they look good and are good to sit on. It is not because porches are suddenly "in," in neo-traditional resorts like Seaside, Florida. On the contrary, those fashions are an attempt at a sort of hot-house re-creation of the civic and domestic values once prominent in small towns, here and elsewhere. The porches of Seaside were built in hopes that people would sit on them and become civil. The porches of Iowa were built because people already were civil. They were a semi-public space where private manners like hospitality, honesty, and kindness prevailed. As such, they had a very desirable image. People wanted to be seen on their porches and be invited to their neighbors' porches. Even presidential candidates conducted their campaigns in those simpler, less expensive days by sitting on their front porches and letting the newspaper reporters and voters come by and chat. Dick Thomas's reflections make us recall these and other facts about old American culture, a culture in which the rest of the United States was more like Iowa. For Iowans to be coming back out to the front porch, and not hiding in patios and backyards, is for them also to have become more proud of their past. So "on the porch," the tourist to Iowa also learns more, touches and feels more, of the whole American past. Finally, although Mt. Vernon has made what Engler might call a "porch theme" for itself, Mt. Vernon is hardly the only porch town. A good example of both vernacular architecture and the vernacular landscape, porches are everywhere in Iowa (Fig. 1.3). So I recommend that you open up Dick's "Porch Peeper's Guide" and go. Or read it, and then add porches to what you look at as you travel. Porches are exactly the kind of subject that makes study of the vernacular landscape so rewarding, because they are both so appealing and so suggestive of life styles and culture.

Iowa cafés also benefit both the tourist and the resident. In Chapter Two, Jon Spayde shows how much there is to be learned from them. They are such an integral part of Iowa culture that in *Prairie City, Iowa: Three Seasons at Home,* an essential modern Iowa book, Douglas Bauer spends many pages describing Prairie City's Please 'U' Well Café and the talk there. The food in cafés is Iowa soul food, as Bauer calls it, and Spayde both describes and defends it beautifully—deliciously. I would further defend café food by saying it is no more repetitive and full of cholesterol and calories than franchised burgers, fried chicken, or pizza. The more important question, as Laura Sayre argues in Chapter Fifteen, is the purity of the food itself, and you are probably safer with local food and you get more local food at local cafés. Spayde also

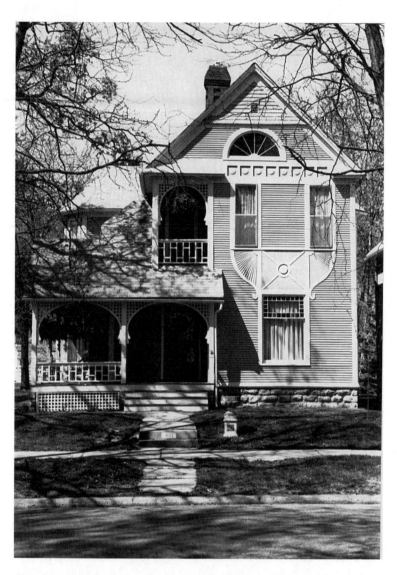

Fig. 1.3.   *Traditional Porches* can be found on older houses all over Iowa. This house, with both downstairs and upstairs front porches, is at 621 Avenue E in Fort Madison. (Photograph by Robert F. Sayre.)

mentions some of his favorite ones, to which I would add Joensy's in Solon, where the pork tenderloins are so big and delicious that even a half-order is more than I should eat, but so irresistible that I do anyway. I smear them with yellow mustard, tuck in as many pickle slices as I can, and eat away (Fig. 1.4). Joensy's is also a tavern, a sort of hybrid between the local café and the local bar, where you can get a beer with your sandwich and watch a ball game on the TV.

The Wilton Candy Kitchen, just four miles south of I-80, about half way between Iowa City and Davenport, is that rare institution in Iowa, a small-town eatery that is itself a tourist attraction, and I would not mind if there were more. It is a really authentic old ice cream store that is open 365 days a year and has been in George Napoulos's family since 1910. When it shut down a few years ago, there were stories about it in *The New York Times,* and not long afterward, it reopened!

Frankly, many cafés look as if they are in a bad way, victims of both the declining rural population and competition from the more efficiently-managed franchise operations. We tourists—and let us be clear: nearly everyone in America is now a tourist at some time—have a responsibility to patronize the local businesses, the ones that do not have national advertising, a standardized product, and standardized service. We have this responsibility and also the potential pleasure of discovering the extraordinary and thus returning a little adventure to our travels. It is partially mass tourism, with its emphasis on the safe and the predictable, all across the country (and around the globe) that has caused standardization and the proliferation of franchised motels and eateries. Local businesses are good too, maybe better. It is so simple to choose the local, and it can save you money. In Nashua just recently, as my wife and I were on our way to Hayden Prairie and then to bicycle the old railroad route between Cresco and Calmar, we found a little "Dairy Shakes" shop that served wonderful chicken salad sandwiches. And being open only in summer, it made its milk shakes with fresh fruit. Our bill for two lunches? With tip, $5.98.

Yet the socializing, the swapping of news, and the talk about work is so essential to people in rural Iowa that it will go on almost anywhere—in hardware stores, at grain elevators, at filling stations, and, these days, at new convenience stores. At certain seasons, like late winter, a farmer needs to talk so desperately that he will visit three or four cafés in one morning, driving over the whole county. Auctions, land prices, cattle prices, deaths, accidents, new

Fig. 1.4. *Café and Tavern merge in Joensy's* in Solon. As the sign on the left indicates, it keeps a tavern's hours—10:30 AM to 10:00 PM—but the announcements and notices on the bulletin board in the entryway reveal that it also performs a café's function as a general community center. (Photograph by Robert F. Sayre.)

equipment, floods, droughts, tax appraisals: all this information must be obtained not just as a matter of interest but for survival. The weekly newspaper is inadequate. Radio and TV are remote. So the coffee circuit is best. It's fast, and it's friendly, and less complicated than e-mail. Thus I recently found an up-to-date convenience store–gas station along Highway 3 in Pocahontas that, in addition to the big glass-fronted fridges full of beer and pop and bottled water for the "in and out" shoppers, had a table in a back corner where the farmers, truck drivers, and elevator men were sitting down talking over their coffee and doughnuts.

How welcome the outsider feels at such places is difficult to predict. I once had breakfast in a tavern—it was all I could find—where six or seven men sat close together at one table, three women at another, and everyone pretended not to see me. Only the waitress spoke to me, repeatedly filling my cup with miserably thin coffee that tasted of salt.

A time when one definitely is welcome in an Iowa town is during the annual fair or festival. This is when a town is on display: the band marches, the firefighters aim their hoses at sliding barrels, the local cakes and pies are for sale, and people try their luck at bingo and raffles. Even the animals get washed and combed and shown off. Yet for all the novelty of such days, they are also steeped in custom. People are friendly, but playing roles. They are spontaneous and lively, but also at moments bored. Beneath all this, as Hanno Hardt notes, is a very profound, conscious and unconscious sense of community. The visitor—and the viewer of these lovely and brilliant pictures—thus has a momentary opportunity to join in it.

Another event or subject that may cross the cultural divide between visitor and outsider is sports. At a café or fair you can start with a comment on Hawkeye or Cyclone football, basketball, or wrestling, and then ask about the local teams and even begin swapping stories. Baseball reminiscences, I find, are the best, because it is still the favorite rural Iowa game. Just look at how carefully the ball fields are maintained all across the state. Even little towns that have lost their schools to consolidation still cut the grass and paint the bleachers at the ball field. Of course, these parks aren't for tourists, unless the tourist is a baseball fanatic, like Jim Harris of the Prairie Lights Bookstore in Iowa City, but they definitely draw the local fans. Whole families go to Little League and Babe Ruth League games. Town teams play before good crowds. And high school teams, both boys baseball and girls softball, play all summer long. When classes end in June, high school baseball seems to be just warming up. Hot nights in July, people gather on the edge of the arc lights with their picnic coolers and folding chairs. August brings the state tournaments. And then the winning town puts up a sign on the edge of town advertising the victory (or adds it to the existing sign) (Fig. 1.5). Doug Bauer provides his own baseball reminiscences here, in Chapter Five, "The Infinite Outfield," and he is by no means alone. Every person in the state, I think, has a baseball reminiscence . . . and has his favorite (or least favorite) ball field.

My own favorite, though I have never played on it, is at Balltown, behind Breitbach's Bar and Restaurant. Breitbach's is

Fig. 1.5.   *Signs and Symbols of the Paton Churdan Rockets,* outside the High School used by the two towns of Paton and Churdan in Greene Co. Victories in the state high school athletic tournaments are causes for town pride all over Iowa. (Photograph by Robert F. Sayre.)

"the oldest bar in Iowa, opened 1852," with farm food so good and plentiful and inexpensive that there is often a wait for a table, so while you wait, walk to the little ball field—yes, the Balltown ball field—beyond the parking lot. It's on a high bluff above the Mississippi, and the low outfield fence is the last obstacle between home plate and Wisconsin. Then, as you look down on the cows far below and the bluffs across the river miles away, turn and imagine a home run hit hard and high, with a west wind behind it. Here the rules and routines and customs of baseball promise the transcendent.

PLACES OF HISTORY

Baseball brings to mind the old Iowa, not just the tourist Iowa, and there are few other states where you can see so many remnants of late-nineteenth- and early-twentieth-century American life. Indeed, the more the landscape changes around larger towns and cities, the less it changes in the places people have abandoned. The "Lost Towns" that John Deason looks for (Chapter Six), the cemeteries that Nina Metzner likes to visit (Chapter Seven), and the country churches that Pat Eckhardt writes about (Chapter Eight) are fascinating relics of the Iowa that was.

All three are also very suggestive sites for meditation and reverie. Read a little, for instance, of Oliver Goldsmith's "The Deserted Village" (1770), his lament for the lost villages of England over two centuries ago, and then try to measure the difference.

> Sweet Auburn! Loveliest village of the plain,
> Where health and plenty cheered the laboring swain,
> Where smiling spring its earliest visit paid,
> And parting summer's lingering blooms delayed: . . .
> Sweet smiling village, loveliest of the lawn,
> Thy sports are fled, and all the charms withdrawn;
> Amidst thy bowers the tyrant's hand is seen,
> And desolation saddens all the green: . . .

"Auburn" was Goldsmith's name for villages like Lissoy, Ireland, where he grew up, that were the victims of the eighteenth-century agricultural revolution, primarily the enclosure acts, that confiscated the common land on which the peasantry had lived and turned it over to the "tyrants" who converted it into vast fields and estates. This leads up to the famous lines,

Ill fares the land, to hastening ills a prey,
Where wealth accumulates, and men decay;
Princes and lords may flourish, or may fade;
A breath can make them, as a breath has made;
But a bold peasantry, their country's pride,
When once destroyed, can never be supplied.

Are John Deason's "Lost Towns" like Auburn? The question does not get asked very often because Americans do not talk about "villages" and "swains" and a "peasantry." The very language of Goldsmith's lament seems demeaning and archaic to American ears. Since our language does not make such a distinction between classes, between the "lords" and the "swains," it is also more difficult to assign blame. If we all began as members of only that "bold peasantry" (farmers, workers, townspeople), we don't feel so sorry for the ones who failed or stayed behind. Nor do we feel much has been lost. Mostly we feel a lot better off. The majority of young Iowans have left farms and small towns not because they have been driven off but for better opportunities elsewhere.

So it is harder to identify that "tyrant's hand." Is a rerouted highway or railroad a "tyrant"? Or is the "tyrant" bigger farm machinery? The automobile? Chemical agriculture? Or is it those opportunities in another place that draw people away?

And yet there is a sadness about the schools that have closed, the "sports" no longer played at recess, and the empty buildings. The little cemeteries and churches may someday be gone too. Like Goldsmith, we also are concerned about the condition of the land itself. How "fares the land"? Terry Evans, the Kansas photographer, has taken aerial pictures of tiny Kansas cemeteries that are completely encircled by huge modern wheat farms. How much longer will they hold out? The long shadows of the evergreens on their borders look like tongues of flame or the ridges of a crown, perhaps a crown of thorns. Such, Evans seems to say, is the end, the nobility, and the martyrdom of the men and women buried there. Will we feel the same concern about the land when such human relics are gone?

Nina Metzner's fascinating observations of the cemeteries of Iowa are equally sharp. She can identify the suffering. She can put the names and inscriptions and symbols together and spot the prejudice, the injustice, the vanity, or the humor (Fig. 1.6). She also invites us into that bygone world of early Iowa, silently invoking Thomas Gray's "Elegy Written in a Country Churchyard":

Fig. 1.6. *Tombstone Icons* are changing. Where people once chose images of lambs or angels, they now are likely to have pictures of their farms, tractors, and trucks, or, as on this stone, their professions and the companies they worked for. (Photograph by Nina Metzner.)

> The curfew tolls the knell of parting day,
> The lowing herd wind slowly o'er the lea,
> The plowman homeward plods his weary way,
> And leaves the world to darkness and to me.

However, neither Deason nor Metzner indulge in the moralizing and the morbidity of Goldsmith and Gray. Deason's sympathy is with the survivors who still live in Iowa's "deserted villages," where age and isolation have encouraged them to become more individualistic and self-reliant. They tell their stories, which he feels honored to learn. He is trying to recover places which have literally been erased from the map, places which he (and we) would otherwise not know about. So he does not impose himself or his ideas on them. Nor does Metzner unduly impose her interpretations of early Iowa on the dead in Iowa cemeteries (as Edgar Lee Masters emphatically did in *A Spoon River Anthology*, that classic of the Illinois Graveyard School).

Will Iowa's lost towns, cemeteries, and churches someday become tourist attractions? Lost towns do not seem likely to, for once they are "found" they are no longer "lost." But think how some western mining towns have been turned from "ghost towns" into tourist bonanzas. Think how famous some cemeteries are, though mostly for the fame of the people buried there. Churches, however, are the most likely to receive this treatment, and Patricia Eckhardt clearly wants us to know more about them and to visit them. She is a leading authority on their architecture and has written applications that have placed many on historic registers.

What Patricia Eckhardt's work also points out is the importance of religious denominations and church culture in the history of Iowa. I know of no published state history that does justice to them. You cannot look at the variety of churches in nearly every city and town or take her "Pilgrim's Road" from McGregor to Dyersville, looking at the imposing German Catholic churches in those towns, without wondering about the people who built them . . . and paid for them (see Chapter Eight). In 1890 how many people were in the congregation of Saints Peter and Paul in Petersburg, today an unincorporated town of maybe one hundred people. That beautifully proportioned stone church, with its lofty central tower facing east and two flanking towers facing northeast and southeast, can seat nearly six hundred worshippers. It is a farmers' church, with lush fruits and vegetables framing the saints in its stained glass windows. The wealth of the soil, the prosperity of the nineteenth-century German settlers of Bremen Township, Delaware County, and their devotion to their farms are all expressed in that church. No serious historian can overlook such forces. What became of them?

NATURE'S PLACES

Where the settlers of Iowa, like the German farmers who built Saints Peter and Paul, valued land for its fertility and built a landscape of fields and farmsteads, Americans today value land that is picturesque and fun to play in. The settlers wanted land to grow things in; the contemporary suburbanite wants vistas to look at and exercise in. As we have shifted from an agrarian society, where most contact with nature was in work, to a suburban society, where most contact with nature is in the form of leisure, there has been a great corresponding change in what we think is good country and a good place to live. We are no longer a nation of farmers but of joggers, skiers, and mountain bikers. Perhaps I exaggerate. We are also a nation of golfers and TV viewers. But even the images of nature projected on TV—from golf courses to Caribbean cruises, from African safaris to Australian reefs—cater to this suburbanite's and vacationer's ideal of nature. Attractive, interesting nature, to the modern American, is not farmland. And this is the reason, I would argue, why Iowa is "boring." There is no place to play, at least not in pricey modern terms. What are you going to do in Iowa with your sea kayak?

I first became personally aware of this dislocation between the Iowa landscape and modern recreation when I wanted to learn Scuba diving. My goal was to explore tropical reefs, but I started with a course in Scuba diving in the University of Iowa swimming pool. In December, at the end of the semester, however, came the deep-water dive—the final requirement for getting my certification—and I dropped out, chickened out I maybe should say. The dive had to be done in an abandoned rock quarry, where the air temperature was near zero and the visibility nil at the dark bottom of the quarry. Scuba diving in Iowa is highly skilled professional work, done by brave men who search for drowned bodies in dark quarries and dirty rivers. It is not recreation.

What the modern Iowa recreationalist has to do, therefore, is; one, adopt different sports, and; two, become aware of the past and present of nature in Iowa, so that; three, he or she can look forward to a more diverse array of future activities. The Iowa recreationalist must, in other words, try to use and see the landscape differently.

The leading example of adopting a different sport has been the taking up by thousands of people of bicycling. This great movement began in 1973 when Donald Kaul and John Karras initiated the *Des Moines Register*'s annual ride across Iowa (RAG-BRAI®).[2] Before that, recreational bicycling seemed unthinkable. Bikes were for kids and a few New England college and university professors, who pedaled serenely to classes on their ancient Raleigh three-speeds. But since 1973, tens of thousands of people have taken up the sport. Other factors have encouraged them—improvements in bikes, the national fitness movement, the build-

ing of bike trails, and, for a time, gasoline shortages. No movement or change in taste like this happens from just one cause. But
the result has been a highly popular new way of getting into the
Iowa landscape. It has, in addition, been popular with both the
locals and the tourists.

A similar success has been cross-country skiing and, for many
other folks, snowmobiling. These sports haven't brought in as
many outsiders as RAGBRAI—we don't have Minnesota or
Wisconsin winters—but they have given lots of Hawkeyes a way
to enjoy ice and snow and reason to quit complaining that there is
nothing to do.

Becoming aware of nature's past in Iowa and its potential
future is a different kind of recreation. It is generally less physical
and more intellectual, for it requires reading; looking at old maps;
learning subjects like botany, zoology, and geology; and consulting
many kinds of old records, from surveyors' notes to train sched-
ules. But hiking and searching the countryside are essential too, as
illustrated by the hundreds of people who have gone out looking
for prairie remnants or explored old railroad routes, with the goal
of making them recreational trails.

This is, in fact, a special Iowa and midwestern activity, and I
am not aware of equivalents elsewhere. Prairies were the landscape
of this part of the country, and they were almost totally destroyed,
so that just locating the remnants of one was a life-time vocation
and avocation. Early leaders of this sport, or cause, in Iowa, were
Bohumil Shimek of the University of Iowa, who realized that some
of the best prairie remnants were on railroad rights-of-way, and
Ada Hayden of Iowa State University, whose doctoral dissertation
was on the ecology of prairie plants. Later Professor Hayden gave
many public lectures on prairies, illustrating them with photo-
graphic slides she had made on field trips and then hand-colored.[3]
Following in the paths—or off the paths—of Shimek and Hayden
have been scholars and amateur botanists from all over the state.
In western Iowa Bill and Dianne Blankenship have traipsed
through the Loess Hills. Professors Paul Christiansen at Cornell
College and Daryl Smith at the University of Northern Iowa have
been teachers of new prairie preservers. Glenda Buenger and Mark
McAdams in south-central Iowa recently made major discoveries
in the Eddyville Dunes along the Des Moines River. Their son
called their drives and walks in search of prairies "prairie-
scoping." As of 1997 the Iowa Prairie Network had four hundred
members.

Carl Kurtz is one of the leaders of this movement. He and his wife Linda have travelled all over the state searching for prairie remnants. They have collected prairie seed and transformed part of their family farm into a seed nursery, where they grow prairie grasses and flowers and harvest the seeds for sale to other restorationists. As a nature photographer, he has also photographed Iowa prairies, marshes, and wildlife, and in this way brought his discoveries and perceptions to other people. His pictures in Chapter Nine are just a tiny fraction of his work, and, he might add, just a tiny fraction of what is to be seen in Iowa by anyone who trains himself or herself to search and to see.

The conversion of Iowa to farmland entailed plowing up millions of acres of prairies and marshes, and it also took an enormous toll on birds and animals. James J. Dinsmore's book, *A Country So Full of Game*, describes the now almost unbelievable plenitude and variety of wildlife in Iowa before Euro-American settlement, and tells story after story of the hunting, trapping, and wanton killing which largely destroyed it. There were not only buffalo, wolves, and coyotes, but bears, wild cats, beaver and other fur-bearing animals. There were prairie birds like prairie-chickens, quail, and ruffed grouse, and millions of shorebirds and waterfowl. Ducks like blue-winged teal, mallards, and canvasbacks were shot not just for sport but for sale to expensive restaurants in Chicago and New York. Some teams of market hunters shot an average of 14,000 ducks a season, the season running from mid August until the lakes and marshes froze in November.[4]

But some animals and birds have in recent decades returned to Iowa. Indeed, some, like deer, are more abundant than ever, thanks to the game policies of the Department of Natural Resources and changes in vegetation that provide new habitat. The more we observe such changes, the more we learn about the capacity of some wildlife to adapt to the landscape of humans. Looking at snow geese, eagles, swans, and pelicans, James Dinsmore describes some of these adaptations in Chapter Ten. As these birds take to the field to glean corn or adapt to artificial reservoirs they become, in a way, part of the ordinary, man-made, and vernacular landscape. His "A Wild Bird's Eye View of Iowa" tells where to see them in different parts of the state, northeast, west, and central, and the best times of the year for viewing.

My own interest in the historic natural landscape has been in prairies, railroad routes, and lakes. I chose to write about lakes here (see Chapter Eleven) because they are, I believe, the least known feature today, even though in the late nineteenth century, in the age of Dinsmore's market hunters, they were famous, or infamous (if one was farming near them). Recent floods, beginning with the catastrophic floods throughout the upper Midwest in 1993, and then the floods in North Dakota in 1996 and in northeast Iowa in 1999, should make us want to know more about them and reconsider the whole program that Iowa and other states have followed for over a hundred years of draining lakes and marshes. Can the flood control dams and impoundments like Lake McBride, Saylorville, and Rathbun ever be as effective as the natural lakes and marshes? The artificial lakes were also promoted for recreation, but how long will they be good for boating, or for flood control, as they fill with silt from erosion? The answers to these questions are difficult, partially because they are so often couched in technical terms and measurements, while slighting the physical realities of the land and its water. Therefore, in addition to the technical data, which was often grossly distorted by the advocates of dams, we need to see the sites of the drained lakes and their surrounding marshes. What did the lakes look like? What was their visual effect on the surrounding country? As we look around the vast "Lost Lake Country" of north-central Iowa, we can also see how ineffective drainage often is in making fields available for farming. Drainage inlets are usually surrounded by circles of wet, black earth where crops don't grow. Ironically, where it is effective, it simply contributes that much more water to a "flash flood" somewhere else (Fig. 1.7).

Closer observation of the Iowa landscape, therefore, should be more than just a recreational interest. We need it for making policy and protecting farms, factories, and homes. But we can use our recreational time to do this observing and to read experts like James Dinsmore and Jean Prior, whose book, *Landforms of Iowa,* is a beautiful explanation of Iowa geology for the non-geologist. Her account in Chapter Twelve of the controversies surrounding the determination of the highest point in the state teaches us, in passing, about glaciation and how glaciers not only smoothed Iowa but left the kames, which are *some* of its highest points, even if not *the* highest points. In the end, she asks, what is a "high point"? By seeking to find the highest point in the state we learn about the forces that shaped the land. But by focusing obsessively on such a question we neglect many other beautiful places that may not be quite as "high" in feet and inches but provide spectacular views and may teach us about other geological forces. Her descriptions of these

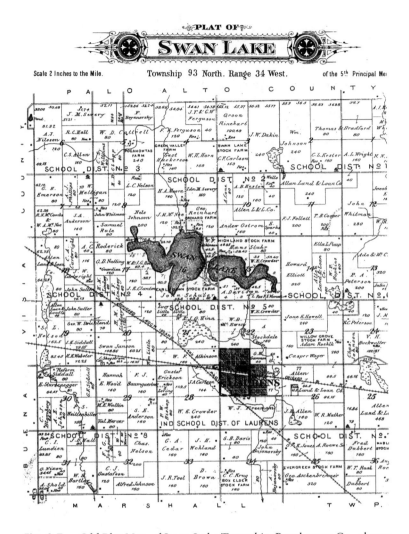

Fig. 1.7. *Old Plat Map of Swan Lake Township*, Pocahontas Co., shows Swan Lake, before it was drained in 1911. It is now corn fields, but the county road still follows the old route between the two parts of the lake (the one on the east was also called Muskrat Lake, or Rat Lake) and along the eastern and northern edges of Swan Lake.

places, both the past and present high points and the other scenic points, is an invitation to go look around. She even teases us with one "high point" that is underground. In the 1960s, when I first heard of the controversy Jean Prior recounts, I thought it was silly.

Her story shows why to many other people it was not and how it has been given an instructive conclusion.

TOURISM, COMMERCE, AND THE LANDSCAPE

To come back to Mira Engler's point, tourists themselves are having an increasing effect on the landscape they visit. The "theme town"—and there are now dozens of them, mostly along the Interstates, but others are to be found all over the state—is not a natural attraction, like Ocheedan Mound, or a pre-existing and independent cultural resource like a beautiful church or an interesting café. It is a specially designed or redesigned site promoted just for tourists to see and, in the current phrase, "to experience." Unquestionably, some are popular and add dollars to local economies. Some are also interesting and creative, some are not, and some are simply an exploitation of the citizens or the tourists, or both.

But I want to sidestep the question of which are which, first, because Ms. Engler herself takes that up and, second, because answers will still be partially subjective. What I would rather do is accept "theme towns" as examples of how tourism has affected the landscape and now conclude with some speculations, suggested by the final two chapters in this book, on what tourists and consumers themselves might do to affect the Iowa landscape. How can they be active, and not just be the passive receivers of whatever is spread out for them? How can they vote with their feet (and their pocketbooks)?

My own chapter on hardware stores, I must say, was not written with this question specifically in mind. (See Chapter Fourteen.) I simply recognized hardware stores as a wonderful illustration of the ordinary Iowa landscape. They were ubiquitous. They were essential. And yet people took them for granted and did not think about them very much. I also realized that I liked them, and so thought that visiting a lot of them, in different parts of the state would be fun. As soon as I mentioned the project to friends, I learned they felt the same way, and that confirmed my hunch: this was a good topic.

The further I went with it, however, the more I realized that hardware stores were both examples of the vernacular landscape and culture and also crucial agents or influences in it. The old-fashioned "general store" type of hardware dealership still had chairs in the back and a coffeepot around which folks could gather.

The suburban stores were examples of efficient consumer service. Other rural and small-town stores carried the goods that people in their area needed, thus telling something about that area.

But as agents or influences in the culture, the hardware stores also facilitated things. Some made it possible for people to fix their small appliances, rather than throw them away. They gave people the advice and sold them the tools and supplies with which to do things themselves. They were the essential toolboxes in the vast do-it-yourself culture of the United States—a culture that may be particularly strong in Iowa because of the necessary self-reliance of farmers and people in rural areas. What hardware stores sold could show up the very next day on someone's front lawn.

The consumer's choices, however, still make a great difference. By going to hardware stores, rather than discount stores, the consumer keeps the hardware store in business. By learning to fix something, he or she cuts down on waste. And by choosing one product or procedure over another, the consumer contributes his or her bit toward how things look and work.

Nowhere, I felt, is this more crucial than in lawn care, a big business for most Iowa hardware stores and one that now has a known effect on air and water pollution, not to mention noise pollution and the retention or infusion of water in the soil. The cosmetic turf grasses we currently use require lots of fertilizers, weed killers, watering, and cutting. Their shallow root systems do not hold the soil or soak up nearly as much water as prairie grasses. They are cool-season grasses that are not meant for prairieland summers.

Iowa home owners can cut this pollution and improve infusion by changing the way they care for their lawns—by planting different grasses and ground covers and using different fertilizers—decisions that are, in the last analysis, made at hardware stores and in turn affect what the stores stock. Tourists also can have an effect. After all, they are homeowners too. And their aesthetic and recreational judgments have a direct effect on what is done at the towns, restaurants, and bed-and-breakfasts they visit. If their goals shifted from theme towns to prairie restorations and bike trails, the effect would be felt.

Aldo Leopold provided an ideological justification for this aesthetic when he proposed in the 1940s that native prairie be planted around the restored Agency House in Portage, Wisconsin. A lot of money had just been spent to fix up and refurnish this frontier Indian agent's mansion to its 1830s condition, he noted, only to "set it in a landscape monopolized by stowaways from Asia."[5] Visitors to Iowa historic sites have a right to be equally critical. They also have a right simply to be bored and disgusted by dreary, repetitive "landscaping"—the monotonous blue grass, spirea, and evergreens.

In "Outstanding in the Fields" (Chapter Fifteen) Laura Sayre makes this argument all the more emphatically, applying it to our seeing, buying, and eating the products of alternative agriculture. Six years ago, when she began working in alternative agriculture, as an intern at Wes and Dana Jackson's Land Institute in Salina, Kansas, organic agriculture was very rare. But sales of organic

Fig. 1.8. *Alternative Agriculture today* can also mean preserving older agricultural practices, such as bundling grain stalks together in shocks, as is illustrated on this field in northeast Iowa. Note also the western ranch-type bar over the gate, with the weather cock on top. (Photograph by Mutha R. Sayre.)

food have been increasing at an average rate of twenty percent per year, and, as confirmation of its success, a few years ago then-Governor Terry Branstad urged more research on organic agriculture in Iowa. It appeals to consumers because it provides healthier food. It appeals to farmers because it generally brings them better profits, as well as being safer to grow. And it appeals to environmentalists because it does less damage to land and water. One of the most telling signs of the organic farm, Laura points out, is the much greater abundance of wildlife—birds, butterflies, and small animals—to be found on and around organic farms. But the other signs she suggests—and she is a certified organic inspector for the Northeast Organic Farming Association—can be equally telling (Fig. 1.8).

These signs and practices of organic agriculture, as well as other kinds of sustainable agriculture, are as vital to our own health as they are to the health of farmers and their fields. That is why the consumer, both as tourist and as resident, has a right to look for them and to be, as it were, a shopper on the road and in the country as well as in the grocery store. The good traveler in Iowa should expect the best in all things, and this book is intended to help the traveler look for it. But travelers should be particularly demanding in food. It is their right, and their hosts' Iowa birthright. With such standards, a tourist has a good impact and can be a true eco-tourist.

NOTES

1. Efforts are now underway to restore the Wright bank and hotel building.

2. See John Karras's account of that first ride in "Iowa: Bicycling Heaven," in *Take This Exit,* pp. 298–313.

3. Shimek wrote about prairie remnants on railroad rights-of-way in "The Persistence of the Prairie," *University of Iowa Studies in Natural History,* vol. 11 (1925), pp. 3–24. An account of Ada Hayden's work is in Rebecca Conrad's valuable history of Iowa state parks and preserves, *Places of Quiet Beauty: Parks, Preserves, and Environmentalism* (University of Iowa Press: Iowa City, 1997), pp. 179–89.

4. James J. Dinsmore, *A Country So Full of Game: The Story of Wildlife in Iowa* (University of Iowa Press: Iowa City, 1994), pp. 154–n55.

5. See "Prairie: The Forgotten Flora" in *Recovering the Prairie,* ed. Robert F. Sayre (Univ. of Wisconsin Press: Madison, 1999), pp. 161–63.

❧ Part I. ❧

A Place of Customs

❦ 2 ❦

Iowa Cafés

Jon Spayde

FOOD AND BEYOND

I'm going to assume at the outset that the search for a wonderful Iowa café is a quest for something even more important than chunky sweetrolls, or scrambled eggs and home fries, or prime rib with mashed potatoes. I'm also going to assume that in looking beyond food, we are also looking beyond the first and most obvious level of "atmosphere"—coziness, cuteness, the sense of having been returned to a so-called simpler time, and so on.

Not that these qualities don't count; all restaurants trade in them. But they're peripheral to the most important thing that really careful Iowa café connoisseurship lets us sink our teeth into: knowledge. Knowledge about ourselves as midwesterners and as Iowans. Knowledge of what we Iowans are like as a people, how we like to spend our time together, what we value most.

By a café I do not mean, of course, Burger King, Donut Land, Happy Chef, Boston Market, the deli counter and molded-plastic tables at a Hy-Vee grocery store, or any other chain eatery—although grocery deli areas often do take on something of the ethos of real cafés, complete with coffee-nursing retirees and authentic café banter. They prove that, on one level, the café is as much a style of interaction among patrons as it is a physical place.

But the cafés in which Iowa café culture thrives the most are not just independently owned, they're local in every sense. They may be Main Street businesses, located right in the middle of town—even in the middle of very tiny towns. (Don't, however, assume that every Iowa town has its café; the many pressures on our rural and small-town landscape—depopulation, falling farm income, "development" at the peripheries of the larger towns and cities—have pulled even the most basic businesses out of many proud towns—but that's another story.) They may be steak houses or catfish palaces at the town's edge. They serve food made on the premises, they are not decorated by restaurant consultants, and their owners are present (often working in the kitchen).

The purest kind of café is open during the day. It keeps the working hours of working people and offers daytime diversion for

Fig. 2.1.   *Menu Board* in the Uptown Café and Lounge, Charles City, is a billboard as well for local businesses. (Photograph by Robert F. Sayre.)

the retired. The ordinary concerns of the day flow in and out of the café's doors. The atmosphere of a special occasion, of removal from dailiness, that even the humblest dinner-only restaurant tries to provide is foreign to the spirit of this kind of café. For the gainfully employed, it's a place for interim reports on how the day is going; for the retired, it's a forum for remembrance, mostly remembrance of the work and play of their daylight lives. "More farming and fishing goes on in this darn place than out there on the land," one old gentleman told me in a Fairfield café a few years ago.

What flows along with the talk in a café is, of course, coffee itself, the flavorless but caffeine-rich traditional American vacuum-can blend. In an era of proliferating coffee shops and booming elite-coffee consciousness, our cafés stick with the old stuff. And, of course, the point of coffee in a traditional Iowa café is not its "nose" or its taste or where in the Zimbabwean highlands it was grown, but its *endlessness.*

Depending on the place, anything from fifteen to fifty cents buys you a bottomless cup. The server's vigilance over how much of the brown stuff you have left in your cup, and her or his promptness in topping you up again, is a primary gesture of hospitality, and the ritual of pouring and repouring—welcoming and re-welcoming—is enacted again and again as the morning and afternoon creep by. Café coffee exists more to be poured than to be drunk, an always-reliable bargain for a thrifty people and a symbol of a source of largesse that, unlike the weather or commodity prices, never disappoints. The cup, resting at the left or right hand, is a seemingly immovable guarantor of conversation long continued, always renewed, never the same and yet never strikingly different from itself.

At the same time, of course, a café in the Iowa sense always serves real food, too. While cafés in the urban mold—with espresso drinks, and not a lot to eat beyond biscotti, muffins, and scones—have made inroads into urban and even small-town Iowa, our traditional cafés are still places to eat heartily. They offer the same staples that have been on the menu since time out of mind: the egg-and-griddle-cake breakfast array; straight-forward sandwiches and soups; and if dinner is served, it's bound to be those redoubtable old carnivore dreadnaughts: strip sirloin, prime rib, ham steak, fried chicken, batter-fried channel catfish, and so on.

It's the fare that has been marketed as "comfort food" since urban foodies created the retro-diner in the early 1980s and restored mashed potatoes, chicken pot pie, and apple pie à la mode to the sunshine of elite approval. Rural America, of course, has not needed to revive what it has never stopped preferring.

All this brings up the unbelievably touchy question of rural "backwardness" versus urban "edge," and rural cafés are a fascinating vantage point from which to think about it. As we'll see a little further on, Iowa cafés haven't allowed the seismic changes in American eating habits in the last thirty years or so to pass them by entirely—what I call tearoom-style cafés have sometimes introduced urban fare like lightly sauced pastas and imaginatively seasoned chicken breasts, for example.

Fig. 2.2. *The Apple Basket Grill,* on the east side of the Poweshiek County Court House Square in Montezuma, is not open for coffee. But as the checkerboard front and the invitation on the window announce, it does have the friendly atmosphere of a café. (Photograph by Robert F. Sayre.)

But in most places, and particularly in most small places, the post-Julia Child "foodie revolution" that food writer/philosopher Jeremy Iggers details in his 1997 book, *The Garden of Eating,* may as well never have taken place. There are a slew of familiar, not to say stereotypical explanations for this, and some of them probably have some merit, as far as they go: Rural people and rural social structures are resistant to trends; rural people are "honest" and like "honest," more or less unadorned food; and so on.

But if you use your ears as well as your taste buds in an Iowa café you'll get a clue to the deeper meaning of the year-after-year familiarity of café food. Café eaters know one another. Café talk is laconic, easygoing, familiar, sharpened now and again with a kidding edge ("Carl, I wish I had a job like yours—nothing to *do* all day!").

But most of all, café talk is commemorative; it brings the distant or the recent past back into the minds of those present. I heard three retired farmers in a Northwood café discussing the difference between rural social life in the 1940s and today with a precision and aptness that a sociologist would envy. ("The combine killed the old group threshing. It isolated the farmer by himself out in the field, and that changed everything," said an old gentleman in a Pioneer Hy-Bred cap.) In a café-cum-tavern in Millersburg, I heard a jolly middle-aged woman detail the mild beer-induced indiscretions of a male friend—present at another table—in that very establishment the previous night. Laughter ran around the place.

Because the café is not entirely a place to "go out," but also (and maybe more importantly) a place where the community re-encounters parts of itself night after night and where collective and individual histories are recounted, it stands to reason that the food that makes this communion a genuine ritual should be, to a great extent, ritual food. And ritual food doesn't change.

The trend-conscious urban restaurant takes its diners on a voyage out—to Europe or Asia or North Africa, to New Orleans or New Mexico or to some realm of ideal (that is, ever-changing) cosmopolitanism. The Iowa café takes eaters on a trip back into the social body and shared time; and, since absolute strangers are rare in these places, it's a group trip. Urban eaters of the foodie revolution can savor exciting tastes, but by and large they have to do without this powerful shared experience, this good natured, unsolemn communal-ritual dimension of breakfast, lunch, and dinner.

The traditional menu also allows for another ritual function: competition. The *Des Moines Register*'s yearly readers' poll to determine the best cinnamon rolls in the state (often, though not always, the *largest* cinnamon rolls in the state as well) is only the most visible example of this agonistic spirit where café food is concerned. Catfish, prime rib, New York strip steak, tenderloins—the limited menu provides a standard of comparison from town to town, and if the competition doesn't have the intensity of football or wrestling rivalries, it nevertheless allows for connoisseurship.

And true connoisseurship it can be. Simplicity and predictability of fare are by no means the monopoly of what some writers are pleased to see as a "debased" and "plastic" middle American culture. Their various high culinary traditions aside, most Europeans spend most of their eating time savoring very simple food, much of it (as vegetable-hungry American tourists soon discover) of the meat-and-potatoes variety. The best *steak-frites* (steak and fries) or *poulet rôti* (grilled chicken) in a Paris brasserie is no more complex than a really excellent prime rib in a little spot in Hardin County. A perfect slice of Spanish ham, enjoyed in a noisy corner bar in Madrid, is no fancier, or tastier, than a smoked-on-the-premises Iowa slice. That staple of the Japanese restaurant lunch, *tonkatsu* (pork cutlet), is nothing other than our own iconic breaded tenderloin (novelist Doug Bauer calls it "Iowa soul food") without the bun and with a little soy-based dipping sauce on the side.

When the American urban foodie revolution, with its insistence on kaleidoscopic variety, identified the foreign with the fashionable, it obscured the stable, predictable, ritual dimension of all cuisines; luckily, enlightened American food writers like Jane and Michael Stern (in their various and uniformly excellent *Road Food* books) have re-cemented the connection between our perennial favorites, like those on offer in every Iowa café, and world traditions of comfort food.

SPOKEN SPACE

When it comes to the physical attributes of an Iowa café, it's not easy to generalize; of course, they come in all sizes, shapes, ceiling heights, degrees of illumination and decor. But I insist that we establish a sort of base line by concentrating first on what I am sure is the purest type: the small, small-town café, the establishment that's managed to survive in one of the remotest corners of the

Fig. 2.3. *Iowa Cafés* occupy all sorts of buildings. As the signs here show, the HOMESTYLE CAFÉ in Brandon, between Cedar Rapids and Waterloo, took over the Farmers Savings Bank, which suggests that cafés are possibly more important than banks and also more enduring! (Photograph by Robert F. Sayre.)

rural landscape; a place that may be called The Hometowner or the Koffee Kup, plunked right down at the intersection of the two main (or only) streets in town.

This is typically a building a lot longer than it is wide, with a lunch counter not right in front by the window, but about midway in. (In cafés as well as in bars, Iowans do not like to be seen by busy passing neighbors sitting idly with a beverage in front of them.) In the winter, a couple of snow shovels lean near the door, ready for use on the sidewalk in front of the place.

Inside, the light is not particularly bright; and what you can see in the light is a miscellaneous assemblage of amenities in a wide-open space; there's no crowding in here. Near the door, maybe a couple of pinball machines or video games. Pushed up against one wall, a pair of simple steam tables that will come into use at night to keep the catfish or the meatballs warm. On the wall behind the breakfast-and-lunch counter and all around the veteran-but-not-antique cash register (it's electric but not electronic) there's a wonderful miscellany of stuff: A big poster with the football or basketball schedule of the Hawkeyes or Cyclones (or both, in certain locales). Self-effacing joke placards ("Gossip has to start somewhere. Why not here?" "This is a non-profit business. It didn't start out that way, but that's how it's turned out"). Maybe an aging portrait of a twelve-point buck standing solitary and noble in a forest clearing. Clusters of commercial snacks: beef jerky in big clear cylinders, racks of chips, candy bars in tipped-forward boxes. If the place is small enough to function as a bar too, there'll be a brace of bottles against the wall.

On the opposite wall, a bulletin board crowded with for-sale-by-owner notes, lost pet notices, and auction announcements. The plywood panelling that covers the wall is adorned with a few colorful, randomly placed cardboard seasonal decorations of the type you can get at the drug store or the card shop: leprechauns, bunnies, Santas. Elsewhere on the wall a lighted-at-the-sides sign advertises lunch and dinner specials, hand-lettered in glowing colored chalk.

The ample floor space of the café is given over to rather functional-looking tables and chairs, which may or may not match. There are no "two-tops" (tables for two); every table is intended for a quartet of diners at least. In back, in plain sight, are stacked chairs, a table on its side, maybe even a mop tucked into a plastic pail of clean water.

This is the Iowa café at its most basic. What sort of "experience" is it? Well, not much of one, I suppose, if one's standard is metropolitan—restaurant as theatre, atmosphere as carefully engineered magic. But let's pay attention. If our café is not theatrical, it is nonetheless eloquent. And I use the word eloquent—which refers to the flow of speech—for more than one reason.

I've already suggested that the Iowa café is as much a place for the voice and the memory as for the palate. Let's push the point even deeper. In one of my favorite cafés in northern Iowa, this placard, hand painted, adorns one wall: "There's not much to see or do in a small town, but what you hear in here will make up for it." An apt and revealing thesis about small-town life boiled down to one

Fig. 2.4. *The Uptown Café and Lounge* in Charles City illustrates that some cafés also provide beer, wine, and liquor—although still in a safe and neighborly environment. (Photograph by Robert F. Sayre.)

sentence. We Iowans may not be as renowned as Southerners, New Englanders, or Westerners for the grain and rhythm and music of our talk, but who can doubt the pleasure we take in it, its sly and understated humor, the way it turns aggression into kidding, admits satire and world-weariness but turns them both into wry affirmation of the pleasurable regularities of life? Small-town talk really does offer a luxuriance and an intricacy that, for the sympathetic listener, amounts to a special kind of tourist attraction.

The closer you look at the café—even the café as a physical place—the more you can find in it the qualities of Iowa talk. Is it too much to suggest that we can sense in the café's look and feel some of the same qualities we can find in the stories we'll hear at its counter and tables?

Fig. 2.5.   *High School Class Pictures* adorn the walls of the back room of Brandon's HOMESTYLE CAFÉ, providing nostalgia for residents and for visitors too. The cabinet holds athletic trophies. (Photograph by Robert F. Sayre.)

The overall functionality of the café's look is overlaid with elements of decor that correspond to time-honored topics of café conversation: the college sports posters, the bulletin board notices that detail the passing of goods from hand to hand and the fate of farms. The informality of the layout of the place, that seems to recognize no single perspective or organizing principle, but lets elements coexist in a peaceful jumble, is—as students of popular art and architecture say technically—vernacular. It's even colloquial. It respects and resembles the flow of incident and anecdote in informal talk. The space rambles the way a gentleman of leisure in a feed cap rambles.

Nothing in the decor is professionally executed, nothing is

designed to surprise, and nothing refers to special tastes. Still, there is genial, even whimsical decor here and there, and a desire to go beyond, if not too far beyond, the functional—a match for the reticent but lively rhetoric of Iowa talk, which embroiders, but with economy, resisting the full baroque complexity of Southern storytelling or the staccato, insistent urban East Coast boast-and-brag.

Most important of all, café talk is often about work and workmanship; and the café refuses to hide its nature as a place where everyday work is done. Remember those snow shovels leaning by the door; the idled steam tables and extra chairs and mop in plain view? In fact, the unhiddenness of work, the informality that expects all diners and coffee drinkers to both accept and respect the evidences of everyday labor, is for me the hallmark of the "pure" type of Iowa country café.

With this benchmark in mind, we can look at some other café styles—fancier, showier, more theatrical in varying degrees—with an eye toward seeing what they "say" about aspects of Iowa.

THE TEA ROOM STYLE

The next-fancier style of café is the kind in which a permanent decorative scheme is present in some or most of the space. As often as not, the theme follows one or more of the conventions of bed-and-breakfast decor. Antique toys, dolls, or stuffed animals adorn shelves; gingham- or calico-patterned curtains are gathered primly at the windows. In this hybrid café, however, the designing hand does not take over totally. There are still likely to be snow shovels leaning by the door, idled restaurant equipment left in plain view. The café is moving toward an awareness of patrons as guests or consumers, not just members of the extended family represented by the very small town; and of course, such cafés are likely to be found in somewhat larger communities. But something keeps the café from losing the signs of kinship with daily work life and ordinary daily talk.

There's also a sort of gender balance in play; the artifacts of the conventionally "feminine" bed-and-breakfast culture of lushly comfy Victoriana and Edwardiana modify, but don't overwhelm, the conventionally "masculine" feel of the mostly functional tiny-town café. (It's important to note, though, that the more traditional kind of Iowa café is by no means a solely masculine space; in it, female owners, cooks, waitresses, and patrons maintain a vivid presence—the presence of the energetic, hardworking, self-reliant rural woman, ready and willing to trade jokes and insults with men.)

And, of course, the presence of the signifiers of "rurality" (those calico curtains; maybe a butter churn) mean that the café is consciously taking part in that widespread retailing of a highly artificial and conventional image of the American countryside that goes on in countless gift shops, B-and-B's, and tea rooms throughout Iowa and other parts of rural America. This image, which owes more to the photo spreads of magazines like Meredith's *Country Home* than to any real attempt to recreate a past that Iowans remember, is less an expression of the café's identity and rootedness than an attempt to give it sophistication.

The apotheosis of this approach to café decor can be found, of course, in the tea rooms that have sprung up in Iowa in the last fifteen years or so. Unapologetically (conventionally) feminine, these flouncy, lacy, over-adorned establishments—really extensions of bed-and-breakfasts—are like installation-art pieces in which women collage together images of an ideal feminine sensibility. Tea rooms are at the same time powerfully self-expressive and extraordinarily self-conscious—that is, conscious of the customer as participator in an ethos and an experience that the tea room attempts to provide.

In other words, by their greater attention to decor (whether they attempt a professional-looking unity of motif or simply overwhelm with miscellaneous flounces and furbelows), tea rooms do what most conventional restaurants do: create a theatrical experience by banishing objects that refer to the actual production of food as work. Fantasy and magic surround the diner—a hometown fantasy and magic that are still far away from the conventionally sophisticated scenic effects purveyed by restaurant consultants and designers in the metropolises and the malls (of which "entertainment dining" à la Planet Hollywood and the Rainforest Café are the annoying extremes).

It is, of course, no accident that tea rooms and tea room–influenced cafés are among the places where the hold of the conventional café menu has been broken, allowing in metropolitan aliments like biscotti, pasta primavera, and French-style omelets. And even a hybrid café—one that is hesitating between the world of the tea room and the ethos of the bulletin board and lighted-chalk sign—is likely to have a lonely commercial flavored-espresso machine, rarely used, but present as a signal of aspiration.

Fig. 2.6.   *A Sign of Change* in Iowa cafés is the Dutch East Indies Coffee Co., in Pella, where you can get espressos, cappuccinos, and lattes as well as the traditional java. It also serves Italian sodas. (Photograph by Robert F. Sayre.)

THE "REAL RETRO" CAFÉ

An alternative to both the plain-spoken hometown café and the tea room is the "real retro" diner—an eatery that's caught between old and new, between being uncomplicatedly itself and joining the twenty-year-old retro trend. It may be a handsomely refurbished classic candy-and-lunch-counter place (like the impressive Princess in Iowa Falls) or one of the several cafés that trade in early-rock-'n'roll nostalgia, complete with 45-rpm records on the walls and Bill Hailey, Buddy Holly, and Gene Vincent on the sound system. In contrast to the tea room's bizarrely imaginative never-land of mixed ruralia and Victoriana, these cafés aim at evoking a somewhat more historically specific, and closer, past—the thirties, forties, or fifties.

And as cafés that have, in all likelihood, ignored restaurant trend-mongering for most of their lives, they have required very little retro-ing to be retro—just the emphasizing, here and there, of the privileged signifiers that prove that the café is self-consciously cultivating the past, not simply, boringly stuck in it. This usually requires simplifying and theatricalizing the restaurant experience. The restored gem from the forties is decorated with posters from the appropriate *Life* magazine covers and movie posters; while big, garish posters of the Hawkeye lineup for 1999 are banished, as are bulletin boards and anything else that would break the retro mood.

OUT THERE AND BACK HERE

As I've been suggesting, the essence of Iowa café connoisseurship is a feel for the struggle between restaurant as nearly unconscious register of community life and restaurant as theater. It's rare to see this struggle completely resolved in either direction. In the most straightforwardly local, not-trying-to-impress café there is always some effort to make magic, even if it's represented by a twelve-point buck in a clearing and a few cardboard leprechauns. And in the most self-consciously fancy and magical place, whether it's a painstakingly restored lunch counter or a super-femme tea room, there is bound to be some record of true community life. These are, after all, locally owned places; it takes a highly-paid consultant to create a restaurant so seamlessly theatrical that it belongs absolutely nowhere.

Our Iowa cafés, then, always oscillate between the two poles of "out there" and "back here," between some sense, however faint, of a utopian, playful space beyond daily cares and a comfortable gathering place for the ritual reinforcement of community bonds. Chain restaurants avoid this tension entirely, because their intended customer is a mobile, automobile-borne consumer who is looking for an infinitely-reproduced, always-the-same food product in a changing landscape.

I don't think that it takes very much imagination to see in this ambivalence about café meaning and café atmosphere a wider ambivalence about modernity and the outside world. The retired farmers I overheard in Northwood, with their elegies about the coming of the combine, were voicing second and third thoughts about the hunger for modernity, "advance," and up-to-dateness that has differentiated midwestern rural culture from that of the South, New England, and the pastoral West from the very beginning.

Despite periodic "New South" enthusiasms, no one below the Mason-Dixon can forget that participation in the modern national economy was forced upon them by the bloody misfortunes of war. From Thoreau's skepticism about the telegraph to today's "Keep People Out Of Maine" movement, rural New England has usually cast a cold eye on the prospect of joining the great national consensus about the modern. And the closest thing to our national epic is the complex tale of the settling, nationalizing, and technologification (via the railroad) of the West—a process that is broadly tragic, if by tragic we mean that it is seen to be both sad and inevitable.

And then there's the Midwest, and in particular the most iconically midwestern of states, Iowa. Tied from the nineteenth century on to eastern economic interests, seedbed of industrialized agriculture, painfully unwilling to seem behind the times, Iowa's relationship to modern trends beyond its borders has been one of acceptance. Resentment or resistance to modernity has been quiet, secret, even furtive, while towns trumpeted their up-to-dateness and farms accepted more and more modernity: the combine, fence-to-fence planting, hybrid seed, and perilous participation in the global marketplace.

Today Iowa is coming to terms more and more with the post-industrial (practically post-agricultural) economy of globalism, the growth of information industries, and the marketing of *experiences,* of which the most important sector by far is travel and tourism. The Dyersville "Field of Dreams," Iowa's most heavily touted tourist destination, demonstrates both the attraction and the dilemma of tourism: when you sell your homeplace as an experience for outsiders, it is never enough to let the place play itself. It needs to be clothed in colors of sufficient generality and mass appeal not only to draw visitors, but to be recognizable to them as the commodity they have come for. (The "Field of Dreams" has both of those bases covered by virtue of being the from-scratch creation of the movie industry, with Iowa atmosphere attached.)

The modes in which Iowa is now selling itself to outsiders— haven of a nonspecific rural nostalgia, signified by the decor of B-and-Bs and tea rooms; treasure house of lapsed architectural styles (like the old Moderne-detailed "real retro" Main Street café)—increasingly mean that she is "playing herself" in ways that evoke not the specific memories of real Iowans, but a sort of faux-national memory made up of Victoriana, Edwardiana; and images of Buddy Holly, the Big Bopper, and Shoeless Joe Jackson. Maybe the most poignant contrast that the differing styles of Iowa cafés have to offer us (as we enjoy our battered shrimp and rhubarb pie) is the contrast between the real memories of living people—eloquently if clumsily enshrined in the "spoken space" of the un-selfconscious café—and the ambiguous sense of place and time created when a café "catches up."

❧ 3 ❧

From Porch to Patio and Back

Richard H. Thomas

Broad front porches were once so common on American homes that we tend to take them for granted. No architectural element is so prevalent in Iowa and so capable of evoking nostalgia and memories of a past America. Iowa might well be called the "Porch State," and the ever-present porches of a century ago tell us something about ourselves. The design of domestic dwellings reflects the prevailing cultural notions of what a "home" should be and of what the owners perceive essential to their life style. Therefore, a house is not only a shelter but also a cultural statement of how personal space and social life are organized. This is especially true of porches, which have through the years been not only decorative but also highly functional—a very important part of the social and domestic life of Iowans.

Between 1860 and 1990 our national life saw many changes in technology, values, population, land use, consumer habits, and social structures. These changes were sometimes rapid and accompanied by tensions between the desire for *privacy* in an increasingly crowded urban environment, and the need to be public enough to enjoy the benefits of *community life*. This dialectic between privacy and community is especially apparent in the domestic architecture chosen by the more wealthy classes, those who were the architectural style leaders and arbiters of culture. But we see additional evidence of this conflict in the housing of other socioeconomic classes which followed the lead of the gentry class, selecting homes which included elements of the homes of their "betters," to use a nineteenth-century term.

The porch, though only one part of the total home, is a fascinating reflection of this conflict between privacy and community. It was, for one thing, a very prominent feature of any house. The Victorian parlor, which also attempted to negotiate the conflict between public and private, ostentation and intimacy, was inside and not visible from the street. Likewise the modern den or family room, which gives more emphasis to privacy. The backyard patio, a contemporary of the den and its outside equivalent in some ways, was also less visible and did, for a time, replace the porch as a popular architectural feature of any fashionable home. But the return of the porch in the past decade suggests that the patio and/or deck have not been adequate substitutes. People also wish to be more public in their leisure, to see and be seen in their homes, and so to be a part of their community. Thus the dialectic of community and privacy is still very much alive, and the porch is the visible expression of it.

A PEEP AT PORCHES

These issues are further complicated by the seemingly infinite variety of porches in Iowa; on farmsteads, in villages, and in cities. Porches can be found on each floor, on the side, on the back, across the front, or wrapped around the main entrance and even set into the slope of the roof. In turn, each had its particular decorative and functional values. First-floor porches tended to be more of a public area and those on the second floor usually more private. But the variations and combinations have to be seen to be fully appreciated. Therefore at the end of this chapter I have prepared "The Porch Peepers Guide," which highlights selected porches in certain towns. Persons traveling to Vermont to see the brilliant fall leaves are known as "Leaf Peepers." "Porch Peeping" is a great way to see Iowa in *any* season of the year!

As you start looking at porches remember a central feature of the changes over the last century is how speed compressed both time and distance. In the late nineteenth century, most gentry-class homes were built on large lots and set rather close to the street and sidewalk. The homes faced the street and were viewed by passersby on foot or from horse-drawn vehicles. One approached and passed at a slow pace, with plenty of time to appreciate an entire house and its intricate ornamentation.

Part of our failure in recent years to appreciate the grandeur of these older homes is attributable to the speed at which we now travel. Many of these homes that have survived are often crowded by newer structures and are surrounded by less open space. At a car's speed of twenty-five or thirty miles per hour and with the distractions of traffic, viewing time is reduced to approximately six seconds. When looking for porches in rural areas, you may pass the house before you realize it has a grand or lovely porch (Fig. 3.1). The nineteenth-century passerby on foot or by buggy had far more time to appreciate the architecture and the ornamental features of the home, many of which were clustered on the porch. Streetscapes were filled with one porch after another and most

Fig. 3.1. *Pine Ridge Farms, 2.5 miles west of West Liberty,* a place where you need to slow down. (Photograph by Richard H. Thomas.)

people walked to work, school, or the neighborhood grocer. The very rituals of daily travel meant the porch was related to the familiar visual environment.

There was sufficient time for passersby to notice the presence or absence of a home's residents on the porch because the porch represented an opportunity for social intercourse at several levels. When family members were on the porch, they might merely wave or exchange trivial greetings to those passing by. Or they might also invite passersby to come up onto the porch for extended conversations. In other words, family members were very much in control of this social interaction, because the porch was an extension of their living quarters or private space (Fig. 3.2). A fence or hedge might also be present to help define the public and private areas. It was not only a barrier but a frame to set off the house and porch, and so was generally kept low enough that visual contact between the sidewalk/street and porch was possible.

Fig. 3.2.   *17 E. 6th St., Wilton,* a place to sit a spell. (Photograph by Richard H. Thomas.)

While the front porch served the function of letting others know that one was available for limited forms of interpersonal exchange, it served many other functions as well. The gentry homes were intentionally designed to provide space for entertaining guests, and large front porches were often the locations of social gatherings. The grand porches of the high Queen Anne style often wrapped around an imposing turret, offering comfortable entertaining space for both the family and invited guests (Fig. 3.3). However, a porch meeting with friends did not require cleaning the entire house and offered social time without formal arrangements. The more formal rituals associated with "calling" did not take place on the porch. Such social rituals were usually conducted in the parlor or receiving hall where things were more "proper." Furthermore, a well-shaded back or side porch provided a cool place in the heat of the day for women to enjoy a respite from household chores—a good place to "sit-a-spell" and break string beans or do a little mending while enjoying a brief breath of fresh air. In Carl Van Vechten's novel, *The Tattooed Countess*, set in Cedar Rapids, two neighbor women gather at the same time, several times a day, on their adjoining porches to observe the neighborhood and exchange gossip. The front porch was an ideal platform from which to watch the world go by. Children considered the porch as part of their play area and were relegated to it when tensions mounted in the home.

Because the front porch was a special zone that mixed both private and public space, it provided courting space, within earshot of concerned and protective parents. Being within the general confines of the house afforded some privacy, yet the watchful eyes of neighbors and proximity to parents kept the space public. The porch swing permitted a courting couple to sit together in an acceptable environment, and many a proposal of marriage was made there.

Two widely known films loved by Iowans use the porch as the setting for romance. In *The Music Man* Marian's front porch and the hotel porch are the settings for the love song, "Goodnight My Someone." The farm front porch in *State Fair* provides a bucolic backdrop for the opening and closing of the movie, which is filled with the adventures of an idealized farm family.

Not all porches were on the front of houses or blended public and private space. Small, upper-story porches had the very practical purpose of providing a second-floor outdoor area for shaking a dust mop or rugs and providing cross-ventilation. (Fig. 3.4.) Sec-

Fig. 3.3. *422 Cody St., LeClaire.* Wave to the neighbors! (Photograph by Richard H. Thomas.)

Fig. 3.4. *202 8th St., Tipton*—for the cool of the evening. Note the two second-floor porches. (Photograph by Richard H. Thomas.)

ond-floor sleeping porches were especially popular in Iowa as they offered relief from the summer heat. And back porches functioned as service entries and private space where the wife and mother could appear outside the house in her "chore clothes."

In the early settlement period of Iowa, the simple Greek Revival "stage-stop" buildings often had an extensive second floor porch off the guest rooms (Fig. 3.5). It could also be reached from the ground by narrow stairs attached to the side of the structure. The later Victorian styles which dominate Iowa popularized the porch, and the humblest homes could not do without some form of a porch (Fig. 3.6). The porch was a pervasive feature that disappeared slowly. Americans seemed to cling to it even as architectural styles changed.

The popularity of the porch in Iowa, as elsewhere in America, was closely related to the influence of Andrew Jackson Downing (1815–1852), who, in turn, spread the architectural gospels of the

Fig. 3.5.   *Old Rural Stage Stop, 4.4 miles west of Plain View,* a welcome rest stop. (Photograph by Richard H. Thomas.)

John Ruskin (1819–1900) and Augustus Pugin (1812–1852). To them architecture was an expression of moral truth. It also had a mission of adding to domestic and civic virtue, by providing safe, comfortable, and attractive homes that were appropriate to the wealth and social status of their owners. In *The Architecture of Country Houses* (1850), Downing asserted that for every class of American there was a corresponding size and style of house— cottages for laborers, farmhouses for farmers, villas for the gentry, and so on. But whatever the style, it included a porch, or veranda, as Downing usually called it, that afforded the occupant a place to enjoy the view, take in fresh air, and relax in the shade. The veranda was a "large expression of domestic enjoyment . . . a place of social resort of the whole family." It was, he believed, the most fundamental adornment of any house, insisting that "to decorate a cottage highly, which has no veranda-like features, is . . . as unphilosophical and false in taste, as it would be to paint a long-hut, or gild the rafters of a barn." (Downing, 120). Porches symbolized civility, manners, and a code of courtesy, which for Downing and his followers were essential to democratic virtue (Fig. 3.7).

The Architecture of Country Houses had an enormous impact, which came during precisely the same decades when Iowa was being changed from rolling prairie into farms and towns. One can still find houses in Iowa that seem copied from its pages. Indeed, what may be the most widely publicized house in the whole state, the little carpenter-gothic house in Eldon, whose long front porch is the background for Grant Wood's *American Gothic,* shows all the signs of a Downing knock-off.

The new women's magazines and home 'help books' of the nineteenth century further contributed to the popularity of porches by articulating a concept of domesticity which defined and limited

Fig. 3.6. *226 Cody St., LeClaire*—be it ever so humble . . . (Photograph by Richard H. Thomas.)

Fig. 3.7. *Penn and Highland, Williamsburg.* Life is good! (Photograph by Richard H. Thomas.)

the role of women, as well as how family life was to be conducted. The properly designed and appointed house nurtured domestic values that confirmed social roles and expectations. To live in it was thus to absorb the values designed into it. Women were responsible for the moral education of family and community, and the porch was a vital part of their domain. On it they could see out and be seen, and yet still be sheltered. On it they taught and learned the proper styles of socializing.

Given this perspective we should not be surprised by the inclusion of a porch or porches on buildings related to women and women's work, such as the care of children, the ill, and the infirm. Handsome porches appeared on college dormitories for women, on homes for orphans and juvenile offenders, on hospitals and asylums, and on "poor farms" for the indigent aged. Acceptable hotels were a home-away-from-home and what more universal symbol of the joy and security of home than the porch? The hotel porch was an advertisement promising warm home-like hospitality (Fig. 3.8).

By the turn of the century, an even greater selection of porch styles was available to the home builder because of a well-established millwork industry, new building materials and techniques, cheap labor, and the publication of house plans in books and magazines. At the same time, young innovative Chicago architects like Louis Sullivan, Frank Lloyd Wright, Walter Burley Griffin, and Barry Byrne were searching for a new architecture that would become distinctly American. Architects from the emerging Prairie School all found clients in Iowa for commercial and private buildings, and the Rock Glen area of Mason City has a remarkable collection of homes by Griffin and Byrne.

The Prairie architects, however, had no time for porches or elegant entrances and were anxious to accentuate the more private aspects of domestic life. They associated front porches with the

Fig. 3.8. *Manning Hotel, Keosauqua,* a promise of hospitality. (Photograph by Richard H. Thomas.)

excessive ornamentation of the Queen Anne and other European-dominated styles that they were rebelling against. Their young clients and contemporaries were at the same time rebelling against the rigid domestic proprieties that were sometimes symbolized by gossipy mothers and maiden aunts sitting in rocking chairs on front porches. The two women on their porches in Van Vechten's *The Tattooed Countess* were small-town busybodies, emblems to him of domestic oppression. Prairie architects helped lead Americans off of front porches and into sheltered back porches and patios, which they turned from places of work into places of relaxation. But styles did not change rapidly, and many of the wealthy and cultured gentry in Iowa continued constructing homes with elaborate front porches. In Mason City, too, the recently restored Queen Anne home of Meredith Wilson stands among other Victorians, with front porches—only a few blocks from the Prairie School houses in Rock Glen.

Part of the resistance to abandoning the porch as an essential element of the home can be attributed to the primary group relationships that permeated both the large and small communities. In urban areas the "row house" presented a streetscape of blocks of small porches with uniform set-back and almost identical design. Summer evening visiting was possible while the children played in the streets and small yards. Americans valued knowing their neighbors and being known by them. The porch was a place to be seen while still within the perimeter of one's home or private space. It had an additional advantage of being a platform from which to observe the activities of others. The porch, therefore, facilitated and symbolized a set of primary group relations and a strong bond to the community, which nineteenth- and early-twentieth-century Americans supposed was the way God intended life to be lived (Fig. 3.9).

DECLINE, OR FROM THE FRONT PORCH TO THE REAR PATIO

It is too simple to say that the porch disappeared because the fickle population was tired of the Victorian forms and wanted something new and different. The decline of the porch can be attributed to many factors. The enormous growth of urban areas made land values rise dramatically. Buildings were placed closer to the streets and, with the invention of the elevator, became much taller. Thus, the disappearance of a substantial-sized yard and porch.

Fig. 3.9. *415 N. 2nd St. West, Mt. Vernon,* here in God's country. (Photograph by Richard H. Thomas.)

The nation became more urban in other ways as well. Population density fostered an emphasis on privacy among the new managerial middle class. The social values of community—so identified with the porch—were being rejected by the new urban culture which sought privacy and anonymity amidst the press of large impersonal forces.

Another factor working against the continuation of the porch was the erosion of the moral underpinnings that had rationalized much of Victorian architecture. By the end of World War I, Downing's moral philosophy and architectural vision had proven inadequate. His morally-based architecture with its claimed civilizing capacity, had not stopped the barbarism of war or the disintegration of families so evident in urban America by 1920. As Downing's influence waned, so did the porch. The porch fell to pieces along with the rest of Victorian culture.

American homes also began to reflect the change in family size and the trend away from clearly formal rooms. The expanding managerial middle class wanted more efficient and more economical housing. They chose the plainer, more informal Craftsman style over nineteenth-century opulence, and modest bungalows and prefabricated homes over inefficient and costly Victorians. Still, most of these more modest structures preserved the tradition of the front porch, if only as a pleasant entry to the house and a place for introductions. The Craftsman bungalow reveals the tenacity with which the porch hung on in early urban and industrial America (Fig. 3.10).

The building boom in the 1920s and the new spirit of the decade encouraged the adoption of revival styles. Spanish Mission homes appeared on the prairies of Iowa, and English Tudor homes dotted the streets of small towns. These styles often included courtyards and small outdoor entertaining areas called patios (a Spanish word) at the rear of the house. However, Georgian Revival

Fig. 3.10.   *424 1st St. West, Mt. Vernon*—an all-American porch. (Photograph by Richard H. Thomas.)

houses demonstrated their grandeur with large front porticos. Homes were set back farther from the street, and the driveway and garage became important to accommodate the growing number of automobiles.

After World War II the population explosion, a vigorous post-war economy, national demand for housing, and large federal subsidies for veterans all contributed to a massive building boom. Unlike the railroad suburbs of an earlier time, this new automobile suburbia was driven by a need for moderately priced homes that lent themselves to mass production. In these new planned communities, land was costly, labor expensive, and architects were often the employees of large development corporations whose profits came from standardized plans and construction methods.

The resulting "bedroom communities" often lacked established social structures and the ingredients for building a sense of community among neighbors. The alley disappeared and the cul-de-sac ensured a degree of isolation from traffic and from passing neighbors. The car was essential to almost all aspects of economic and social life. Thus, the double garage moved to a dominant position on the front of the house where the porch once reigned supreme. Houses were set back a considerable distance from the street, and the paved driveway and large lawn pervaded the view from the street. The residents were generally of the same age and economic status, creating a bland social environment. High mobility rates meant rapid neighborhood turnover and loss of community.

Many suburbanites were refugees from the city seeking single-family dwellings, which would maintain the privacy afforded by the anonymity of urban culture. One way of achieving privacy and providing outdoor space was the patio. Like the front porch, the patio was an extension of the house but far less public. It was easy to hail a passerby from the porch, but exceedingly difficult over the high fence which often surrounded the backyard patio. Even if the patio was open on several sides, its location in the rear of the house provided privacy and created barriers to the public contacts once facilitated by the front porch.

Once the porch provided an elegant sense of entry into the home. In the new suburbs the front entry was only slightly more elaborate than the other entrances. With the disappearance of the porch any grand sense of welcome was gone.

It should be noted that many architects were able to find patrons among the new upper economic groups who were anxious to separate themselves from the prefabricated or mass-produced communities and wanted homes that reflected their individual tastes, life-style and status. Professionals, particularly doctors, lawyers, and rising business executives, could afford both innovative architects and enough land to ensure privacy. In many of these homes, the patio achieved a prominent place at the rear of the house and opened onto a large landscaped area with a commanding view of the city or countryside. Front porches might be included, but they were largely ornamental.

THE RIVAL, OR BACK TO THE FRONT PORCH

The past decade has brought an amazing renaissance of the porch. The designs of architects associated with the "New Urbanism" celebrate the porch as an important element in developing and enhancing a sense of community which they believe has been lost and is in need of recovery. This "neo-traditional" movement is led by the architectural firm of Andres Duany and Elizabeth Plater-Zyberk of Miami, Florida. They have designed more than a hundred New Urbanist projects. Behind much of their thinking is the increasing wave of concern about urban sprawl. But essential to their town plan and home design is the necessity to revive older patterns of towns and neighborhoods. These new communities intentionally attempt to revive the "village"—homes clustered around a center of civic life. Among their planning principles are a density of five to six units per acre, an abundance of public space, and mandatory design codes and zoning controls to create and preserve harmonious streetscapes. Homes in these communities take their design from older styles with porches, gables, and dormers. Houses are close together and set near the street with walks and generously scattered small parks. Sales brochures show homes with walks and porches while trumpeting the values of true community living. Porches are again celebrated as a place for informal interaction and as symbols of a neighborhood where people enjoy a common life. While the future of such developments is not clear, these new communities are doing well in Florida, Tennessee, California, and Maryland. One such effort is underway in Ames and another in Iowa City. Critics of the neo-traditional movement charge that Americans are not yet willing to live in what they call "theme parks," or to dispense so readily with their cars and their privacy.

Meanwhile, back in Iowa's older small towns, evidence of a renaissance or re-appearance of porches is abundant. The case of

Mt. Vernon, Iowa is illustrative. This college town of slightly more than three thousand has three historic districts listed on the National Register of Historic Places. One of the districts features the entire campus of Cornell College and the historic homes surrounding it. Cornell College is the only entire campus found on the National Register. Another is a charming residential area with homes all constructed around the end of the nineteenth century. The third is a small commercial district. Popular support for historic preservation is evident even to the casual observer. In the past two decades civic pride and action have made historic structures a tourist attraction.

For several years Mt. Vernon sponsored an annual Parade of Porches to display the charm and grace of the town and its variety of porches (Fig. 3.11). Each year a different area of the town was featured (Fig. 3.12). A published guide detailed historic and archi-

Fig. 3.11. *2nd Ave. and A St., Mt. Vernon,* displaying charm and grace. (Photograph by Richard H. Thomas.)

Fig. 3.12.   *Hilltop Dr., The President's House, Cornell College, Mt. Vernon*—where elegance matters. (Photograph by Richard H. Thomas.)

tectural aspects of each porch. Community artisans displayed their wares on some porches, and local musicians provided entertainment on others.

At the same time a concerted effort was made by the city historic preservation commission to encourage and help homeowners restore or rebuild porches on historic homes. In the past ten years more than twenty porches have either been restored/rebuilt or added to homes where they were missing (Fig. 3.13). As in many other communities, between 1945 and 1978 the trend had been to remove porches. The restoration of porches had more positive impact on the visual ambiance of the town than any other single project. The success of the historic preservation movement in small towns like Mt. Vernon, has greatly contributed to civic pride and the quality of life.

Porches of the neo-traditional movement and the restoration/ replacement of porches by individual property owners continue to show the power of the porch as an element in the social matrix. Manufacturers and suppliers have been quick to follow this trend, and currently all the elements for building and maintaining a porch are easily available at reasonable cost. Despite air conditioning, hurried commuter life, and the more easily built deck or patio, we continue to be fascinated by the porch. Today we can have both porch and patio, but the increasing popularity of the porch (old and new) suggests that Americans are reassessing the values identified with it. The revival of the porch in our time comes without the full scope of Victorian morality, yet sees the community-building and civilizing potential of the porch. The current interest in porches also coincides with a rise in the status of women, stressing equality rather than domesticity.

If a man's (or a woman's) home is his or her castle, then the porch was an open drawbridge across which the owners passed in their daily transitions from private castle to public world. The

Fig. 3.13. *205 2nd Ave. North, Mt. Vernon*, a porch restored with care. (Photograph by Richard H. Thomas.)

modern home designed without a porch gives the impression of a closed castle with the drawbridge up, suggesting that the royal family is tired of the world and seeks only the companionship of immediate family or intimate peers. But the fact that the front porch never fully disappeared in Iowa and that Iowans lead in its revival suggests that many Dowingesque values, such as a sense of community, informality, and a love of the sheltered outdoor life have survived here too. Iowa is still the Porch State.

In this transition from porch to patio and back are further lessons. Nineteenth-century families were expected to be public and fought to achieve their privacy. Some of the nineteenth-century sense of community was achieved because of this expectation for forms of social interaction that the porch facilitated. Twentieth-century men and women have achieved a high degree of privacy in the patio, deck, or condominium balcony, but in so doing have lost daily touch with their communities. In their hurried flight from commuter vehicle to the sanctuary of the home (now often through an attached garage), they have little time for informal neighborhood contacts, without which a sense of community is difficult to establish and maintain. The current revival of the porch suggests that our need for a sense of belonging has returned to our consciousness, and we are willing to look again at our past with a fresh perspective.

The tension between the need for privacy and the desire to belong to a community is always with us. Resolution of this ever-present conflict will continue to be reflected in the design of whatever we call home. Meanwhile, enjoy Iowa's porches in their grand and simple elegance.

THE PORCH PEEPERS' GUIDE TO IOWA

Where to Look
Choose any road off the Interstate system. (Its noise and traffic discourage the use and building of porches.) There are many excellent farm homes testifying to Iowa's long agricultural prosperity. Small towns are usually a treasure chest of opportunities. You can't miss.

How to Peep
Don't be in a rush. Remember, the porch was meant to be viewed at either a walk or a slow horse's pace. However, don't linger too

long as some folks may wonder if you are casing the place. Let your eye take in every detail (i.e., brackets, spindles, "skirt" or dressing between the porch floor and the ground, roofline, windows and doors under the porch, as well as the mass). What type of porch are you seeing? (Wrap around, side, back, screened, half or full front, entry, etc.) What furniture is on the porch—does it look "lived on"? What can you see from the porch? Would you like to be seen on this porch? Is the porch inviting—would you like to sit on it? How close is the house to those adjacent? Look for other porches in the neighborhood as they usually are seen in groups.

Beginning Peeping (Peeping 101)
Porches referred to in this chapter with viewing comments for Peepers:

1. Pine Ridge Farms, on U.S. 6, 2.5 miles east of West Liberty
   - House includes a "carriage port" or covering for carriages—large cone-shaped roof on west
   - Symmetrical with balanced cones on east and west corners
2. 17 E. 6th St., Wilton
   - Entrance and sitting porch
   - Note roofline, spindle work, and curve
3. 422 Cody St., LeClaire
   - Queen Anne style with porch wrapped around turret
   - Note wooden fence along sidewalk—low enough for informal contact
4. 202 8th St., Tipton
   - Second floor porches off master bedroom. Left small porch for airing clothing and ventilation. Right larger porch is sitting area, usually above the summer insects
5. Rural—4.4 miles west of Plain View on Iowa 130
   - Stage coach stop on Davenport to Tipton route
   - Locally made brick now painted white.
6. 226 Cody St., LeClaire
   - Observe fence and location high above street level
   - Modest even for mid nineteenth century
7. Penn and Highland, Williamsburg
   - Magnificent Queen Anne with large porch wrapping around two sides and a turret
   - Well preserved and good color selection for Victorian exterior

8. Manning Hotel, Keosauqua
   - Dramatic two-tier veranda
   - Hotel since 1890s
   - Small early river town that has been by-passed by most major historical movements
9. 415 N. 2nd St. West, Mt. Vernon
   - Two-sided porch on a basic Four-Square home from 1900
   - Characteristic of porch functions and social aspects of the period
   - Rebuilt using as much original material as possible
10. 424 1st St. West, Mt. Vernon
    - Classic Midwest bungalow
    - Constructed of stucco, a popular building material in Iowa
    - Also found in brick and wood
11. 2nd Ave. and A St. (southeast corner), Mt. Vernon
    - Excellent preservation of the original porch
    - Landscaping, color and design show full integrity of the style
12. Hilltop Dr., The President's Home, Cornell College, Mt. Vernon
    - Dominates highest point in the town
    - House has a distinguished history from 1840s. Shows how older homes have been "lived in" and reflect changes over the years
    - Porch is recent addition based on styles at the end of the nineteenth century
13. 205 2nd Ave. North, Mt. Vernon
    - Home of Civil War veteran, civic leader, and philanthropist
    - Porch totally reconstructed from photographic evidence and family records
    - Well set on large corner lot with existing carriage house

COMMENTS ON CITIES CHOSEN FOR THIS ESSAY

The communities selected for this essay were picked because they have many good and easily accessible historic resources. As noted, any road in Iowa is a "good hunting ground" for Porch Peepers.

LeClaire
This is a very old river town where many pilots lived in fine homes. It was also home to William Cody (Buffalo Bill), and there is a

good local museum commemorating his youth and career. Excellent porches along highway U.S. 67 (Cody Street).

Wilton and West Liberty
These towns along historic route U.S. 6 are characteristic of small, prosperous, agricultural trade centers that have added industrial plants in recent years. Excellent porches and Victorian homes, especially in the north section.

The Old Davenport to Tipton Trail
The trail is now Iowa 130 and a delightful drive that passes by historic and modern farmsteads.

Tipton
A county seat town of three thousand, Tipton could well be the Porch Capital of eastern Iowa. You can't miss by going a few blocks in any direction from the court house.

Mt. Vernon
Mt. Vernon is most unusual among Iowa small towns in the number of properties achieving national status. The long interdependence of town and college marks the visual environment. The topography of the hill provides an especially lovely setting. It is a nice place to see splendid porches and Iowa historic preservation at work.

Williamsburg
This is a small town with graceful porches (especially on the west side) and a charming commercial square.

Keosauqua
Keosauqua is an old town on the Des Moines River. Hotel Manning is located in a pastoral setting along the river. This charming community is set in a historic area that includes Bentonsport and Bonaparte, both with wonderful historic properties dating from the 1840s when the Des Moines River was a major artery for settlers.

Grinnell
Grinnell is a prosperous college town with many fine porches, including The Cottage, a Grinnell College women's residence dating from the late nineteenth century and recently restored.

Mason City
This is a real Iowa treasure with its remarkable Prairie School homes and high Victorian porches. A rare combination of agriculture and industrial wealth has created a community of architectural excitement. A must-see area. See the home of Meredith Wilson.

STRATEGIES FOR PEEPING

Experienced Peepers sometimes consult bed-and-breakfast guides as they feature Victorian homes—a good source for wonderful porches. Bed-and-breakfasts are often located in communities with an abundance of similar homes. These guides are a good place to look for dramatic examples of high Victorian porches.

Some Peepers look for rural roads and small towns based on regions of the state. The river towns (both Mississippi and Missouri) will treat you to some spectacular porches. Look on the high ground away from the river for the "mansions" of the lumber barons or river merchants, as they liked the view of the river within an easy carriage ride from their places of business. The Mississippi Valley tends to have older homes as it was settled many years before the Missouri Valley area. Both areas have a host of well-preserved porches.

Some regional Peepers like the combination of scenery and porches found in the northeast and west central areas of the State. Any region in the State will produce pleasant rewards. The settlement patterns and agricultural prosperity will be reflected in styles and homes that feature porches.

Whatever strategy you use, you will see magnificent porches in Iowa.

$\gimel$ 4 $\gimel$

Fairs, Parades, and Other Spectacles

Hanno Hardt

Summers are a special time of the year for sampling the spirited celebrations of the solid sense of belonging that exists in Iowa communities. County fairs, the Fourth of July, and numerous special weekends provide ample opportunities for observing such demonstrations of communal strength as colorful parades and exhibitions and generous offerings of homemade food.

From the rolling hills of eastern Iowa, with spectacular views of the Mississippi River, through an impressive vista of farmland that stretches across the midst of the state and to the banks of the Missouri, people here live for the production of annual events that will distinguish their communities once again as the most hospitable places around.

Iowa represents the essence of the local experience, and I always look forward to photographing local events. It is a personal challenge to capture the expressions of a community and to learn about the meaning of a rural life in an era that has become so urban. Taking my camera from place to place, I benefit from opportunities to observe local pride and the willingness of people to show off—at least once a year—with a modest display of talent and accomplishment.

My work has concentrated in recent years on public expressions of celebratory moments in rural Iowa, which are linked across the state by the spectacle of county fairs, beef days, hobo conventions, or lawn chair days that occupy the summer and fall seasons, in particular. There are enough heart walks, wild west weekends, old settlers days, gospel sings, and leisure suit reunions to fill out the rest of the year. But regardless of their origins or circumstances, their size or importance in the region, these annual events are welcome occasions for renewing the sense of community. In fact, they are diversions from the social and political reality of shrinking populations, the demise of the family farm, and the subsequent loss of economic power in many small towns and villages across the state. And they offer the chance for participation among those who are left and frequently involve most of the residents through personal initiatives or a collective expression of solidarity that unites businesses, service organizations, or schools and clubs.

Photographing a local event begins with getting there. For instance, with a drive through the countryside on a warm July morning to the town setting in various shades of green, past the gas station and the new mini-mart vying for passing business on the edge of town, to the worn-out main street, where coffee shop, bank, and post office, located among empty buildings and abandoned stores, draw most of the sparse traffic. Such an arrival can never be too early, however. It is followed by having coffee and a fresh doughnut in the homey café, and an amiable sidewalk chat with local vendors, or a short stroll along main street to check out the photogenic sites. One feels the rising expectations about what lies ahead along the parade route, at the fairgrounds, or wherever the major spectacle of the year takes place.

But most importantly, coming to town is a close-up experience with people. The face-to-face encounter with individuals and their material and linguistic reproductions of specific cultural or ethnic traditions makes these distinctly local events deceptively easy to observe. In fact, because they are local, they are quite difficult to comprehend. Saturated with inside information, neighborly knowledge of people and their relations, and a vocabulary that reflects familiarity; such encounters reveal an utterly private dimension to public spectacles of this kind. They confirm the cohesive nature of the community and demonstrate the personal involvement of people with the events they plan and create so meticulously.

The festivities typically begin when the high school band strikes up a popular tune, the American Legion honor guard raises its collection of flags, and John Deere or Massey Ferguson tractors commence pulling the homemade floats of various organizations and civic enterprises up or down main street and around the block. Led by the sheriff's patrol car with flashing lights, the parade moves past hundreds of people, most of them from neighboring towns and counties, who line the road to cheer on their hometown favorites: pork queens, local politicians, volunteer firefighters, farmers, Girl Scouts, and a colorful assortment of clowns, jugglers, and witches. But this is a social as well. It begins when older folks gather patiently with their lawn chairs and coolers in preferred shady spots alongside main street buildings. Younger folks just stand around or sit on the curb to get a closer look at the passing line of neighbors or friends in the parade. Soon candies will fly through the air and children scramble to collect their treats, while sirens scream, and brass band music floats above the crowd. There are only two ways to spend this day in town—watching the parade or being in it.

But parades are best when they lead up to something else, something even bigger and more spectacular, like a county fair, a rodeo, or at least a demolition derby. Thus, with some luck the activities may quickly shift to the booths and rides at the fairgrounds, where agricultural shows mix with food and games during the day and stock car races or country western band concerts at night. A fairground is the most spacious site in the town. There, business meets pleasure once a year. Tractor demonstrations, livestock competitions, and 4-H club activities take place next to the food stands of service clubs or commercially operated funnel cake booths that have arrived overnight together with shooting galleries, merry-go-rounds, and roller coaster rides. It is a time for contests—the largest pumpkin, the tallest sunflower, the fastest horse, or the oldest tractor, not to mention the best cherry pie. The resulting blue, gold, or green ribbons are proudly tied on livestock or stuck to vegetables, breads, and pies as signs of public recognition and expert judgment of yet another year's harvest. Gratitude and personal pride amidst the competition reflect an appreciation of labor and the generosity of the land.

And so it goes every year with renewed vigor, interest, and enjoyment as long as the thought of pancake breakfasts, rodeos, antique car rallies, or city-wide garage sales rouses residents to reinvent the purpose of their town with another turn of the season.

Fig. 4.1. *Emmetsburg.*

Fig. 4.2. *West Liberty.*

Fig. 4.3. *Solon.*

Fig. 4.4. *Tipton.*

Fig. 4.5. *Middle Amana.*

Fig. 4.6. *West Liberty.*

Fig. 4.7. *Mason City.*

Fig. 4.8. *Mason City.*

Fig. 4.9. *Stone City.*

Fig. 4.10. *Maquoketa.*

Fig. 4.11. *Maquoketa.*

Fig. 4.12. *Corydon.*

Fig. 4.13. *Bellevue.*

Fig. 4.14. *Postville.*

Fig. 4.15. *Solon.*

Fig. 4.16. *Solon.*

Fig. 4.17. *Protivin.*

Fig. 4.18. *Britt.*

Fig. 4.19. *Indianola.*

Fig. 4.20. *Iowa City.*

5

The Infinite Outfield

Douglas Bauer

You see them almost predictably as you drive through the villages of Iowa: baseball fields sitting at the edge of town, occupying a kind of mediating location which separates—or joins—a hem of lawns on one side, a sweep of tilled land on the other.

Depending on the month and the time of day, you'll see the field populated by all manner of players. If, say, you pass by on a weekday morning in spring, there might be a swarm of students in a PE game, crowding the field, too many players for one diamond to hold: four shortstops, twelve outfielders, that sort of thing.

If you find the field on an afternoon in summer, chances are good there'll be a Little League, or Babe Ruth League, or high school game in progress. Now a clearer order and seriousness are evident. There are uniforms. There's only one man or woman per position. And if your car windows are rolled down, you'll hear the undersong of adult voices cheering and instructing, setting a supervisory cadence.

And should you approach the town at night, you might well see, from three or four or five miles away, a cluster of lights at the bottom of the sky. Which often means the field has been given over to adults at determined play; baseball or softball against a team from a nearby town, with all kinds of history, memory, and bragging rights at stake.

Fig. 5.1. *Baseball Diamonds in Iowa* are nearly as common as corn-fields—and are often right beside them. This one is near Cresco, in the northeast; but it might be nearly anywhere. (Photograph by Robert F. Sayre.)

It's the memory of this shared residency, a kind of admirable democracy of recreation, that makes the field so appealing and compelling to me. For like most everyone who's grown up in a small Iowa town, I have memories of the local field in each of its incarnations—as the place we filled for anarchic grammar school games; as the home of the Babe Ruth and high school teams I played on; and most powerfully, as that nearly mythic soil where the town team, the Prairie City Lions, captivated me as a child-hood spectator. Some of the games and some of the players still remain vivid in my mind; indeed, they have grown over time to become the stuff of lore.

There's a man named Harold Timmons who's lived his whole life in Prairie City, except for the eighteen months he spent as a soldier in Korea and Japan. I've been lucky to know Harold, whom everyone calls "Hoop," at two points in my life; first as a child watching him play left field. Then, some twenty years later, on my return to the town to do research for a book, when the two of us spent time together, sometimes talking at my urging about his days in the outfield.

I have described in other places my devotion to the Prairie City Lions Club softball team, to Hoop and his teammates—young farmers and merchants and feed salesmen—who played the game seriously and incredibly well. Well enough, most years, to travel to the state championship tournament in Boone. And I've explained that for me, as a boy on a farm in—to steal from William Gass— "the heart of the heart of the country," the notion of distance and what it defined was something borderless and fluid. So that my worship of neighborly excellence, of the crisp fierce play of the Lions, Hoop especially, was unqualified. This meant the status I gave them was no lower and no less deserving than that of the big league team and its players I also idolized—Al Rosen, Rocky Colavito, and Herb Score of the Cleveland Indians.

Yes, Cleveland. Not Chicago or Kansas City or St. Louis, then the closest cities with major league clubs and so, more logically, the ones I might follow. But growing up, place-ignorant and mercifully dreamy, I perceived every city, every town, to be as far from the farm as every other—and so, obversely, to be just as near. Which is to say, it didn't seem to me as a child that I lived in the middle of nowhere, but rather, in the nourishing anarchy of my imagination, I lived equidistant from everywhere. So the heroes of Cleveland and the heroes of Prairie City were equally grand and equally intimate.

And the local field—where on summer nights I came with my father and much of the town to the Lions' games – will always hold a prominence for me above any other. Both for the uniqueness my memories guarantee it, and also for one of its features, which in my experience was typical of small-town fields.

I speak of the fact that there were no outfield fences.

When I think of watching Hoop Timmons play, I see him reacting to a high fly ball, sprinting forward, or to his left or right, a flamenco ferocity in his earth-chopping stride, then settling in and waiting, poised to make the catch. Or—and here is what I'm getting to—turning in immediate response to the thick click of the ball off the bat and hurrying out toward the night, looking back over his shoulder as if, it appeared, he were curious to see if any of his teammates might be coming along. He ran without fear of a collision with a fence and without any hope of the ball bouncing off one and back to him. Speeding into that last dimness of outfield light where from the stands he was suddenly indistinct, he became a kind of visual rumor of frantic pursuit.

As Hoop reached up with his glove, we in the bleachers, squinting desperately, rose in unison and waited breath-held to see if he slowed and pivoted and trotted back toward us, all calm restored for his having made the catch. Or if instead, the ball soaring over his head, he shifted into full emergency overdrive and in the next instant disappeared altogether behind the drape of night. If this happened, it left us suddenly able only to *imagine* him giving chase, the ball hitting the ground—as the batter flew around the bases—and rolling on toward Missouri, Hoop racing after it through the limitless hell of that generic nightmare we all have some personal rendition of: a ball; a finish line; a slowly closing door; forever just beyond our reach.

The nightmarish feeling continued until the ball suddenly appeared again in the black sky, flying back toward the infield. Hoop had chased it down out there in the dark, then turned and spun and hurled it back in. Moments later he reappeared, trudging back into the night-lit world.

Obviously, a scene of such splendid frenzy could not have occurred on a fenced-in field, with all its dimensions precisely measured and a barrier of some sort (even something as modest as a snow fence) making a border that marked the edge and contained the play. The ball is hit into the air. Hoop drifts back, with either room to make the catch or, if not, to look up and watch the ball sail on.

As I said, this infinite outfield was a feature not only of my hometown diamond, but of all the others in small Iowa places where I watched or later played the sport. And though I now see the absence of fences as marvelous, lending itself to trope and metaphor, as a boy I thought quite differently. What I felt then was how much truer my local baseball world would be if a ball might carry far beyond a fence so that the batter, his hit in that instant decisively defined, could slow and assume the studied canter of the home-run hitter rounding the bases.

As I think about it now, this wish for outfield fences had a lot

Fig. 5.2. *Outfield Fences,* where they exist, are favored places for advertising, just as in most major league parks. This is the Elkader ball field in Clayton County. (Photograph by Robert F. Sayre.)

to do with my obsessive interest generally in the costumes and trappings and details of sports. Plainly put, I felt the need to replicate the original thing exactly, and anything approximate distressed me a great deal. Watching Rocky Colavito on television, for instance, I noted the way he stood in the batter's box preparing to hit, pointing his bat toward the pitcher on the mound, and I counted the seconds he held this pose. (Two and a half on average.)

Or another example: one of the great disappointments of my youth came the day our Babe Ruth League team was forced to play the season's opening game in sweatshirts and jeans because newly ordered uniforms hadn't yet arrived. I was the thirteen-year-old second baseman, it was my first year on the team, and I was set to take the field against Mitchellville. Suffice it to say that I had dreamed of the moment. More accurately, I'd watched it in my mind with a zeal beyond simple fantasy, so that the day I was waiting for had, even before it arrived, become so familiar I wasn't sure whether or not I'd already lived it; whether I was *remembering* or *anticipating* it in all its particulars.

But I did know for sure that in none of the particulars was I wearing a sweatshirt and jeans. And the news that I'd be doing so sent me into a mood of pouting recalcitrance. It seemed a kind of insult to be asked to play a *game* in that attire. (It was an attitude my mother had little patience for: "If you really loved to play, it wouldn't make any difference what you wore." How even to begin to explain it to her?)

I know this kind of careful mimicry of whatever a child worships is not at all unusual, but I do wonder still if my impulse was extreme, helped I'm sure by the relative isolation of my rural childhood. My brother, my only sibling, was born when I was eight years old—when more often than not I filled my days by tapping into my imagination, inventing worlds to enter (many of them competitions) and playmates to go with me, happy bands of opponents. This is in no way a complaint. Indeed, I long ago realized that the job definition, the terms of my daily writing life—imagining worlds and the people who live in them—are just those that define the job of a *child, alone at play.*

Day after day, alone on the lawn on a hot summer afternoon, I'd step up to bat and simultaneously pretend to be the announcer. *He's enjoying a tremendous rookie season. And now he comes to bat with his team needing a big hit. He eyes the left field fence, it's a long poke to left, 340 feet down the line.* My fantasy, then, needed an outfield fence.

I remember other fields I *actually* played on, all of them fenceless. But it's not their open sameness—fittingly as open and as much the same as the rolling recurrence of Iowa generally— which causes them to stand out in my memory. It's rather, because of their individual eccentricities. I recall the field in Mitchellville, where the outfield grass was as tall as a pasture's, so there was always the risk of losing any ball hit beyond the infield which might drop and disappear, deep in the weeds. I can see outfielders searching frantically, like dogs on the scent, ripping up weeds and tossing them aside while the batter sped for third.

I remember the field at Carlisle, where the outfield ran for a distance and then simply dropped off, the earth falling away, so that a player racing after a deep fly ball would suddenly disappear below the horizon, disappear as completely as Hoop going into the night.

I remember a field in a town whose name I can't, which was laid out so that, in late afternoon, the sun shone straight in from left field. Once, in a game, I hit a line drive to left and as I rounded first, both the first base coach and I were so blinded by the sun it was impossible to see what was going on out there; to know whether I had time to get to second. (I was slower almost than it was possible for an otherwise ambulatory boy to be.) So there I was, lurching back and forth, trapped by sunshine between the bases, shouting, "Where is it?", and hearing back a chorus of, "I don't know!" "Go! Take second!" "I can't see it!" "No! Get back!" Finally, I gave up and hurried back to first. Eventually the ball came drifting in, holding me to a record-setting five-minute single.

And here's another memory of another fenceless field. It was at the same time the best and most frustrating recollection of my, shall I say, career: I am sixteen and we are playing the team from Runnells, an even smaller hamlet than my own, a tiny and time-neglected river bottom place four or five miles south of Highway 163 between Prairie City and Des Moines. I remember no real center to the town. I remember passing a grocery, a lumberyard, and not much else as we rode on the team bus toward the field. It was that same flat reachless plain, a swept dirt infield kept tidy as a garden plot, a trig stand of corn in the far, far distance, as though to suggest what further fields, with their even more fragile and necessary hopes, might call us and define us when we were done with games and games were done with us. I had grown somewhat larger and quite a lot stronger by this time, with the occasional ability to hit for power. I mention this in order to describe the storied moment.

The Runnells pitcher, whom I had played against for three years by then, was a big, heavyset fair-haired boy nicknamed Tiny. He was a very good pitcher, but I had hit him well in the past and I'd already hit two long doubles in the game I'm recalling when I next came to bat. (I'm confident that what I've told you to this point is true, but I'm a little uncomfortable in saying now that the bases were loaded and there were two men out. That is how I remember it, but in doing so I'm reminded of all the days, in the midst of some fantasy as I played by myself on the farm, when I created just such scenes and filled them with every last detail to maximize the heroism. *Bases loaded. Two outs. Last of the ninth. Trailing four to one. Full count on the batter. . . .*)

As I stepped into the box, Tiny looked at me and nodded in the way of someone making a decision. Then he turned to his outfielders. And what he did next, to my ego-swelling amazement, was signal them to back up. To move farther back! To position themselves so that any ball I might hit would have almost no chance of going over their heads.

As you might imagine, I viewed this gesture as the ultimate compliment. It seemed at the same time salute and recognition, offering and challenge. And I admit with embarrassment that I can still picture it quite clearly: Tiny recognizing me as I settled in and pointed my bat Colavito-like toward him. Tiny considering the situation and nodding to himself, then turning and motioning to his teammates with a brief, almost clandestine wave, nearly palsied, like a monarch's.

Thinking of it in a slightly different way, what Tiny did was to draw a border in that instant by ordering his outfielders to take some steps back, calculating how far I could hit a baseball and virtually erecting a distant outfield fence—one which I would be most unlikely to clear.

I'm going to continue to trust my memory here and stay with the idea that there *were* two outs and that the bases *were* loaded. (I've no certainty whatsoever of the inning or the score.) And further, that the count was full, three balls and two strikes. And that the idea of hitting a baseball over a fence—as Tiny had turned and, with the instant architecture of his wave, made me see the field as finite—this idea was a kind of tangible concept for the first time in my life. Because, there they were, the outfielders, crouched on the horizon, and hadn't Tiny, with his subtle shooing motion, in effect invited me to try? Hadn't his wave said, "Go ahead, have at it. See if you can hit the ball over the fence"?

On Tiny's next pitch, a slow, breaking ball, high and away, just where I liked it, I struck out. Tiny and his teammates whooped with pleasure and hurried off the field, as I stood there for a moment, unable to move or comprehend what had just happened. For in my mind, I had already hit the ball over the wall. I'd already met the moment I'd rehearsed for years under the easy conditions of my imagination, where the fenced-in outfield was a vital prop. *He's hit one out of here! It's gone! The outfielder's moving back, he's at the wall, looking up, and . . . this ball has left the field!*

And now, as I think about that day, I believe it's true that, without knowing it, I got at least a hint of a central paradox. I had always dreamed of outfield fences. But fences, of course, limit the dream.

Some fifteen years later, I met Tiny again. I was living in Prairie City to research my first book, the same research that allowed me to spend time with Hoop Timmons. Over the course of the year, an issue arose that got me out into the country south of town near Runnells to talk to some farmers. That gray spring morning, making cold calls like a salesman, I drove up a steep driveway, a suburb of hog lots on my left, and got out and walked across the farmyard to a small, fairly recently built, white frame house. I knocked, the door opened and there he stood. Tiny was remarkably unchanged, one of those men who'd already grown into the adult he'd become by the time he was sixteen, seventeen years old.

He gave no sign of recognizing me. So I introduced myself, he did as well, (I hadn't known his given name) and after a few minutes on the subject I'd come to ask about, I confessed that I'd known him when we'd played against each other. Affably enough, he listened to me, and when he didn't respond beyond a kind of general geniality, I began to recall for him the game and the instance I've just described. He continued to listen, and when I finished, " . . . and you struck me out!" he smiled—it seemed with a certain baffled tolerance—shook his head and said he had no memory of it. He said he'd pretty much forgotten that time, those years.

Back in the car, I had a good laugh at myself for being able to summon so well all the vivid business of the incident which Tiny's memory hadn't bothered to keep. And later I began, in an obnoxiously superior way, to think it sad that Tiny, having stayed where he'd been raised, having assumed the farming life which that distant stand of corn beyond the Runnells field had reminded us was waiting, had succumbed to a place-bound seriousness of mind that hadn't retained the baseball games he'd played.

But it seems to me now that the lesson has to do, not with Tiny's forgetting, but with my remembering. And more, with the fact that after all these years what I hold onto is not the strike out. It's the wave. Tiny's opening gesture. A skewed keepsake of memory. That moment of lovely possibility just before the fence went up.

These days, I mostly listen to ball games on the radio. But I listen often here in Boston, having years ago caught the merciless

Fig. 5.3. *Scoreboards* are also paid for with advertising. The Farmers Cooperative Exchange elevator is only a block away from this Prairie City field. (Photograph by Robert F. Sayre.)

and cureless virus of being a Red Sox fan. (Maybe, as I think of it, this is only a logical result of growing up in Iowa, where there seems a fairly similar doomed aspect to the college teams and where a rich pessimism has always prevailed. I recall a banner headline on the sports page when one of the university's basketball teams had lost a game after winning several in a row. It announced, "Streak Had to End Sometime." Well, yes, of course, I thought, but have we all, as this suggests, just been sort of *waiting* for it? Has that been the *point* of the great streak, after all?)

My thought here is that listening to a game on the radio is like watching a game being played on an unfenced field. There is, with every pitch, that suspended millisecond when, unable to see the action, you must wait to hear what's happened and as you do every likelihood fills your imagination. When the game is close and meaningful and the announcer especially poor, it's an excruciating fraction of an instant to endure. You hear the crack of the bat. You hear the crowd respond. And in that eye-blink of time you have no idea what's going on. A ground ball? A fly? A hit? How far? Fair or foul? It often reminds me, as a matter of fact, of those infinite seconds, on my feet in the stands, when I waited to see if Hoop was coming back into view with the caught fly ball, or instead speeding on after it into the flat black world of an Iowa night.

It's often been said, because it's true, that we return to a place, a scene of our youth only to be shocked at how much smaller the

Fig. 5.4. *A Press Box* is essential to the ball field at any larger town. (Photograph by Robert F. Sayre.)

distance or dimension is than we remembered. It's for just this reason that I'm deeply grateful for the infinite outfields of Iowa. For today I can drive past that fenceless expanse on the edge of Prairie City, one kind of field seamlessly becoming another. And with no inconvenient reality to contend with, I can freely picture in my mind how far I hit a ball, or watched one being hit. Without a fence to tell me otherwise, I feel no requirement to square my glorifying memory with the precisely measured evidence. What a gift! How many such chances, how many such places, do we have in our adult lives with their censoring facts?

I'm fairly certain Hoop agrees. One of the days we talked, we fell to reminiscing about the history of the Lions during the time he played, which I discovered corresponded almost exactly to the years I followed them. He retired, he told me, in 1962, the summer before I left Prairie City for college. I didn't ask him when he'd joined the team, for he was integral to it in my first memories of watching him and his teammates and I wasn't interested really in the years before that. I couldn't fathom that a Lions team even existed before Hoop and his peers, so certainly did they as a group put their stamp on the quality of play and on the homely lyricism of the games, the field, the splendid summer nights.

We usually talked while crowded into his tiny jerry-built wooden shed which sat inside an empty grain elevator, one of the several massive concrete silos of the local Co-op. Hoop worked for the Co-op, supervising with an almost parodic fastidiousness the seasonal arrival and continual storage of the area's grain. Sitting between us at all times when we talked was an empty coffee can lined with a layer of corn kernels which absorbed the spat juice from the tobacco Hoop chewed.

Watching him chew, I felt almost as if his ritual of working Red Man tobacco around in his jaw were one of the pieces of my memories he'd kept specially for me, caretaken. He always had a mumps-sized wad in his cheek when he played and one of my earliest attempts at simulating his style was to sneak a tiny nest of the stuff from a Babe Ruth League teammate as we warmed up before a game. What I hadn't known about was the way the tobacco swelled as you chewed. In a panic, I shifted it from one side of my mouth to the other, swallowing a good deal of it in the process. Not many minutes later, as the game was getting started, I was too dizzy to stand and felt my stomach surely about to reject what I'd just sent it. So I hurried to our coach, pleading the mysterious onset of an especially vicious flu. Then I walked around behind the scoreboard, bent over, and my body completed what I'd started. It was the only game I ever missed due to "illness" or injury.

I told this story to Hoop and he nodded and chuckled, recalling a time in the army when he couldn't find Red Man and tried another stronger brand. "Just like you," he said, "I got all white and sick to my stomach. Couldn't stand up. Lord, I thought I was gonna die."

We talked then about the several pitchers who had performed for the Lions, artisans of that strange and astonishing craft of delivering a softball underhanded with velocity and spin enough to make it dip and soar. We remembered one particularly gifted pitcher, in my view the best of them, who was unfortunately prone to sulks and pouts when things went wrong, robbing him of his concentration and control.

And we replayed a few memorable games. A state tournament win in extra innings. (I can still see the cloud of dust that rose from around home plate when Gerald Lovett slid in with the winning run!) The annual series against Percy, our fiercest rival, and, like Runnells, at that point in time a nearby location where life and buildings had once clustered, kept alive by history and complicated genealogy.

As Hoop and I remembered plays and moments, it seemed almost as if the heat of our recollections were making a kind of light that lit the mood and I was very happy inside the wondrous comfort of it. And then Hoop said the thing that makes me think that he, too, has been grateful through the years that the field he played so well was fenceless.

"I guess a fellow never really gets it out of his system," he said. He leaned toward the coffee can, spat and thought and continued. "I go down to the field now and watch them play, and I get to thinking, 'Gol damn, I'd like to try it.' I know, sure as billy hell, my legs'd break down and I'd be so slow and stiff, and I wouldn't be able to hit like I could.

"And yet, I'll be sitting down there in the bleachers, looking out, and somebody'll hit one way out there. And watching it, it'll remind me of some ball *I* hit way back when. And I'll think to myself, 'Hell, I hit them farther than that.' And when I see that in my mind, I get to believing I could still do it."

He shook his head at what he felt to be foolishness and tugged the bill of his cap, pulling it farther down on his bald head. "Now," he said to me, "ain't that silly?"

Fig. 5.5. *Infield carefully raked and lined,* outfield grass cut, the ball field in Auburn in northwest Iowa is ready for the late afternoon game. (Photograph by Robert F. Sayre.)

Imagination and memory, the writer's and the old athlete's armaments. And how the absence of a fence allows one to continue to influence the other.

Yes, I think to say to Hoop. I suppose it's silly. Except that it is not.

Part II.

Places of History

❧ 6 ☙

Lost Towns

John Deason

It's a strange feeling when you first become aware of something that had been right under your nose all the time. Finding your first morel mushroom in the familiar woods you have tromped through for years is one of these revelations. Once you recognize the existence of the morels, then you see dozens of them. Discovering new worlds happens to me all the time, sometimes in the oddest places. It was in 1990 when I discovered lost towns.

I was at What Cheer, trudging through the dust amongst rows and rows of flea market booths on a hot summer's day. I ducked under the shade of a canvas awning, and as I looked through the tools, mason jars, and other oddities, I saw a stack of old highway maps. The smiling service station man with his pump nozzle in hand on the cover of the 1941 Skelly map invited me into his little world of old highways and towns. When I looked at Muscatine County, where I live, I saw a half-dozen towns of which I had never heard. I thought that it must be the heat tricking me. Or perhaps my sense of scale was askew and I was looking at a different county. Nope. These towns were nestled in between towns I knew existed. It was that strange moment of revelation. I could sense my perception of reality changing. I bought the map and resolved to get to the bottom of this mystery.

And thus started a decade of exploration of another world, the world of lost towns of Iowa.

I first tried to find Ardon, ten miles southwest of Muscatine. I followed the Old Burlington Road along the Mississippi River bluffs, and then I cut up through the woods on a gravel road to the upland fields. I figured from the old map that I should be at Ardon, but I saw no sign of a town. I finally surrendered and knocked on the door of a nearby farmhouse. The lady laughed when I asked directions to Ardon. She pointed to the east, over the cornfields, to a solitary house. "That's all that's left of Ardon. The train depot was moved two miles west of here for a township meeting hall. All the other buildings were torn down or moved—the gas station, the store, the livery stables, and the houses. That old house was once the hotel. I guess that seventy people used to live there in the days that the train came up over the bluff and stopped there."

So I found the narrow dirt path between the fields that led to the old hotel. A dozen Rottweilers in cages greeted me when I got out of the car. Someone lived there. The old railroad sign, proclaiming ARDON was set up on posts. Hunters had sent a few slugs through it over the years. No other buildings were around. The road ended right there. There were no railroad tracks, but as my eyes followed the fence row off to the east, I could discern the built up forms of the old grade, now covered with wildflowers.

Later that month I met the lady who lived in Ardon and talked with her about the history of the town. Ardon was formed when the railroad was built, in the late 1800s. The grade coming up the bluff from the Mississippi bottoms below would be the steepest grade of any tracks between Chicago and Denver. To help engines pull their cars up the bluff, a special, powerful steam engine was permanently quartered at Ardon to latch onto westbound trains at the base of the hill and give extra horsepower for the climb. For some reason unknown to me, to get that powerful engine to Ardon, a crew of men worked for a month one winter to move the engine across the fields from Bayfield, five miles to the north. They would lay ties and track ahead of the engine and pull up the ties and track from behind to reuse as they made their way to Ardon. I don't know why the railroad didn't wait until the tracks to Ardon were laid, and then move in the engine. Either way, the trains came, Ardon grew, and then one day the trains were stopped, the tracks were pulled up, and Ardon died.

As I worked on my project, I began to collect older maps of Iowa and to make copies of old maps at the University of Iowa's

Fig. 6.1. *The Railroad Depot Sign for Ardon,* in Muscatine Co. The building in the background, was once the hotel. It is the only building left. (Photograph by John Deason.)

Main Library. I discovered hundreds of lost towns throughout the state. I made it my goal to document at least two of these towns in each of Iowa's ninety-nine counties. As I explained what I was doing to people over the years, some would call these towns "ghost towns." I suppose this came from the term coined for the deserted mining towns out West. I prefer the term "lost towns." My main criterion for calling a former town a lost town is that it not be listed on the current Department of Transportation (D.O.T.) state map. If a town was once on older maps, and has now been deleted from current maps, I figure it has "lost" its identity, at least as far as the D.O.T. is concerned. I also think that the term ghost town implies that people have experienced supernatural occurrences there. Even though people have claimed to have seen ghosts in some of the houses that remain in some of the lost towns I have explored, most of the these towns I would deem to be ghost-free. And many of the lost towns I have found are literally lost from view. All buildings are gone, and passersby at fifty-five miles per hour would be hard pressed to see any trace of a town, unless they had a very quick eye.

Also, the term ghost town implies that only ghosts live there now. Many of the lost towns I visited had people living in them, but there wasn't a large enough population to convince the D.O.T. that a viable town existed. Actually, the D.O.T. has a list of seven criteria, and only if a town can claim at least two of them will it officially be included on the state maps. The seven criteria are: population over twenty-five, a post office, a school, a church, a business, being situated at the entrance to a state park, or having an annual festival or celebration.

In 1999, the lost town of River Junction, in southeast Johnson County, became an official town again, after its third annual Old Settlers' Reunion became a tradition again, after a half-century of being defunct. Because of its proximity to my home, River Junction, or "Stumptown," as some locals call it, was one of the first lost towns I documented. Over the years, I have gone back to take more and more photographs, and to talk with friends I have made there. At one time this town, the first white settlement in Johnson County, had hundreds of citizens, and was bigger than Iowa City. It had a stockyard for the trains that passed through, a brickyard, a whole block of two-story brick buildings downtown, and was platted for fortune. But eventually, Iowa City overtook it, and became the state capital. The railroad lines were abandoned, floods took their toll, and people moved away. The Old Settlers' Reunion, which at one time attracted thousands of people for a week of celebration, dwindled and died. Jerry and Joann Morgan live in a house next to the park where the reunion used to take place. As they became interested in the history of River Junction, the idea to resurrect the reunion became their goal. I attended the first one, using my old wooden 8" × 10" view camera to record the two hundred neighbors, friends, and relatives of people from the past. The next year I dressed up in 1880s clothing, like most of the annual visitors began to do. I am now the official photographer, usually hoisted ten feet in the air on the front bucket of a John Deere to be able to get everyone's face in the photo. Last year I counted over seventy desserts alone at the most incredible pot luck picnic I have ever attended.

One of the joys of exploring these lost towns is discovering the stories that have been handed down over the years. Sometimes, even though a town has lost every building it once had, the neighboring farmers and communities will still remember the stories. When I first came to River Junction, I asked a boy who the oldest person in town was. He directed me to Beulah Watson, who lived in a ranch house with her cats on the north side of town. It took me several visits before Beulah trusted me enough to take her photograph. She told me about her grandfather, John D. Musser, who built the brickyards. He had seven daughters, so he built seven brick houses, one for each of them, as wedding presents. Only one of the houses survives, the one he built for Beulah's mother. She can see it every day from her front window.

As the project grew in scope, I got a grant from the Iowa Humanities Board to help me in my quest. The end result was to be a traveling exhibit of photos and text of the towns I researched in the eastern quarter of the state. Of course, this put a deadline into effect, which can be good or bad, depending on how one works under pressure. For me, the deadline was a great impetus. It forced me to plan out my weekends and do much prior research and map comparison. I began to develop a technique for approaching the exploration of a lost town. Although I was often tempted to write or call ahead to county historical societies to find local historians or "story savers," I rather enjoyed the serendipity of driving into the location of a lost town with no prior conceptions of what I would find. I loved the surprise of rounding a bend and seeing for the first time a lost town that had previously been just a dot on an old map. From there I would find a person at home and explain what I was doing, showing proof of my intentions with photos of other lost towns, a *Des Moines Register* article that had been done at the beginning of the research after I got the grant, and a 1912 copy of *Huebinger's Good Roads Atlas* that was my primary source of lost towns. After getting some stories and history from that person, inevitably I would be directed to other people who knew things, or had scrapbooks, or owned property that was photogenic. I tried to talk to the oldest person living in each town.

At a certain point, I would have to stop my research of a lost town. That point was always a bitter-sweet moment, because I knew that I could go on and on, peeling away layers, finding out more and more information, until, if I didn't stop, I would have enough material to write a whole book on that town alone. I truly believe that every town has enough history to make a very interesting book. Who will write them? I've been to over two hundred lost towns, and I wish I could write those books, but I don't have the time in this lifetime. However, within each county are people who could do this research and write these books. While my project just scratches the surface in most cases, my hope is that it will generate some interest among local historians to begin to write the stories down before they are permanently lost.

A lot of my research was based on information I received by word-of-mouth. Once I was talking with a friend about lost towns, and he asked if I knew of the town on Beaver Island, in the Mississippi River, across from Clinton. A friend of his father had lived there as a boy and told him many stories. In the 1930s there was a grade school on the island, but the high school kids had to go to the "mainland" in Clinton. Since there wasn't a bridge to the island, they used a large flatbottom boat with rows of seats, kind of like a school bus on water. It was connected to a cable and they would pull themselves across. In the winter, when the ice was thick enough, a horse would pull the loaded boat across. During the Depression, the lock and dam system was built on the upper Mississippi. When the pools above each dam filled, the water level rose to such a height, usually only a few feet, that most of the larger islands became too swampy to farm. Over twenty families who farmed Beaver Island were forced to leave. Most of the houses and buildings were salvaged, although a few were just abandoned and left to rot. This old man had told my friend that the school burned down just as the town was breaking up. My friend has a boat at his home in Comanche, just south of Clinton, so he volunteered to take me over there to explore. All the stories from the old man had aroused his curiosity.

As we set foot on the island, a mile south of where the town once lay, my friend warned me that we could encounter wild hogs, whose ancestors once rooted in pens there over sixty years ago. Stories of hunters being attacked by long-tusked boars are often told each fall. (He waited until we were already there to tell me this.)

The island was once five miles long and two miles wide. It was heavily wooded, and since it was closer to Iowa than Illinois, the Iowa farmers in the 1800s claimed the wood. Men from Albany, across the river in Illinois, persisted in coming across the ice and logging in the winter. The animosity eventually came to a head, and two "armies" were formed and met to do battle. These were actually two bands of farmers armed with shotguns and squirrel rifles. As they faced each other on Beaver Island, someone's gun discharged, and all the men scattered and fled to their homes. Later, cooler heads met on neutral ground, and a small portion of Beaver Island was designated as Albany's area to log. The One Shot War was over, with no casualties. Beaver Island is now totally Iowa land.

Our goal that day was to find where the school once stood from the directions the old man had recently given to my friend. After several hours of hiking through high weeds and crossing several creeks, we came upon the former town. No hogs had challenged us. A few abandoned buildings indicated where streets once were. Several stone foundations were visible. As we stood on the walls of one, wondering where the school might have been, I looked into the weeds at the bottom, in the pit that was once the basement. Poking out from dead leaves and weeds were several piles of cast iron forms, each revealing the delicate patterns I instantly recognized—the iron sides of old school desks with the wood of the lift tops and fold-down seats long burned or rotted away. We had found the school.

We sat down and marveled about what life must have been like for a child in 1910 living in this isolated world. Electricity and phone lines connected the island to Clinton. There was a general store and a blacksmith shop. Most of the people farmed their small pieces of land, and probably didn't go to town very often. It would have been an idyllic place for a child to grow up.

On the way back to the boat, we came upon a crumbling house and inside found a large cast iron kettle. Its purpose in the old days was to hold the boiling water used to scald the gutted hogs on butchering day, to make it easier to scrape the bristles off. That was as close to hogs as we got that day, thank heavens.

In some areas of the state, the counties have very few lost towns because of the nature of land development. The land of north central Iowa was the last to be cleared and settled. This area was a vast wetland of small lakes and swamps in the 1800s, so intimidating to travel that even the Indian tribes avoided entering it in certain places. After the art of tiling was perfected, the water was drained off, and farmers moved in. The railroads and towns were built simultaneously, and most of these towns have survived.

In the counties where towns were formed before the railroads came, the towns that were not connected to the lines usually shrank and died.

As I explored Winnebago County, I noted the tiny burg of Delano on the 1912 map. All traces of the town had disappeared, but a farmstead still stood on a knoll overlooking the spot the town once occupied. Rows of century-old white pines protected the farm site. As I talked with the owner, I learned that a famous Iowan had grown up on this farm. Bob Bergland, Secretary of Agriculture under Jimmy Carter, had climbed these trees as a youth. The old outhouse he had used before his father installed indoor plumbing still stood back in the grove, moss on its roof, the door fallen off. The lady who now lived in the Bergland house begged me not to photograph it. It was such a ripe photo op, but I obliged and passed up the chance. The woman also informed me that Terry Branstad, Iowa's governor from 1982 to 1999, grew up just a few miles from this lost town. (Maybe there is something in the water in this county that breeds politicians.)

In the course of photographing over two hundred towns, I often had the problem of choosing one scene to represent the town. Scenes of gravestones or dilapidated buildings, often all that is left of a town at first glance, soon become cliché, with the few exceptions of totally bizarre cemetery art or something in connection with an old building. At first I thought that the quintessential photo I chose for each town should reveal some integral historical truth about that town. I have come to realize that this is a foolish quest. If that does indeed occur, I'll go with it, but often, what is happening right now, at the moment I am there, should represent the reality of that place.

For instance, when I finally got to Lyon County, as far as I can get from Muscatine and still be in Iowa, my goal was to find the town of Granite, two miles from Minnesota and a mile and a half from South Dakota. Just the fact that this town was the farthest north and west was enough of a reason to try to find it. When I did find it, there were several topics I could choose to explore. I could do something with the historic massacre of Blood Creek, a battle between two Indian tribes not long after the first white man arrived. Or I could do something with an old-fashioned harvesting/farm machinery festival that is held there every fall. Unfortunately, this was July. As I talked with one of the few families still living in Granite, I noticed one of the girls playing in the trunk of an old Pontiac, among the horse tack stored there. Instantly, I knew that was the photo. It was just as natural and pure as it gets in Granite. I suppose a person could analyze it for telling details of the town and come up with something, but I accepted it for its immediate spontaneity.

Sometimes I learn pieces of history that are so funny they will probably never be forgotten by the local farmers, even though the town itself has physically disappeared. When I came to the crossroads where Dublin once existed in Washington County, all that remained was a gray, dilapidated Odd Fellows lodge, long abandoned. I recognized it from the "I.O.O.F." letters nailed to the top façade. A side door was open, but I didn't go in. I went to a neighboring farmer and used his phone to call the owner of the building, who still lived in Washington County. He gave me permission to go inside and photograph, and asked me to lock the door when I was finished.

He told me about a contest that the Chicago radio station WLS held during the Depression, promising a honeymoon to Dublin for some lucky couple as the prize. Of course, they didn't say it was Dublin, *Iowa*. The town cooperated with WLS and welcomed the winning couple, putting on quite a celebration for the weekend. I'm sure that story was handed down in their family, just as this story is still told in Washington County. When I took the photo in the upper room of the lodge, I wondered if that was where the honeymoon celebration dance had been held. The only activity there now is done by the pigeons who fly through the broken windows.

One question that cannot be avoided when exploring a lost town is, "Why did this town die?" Sometimes the answer is obvious, sometimes very obscure. The most common cause was whether or not a railroad came to the town. In Sac County the people who founded Grant City probably thought they were wise to choose the banks of the Raccoon River. Someone discovered that there was a pocket of clay ideal for making ceramic tiles near the town, so kilns were constructed and the town seemed destined for growth. All it needed was a railroad. When the engineers came through, buying rights-of-way for the tracks, a problem occurred for Grant City. It was built on the west side of a loop in the river, and in order for the east-west railroad to come through town, two bridges would have to be built. The railroad opted to skip Grant City and go through Auburn, a little town just south of the loop. That decision was the death of Grant City. All major buildings were literally moved south to Auburn, and Grant City was abandoned. The kilns were rebuilt on the northeast edge of Auburn, near the railroad, so the fine tiles could be shipped to places like Winnebago County. An odd elevated cable line was built from the clay quarry to Auburn, to deliver the clay in little carts aerially to the tile works. Today, all that remains is one of the huge, round kilns, sitting in a horse pasture with weeds growing from its roof. I marveled at its construction. The two doors, big enough for a horse to enter for shelter inside, had arched tops, formed from tapered firebricks, laid in a perfect keystone design. I had passed that structure dozens of times over twenty years of visiting relatives, but didn't notice the kiln until it was pointed out to me. Now it has become a landmark I seek with every trip north.

A more subtle but nasty way for a town to die is through political machinations. The town of Moneek in Winneshiek County came so close to prosperity, but missed it by treachery. Early in the formation of the state's government, each county had to choose a county seat for a courthouse. To be chosen county seat, meant a town was assured of success. When the citizens of Winneshiek County voted, the race was between Decorah and Moneek. Decorah was more centrally located, and situated on the Upper Iowa River, a stronger river for mills than the Yellow River, upon which Moneek had been built. Both towns had approximately the same number of voters; however, Moneek had the edge, because the town of Frankville, two miles to the north, would cast its votes for Moneek, and thus be closer to the county seat. A judge from the state capitol came to Decorah to officiate the election. After the polls closed on election day, the ballots, from Moneek and Frankville were being carried in a leather box by horseback to Decorah. The rider was waylaid while crossing a creek and knocked unconscious. By the time he was able to get the ballots to Decorah, the judge ruled that they were invalid. He declared Decorah the winner. Had he been bribed? Did he have friends in Decorah that he favored? Whatever the reasons, Moneek lost, and eventually disappeared. All that remains of a town that once had two mills and a dozen stores is a small schoolhouse in the middle of a cattle lot.

Balesville was a town that died before it was born. Rex Bales owned the land surrounding the intersection of two major highways, 3 and 63, north of Waterloo in Bremer County. In the 1940s and '50s he had built a gas station and restaurant there, and had begun to move in buildings along the streets he built. He owned a busy lumberyard across from the gas station, centered around a

Fig. 6.2. *Kiln for Firing Tiles,* Auburn, Sac Co. This kiln was rebuilt when the tile factory was moved here from Grant City, one mile to the north. Now it is the shelter for an old horse. (Photograph by John Deason.)

massive timber-framed barn. An old dormitory from the county home a few miles to the north was moved next to the service garage, to be used as a hotel. Plans were made to make the town of Balesville. He platted the land into blocks and lots. All he needed was for the county board of supervisors to rezone the agricultural land to business/residential. They refused. It was his opinion that the "powers that be" in several of the surrounding towns feared that Balesville would grow and soon eclipse them, and that they influenced the supervisors to vote against his proposal. Each year he would reapply, and each year he was rejected. He became very bitter, and died a sad man, whose dreams were never realized. When Highway 3 was expanded into a four-lane highway in the mid 1990s, his two-story Victorian house was razed. The old barn was taken apart board by board by a group of Amish farmers and reassembled on one of their farms. Now the intersection, once known as "Dead Man's Corner" because of the many car wrecks that occurred there, has been tamed, and most people speeding by have no idea that the few little houses rotting away on the east side of the road are all that are left of one man's great dream.

Some towns die because of the changing economy. Through a series of events, I came upon the remains of a town that physically resembles what most people imagine when they think of a "ghost town." My discovery began when I drove into the lost town of Iron Hills, in western Jackson County. Maybe a dozen people lived there. The East Iron Hills church still was functioning, its name perhaps indicative of the problems the town had as it tried to survive: a town divided. An abandoned general store still stood, beyond the point of preservation. A woman living across from the store, alone in her grandmother's house, began to tell me the stories of the town. One concerned her grandfather holding off a group of Ku Klux Klan members harassing a local family because of their religious views. We toured the overgrown cemetery, and discussed her relatives as we came upon their graves. She told me about a woman who lived a mile north of town known as the Rattlesnake Lady. I didn't really believe her tales of this woman, until a few months later when she introduced me to Zelma Sager, the Rattlesnake Lady.

In Zelma's kitchen, lining the shelves above the doorways, were blue Mason jars filled with coiled snakes, snake skins, and globs of yellowish snake fat. They were preserved in a pickling solution so she could use them when she was ready, perhaps to make a snakeskin belt or some piece of folksy jewelry. But fat was her favorite item. It could be boiled down in a double boiler until it became clear. She stored this precious, decanted oil in small bottles, and she applied it to her hands at night to cure her arthritis. She claimed she was unable to make her fingers work until she started using it. Now she was even threading needles and making fine quilts.

Fig. 6.3. *Helen Anderson* sitting on the loading dock of the long-deserted Dutton's General Store in Iron Hills, Jackson Co. (Photograph by John Deason.)

As I got to know Zelma and her husband Fay, I learned about a town they owned across the county line in Jones County. Fay's father had been the lawyer in the town of Clay Mills, tucked into a valley on a stream that emptied into the Maquoketa River a few hundred yards to the south. Twenty-seven families lived there at the turn of the century, all employed in some connection with the lime kilns that were built into the bluffs surrounding the town. Lime, before the invention of Portland cement, was a necessary building material in Chicago. It was formed when limestone was

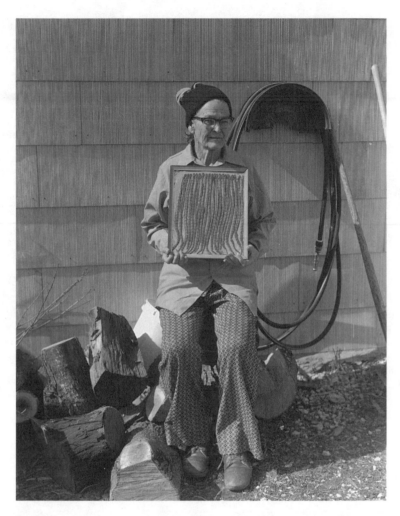

Fig. 6.4.   *Zelma Sager* of Iron Hills, Jackson Co., holding a collection of baby rattlesnakes that had crawled out of the mouth of a huge mother rattler that she had killed. (Photograph by John Deason.)

burned in huge vertical kilns, and it had to be put into barrels immediately before it began to oxidize. This industry required men to quarry chunks of limestone from the bluffs, cut firewood to fire the kilns, make barrels for the lime, and deal with the many horses used to do most of the hauling and delivering. It was a flourishing town. Then, when cement that needed no lime was invented, the lime market ended, and so did the town. As the people began to move away, Fay's father bought their houses and land. Eventually, he moved his law practice to Maquoketa, and ended up owning the whole town of Clay Mills, along with hundreds of acres of wooded bluffs and pasture land around it. A big flood took out the bridge across the Maquoketa River, and the county eventually closed the road that came over the bluff.

When I first got a view of Clay Mills, coming down through the trees into the little valley, I was astonished. No other lost town in Iowa was remotely this well-preserved. It was kind of a secret, known only by the local farmers, and by a small cult of canoeists. When people would canoe down the Maquoketa, they would often paddle up the stream to Clay Mills. Fay and Zelma didn't mind if they stayed overnight in the main house that remained there, as long as they didn't leave garbage behind. When I first saw the house, one wall was covered with the names and dates of people who had camped or had picnics there. This wall is no longer there, since her grandson remodeled the house and turned it into his family's private retreat.

Throughout Iowa there are many lost towns that died when their main source of income left. A common reason in south-central Iowa was coal. Dozens of little towns that grew up around coal mines became defunct when the coal played out. In the northeast counties, lead mines closed, with similar results. Towns that quarried limestone as a building material for Chicago as it rebuilt after the great fire died when there was no more market for stone. Many eastern Iowa towns were centered around water-driven mills, and when electric or steam-driven mills were constructed in bigger cities, or when floods took out the town's only mill, those towns often died.

What is left when a town dies? Often, it is only a cemetery. Sometimes the church connected to the cemetery will continue to serve the local farmers, even though the town has disappeared. St. Michael's Catholic Church in Holbrook, in Iowa County, is a good example of this. After years of dwindling membership, however, it is now closed.

Sometimes, a schoolhouse will remain, used as a voting center or township hall. The schoolhouse that was in Buckland, on the Yellow River in Allamakee County, was bought by an art professor from Cedar Falls and restored for use as his summer art studio. I was surprised to find him and his wife at home during a rainstorm when I was trying to find what was left of Buckland. The

Fig. 6.5.   *Interior of the Now-Defunct Saint Michael's Catholic Church,* in Holbrook, Iowa Co. (Photograph by John Deason.)

polished hardwood floors and soft light coming through the east windows created a luminous glow inside. It was perfect for his painting. As we talked, the rain quietly fell, and then stopped, and the birds began to sing. The idyllic warmth was seductive. They had salvaged this place and made it into paradise.

At the town of Buena Vista, on the banks of the Wapsipinicon River in Clinton County, I found an old barn, where a man had

Fig. 6.6. *John and Mary Lou Page* at home in the old "16 School" near Volney in Allamakee Co., along the Yellow River. They bought it years ago to use for John's summer painting studio. He is a retired art professor from the University of Northern Iowa. (Photograph by John Deason.)

once hanged himself because of a broken love affair. The barn has since been demolished, I believe. Another trace of the town were two concrete-filled steel buttresses that once supported the bridge that connected Buena Vista to Scott County. And finally, I found the lot where the old hotel once stood, now just a pasture filled with deep holes. This mystery was explained to me by a man who lived in a trailer down river from where the bridge had been.

Apparently in the 1800s, the hotel was a popular roadhouse for the federal soldiers that would travel the few roads, called dragoon trails, that existed in Iowa. Once, when these troops were delivering a gold shipment to Ft. Atkinson up north, they stayed overnight at the hotel. Sometime during that night, the gold was stolen, and since no traces of horses could be found, and the gold was quite heavy, the popular myth arose that it had to have been buried nearby. A half-century ago, a man bought the old run-down hotel as his residence, and became obsessed with finding the gold. He spent years digging holes in the ground trying to find the box of gold coins. Twenty-five years ago, he died when the building burned down. Investigators poking through the ruins found the melted mass of a glass jar and the only two gold coins he had ever found. These coins had obviously been lost by people who had visited the hotel over the years, but they were enough to fuel his rabid quest for riches.

As I have explored Iowa for lost towns, I have met the nicest people. Only rarely have I met someone who didn't want to talk about their little town's history. I was in the lost town of Bentley, in Pottawattamie County, talking with an elderly man sitting in a chair behind an ancient cash register in the office of a gas station that was straight out of the 1920s. I think he didn't care if he sold any gas or not. He was just having fun talking with people who stopped by. I asked him if anything newsworthy had ever occurred in Bentley. He thought for a moment and then spoke. "I guess it would be the time the guy who lived in that house over there across the road shot the moose." A few years earlier a misguided moose had wandered down from Minnesota and began to live in the woods around the area. Reporters came out and did stories on the wayward moose, and people in the area kind of adopted it. Well, the man to whom he referred got a deer hunting license that fall and went out and shot the moose and was going to get it stuffed. He told people he shot it in self-defense, but since the bullet had entered the moose from behind, no one really believed him. He got a bad reputation as the moose killer. Eventually he sold his house and moved out of the area. People in town still talk about that moose.

I was up in Buchanan County late one afternoon exploring the lost town of Bryantsburg. I saw two middle-aged couples digging clumps of irises out of the weeds and putting them in cardboard boxes. This was rather odd, I thought, so I stopped to talk with them about what they were doing. The one couple lived there and farmed the land around the former town. The other couple lived in Hazleton, three miles to the north. They explained to me the story

Fig. 6.7. *Iris Gatherers in Bryantsburg,* Buchanan Co., dig bulbs to plant in a Hazelton park in honor of the man who once lived in the house in the background. The two bachelor brothers who had lived there raised bees and irises. When the brother who raised bees discovered that someone had stolen his hives, he died the next day. The other brother died shortly thereafter. (Photograph by John Deason.)

of the two bachelor brothers who had lived in the little abandoned house in the overgrown apple orchard beyond where they were digging. These two brothers, who were in their eighties, each had a passion. One loved keeping bee hives and harvesting honey. The other loved growing hundreds of varieties of irises. One winter morning the honey-loving brother looked out the kitchen window and discovered that someone had driven in and stolen all of his hives. He had a heart attack and died within days. The other brother, perhaps despondent and stressed from the events, died soon afterward. The doctor said that he had given up on living.

Years had passed since that time, and now the place was overgrown. Weeds threatened to smother the irises. The two couples I was talking to had come up with the idea of saving the irises and replanting them in a special plot in the town park of Hazleton as a memorial to the two brothers.

It seems that every little lost town I have gone to has some sort of story to be found, if I just take the time to ask the right person. I feel that I am like the people rescuing the irises, but instead, I am rescuing stories and photographing places before they disappear. It is amazing how quickly things do disappear. Back in Jackson County, I learned that Zelma and Fay Sager had passed away just several years after I had met them. And the woman who introduced me to Zelma, Helen Anderson, had died in a car wreck driving back to Iron Hills from her job. I feel fortunate to have met them. Buildings I have gone back to photograph are sometimes gone. There is a leaning, wooden grain elevator just north of Tipton. I have watched it lean more and more each year. I am making a point of going there this summer and photographing it. I hope that it is still there. And I hope I can find someone who can tell me some stories about it.

7

The Soul of the Heartland: Rural Cemeteries in Iowa

Nina Metzner

Take a drive across Iowa during the summer and you might not even notice them. They are a sight so common, so much a part of the landscape, they can nearly be overlooked. The long rows of headstones flash into your peripheral vision as you motor past but never really register unless you're actively seeking them. By July and August some of them lie hidden behind the lush green corn and soybean fields, invisible, unless you know where to look. In the deep chill of an Iowa winter they are little more than snowy mounds, part of the gray and white landscape that includes fallen corn stalks poking through an icy crust, dried hay bales, and frozen flower beds. But in the fall, and again in early spring, the red and gray stones stand out against the raw black dirt and brown grasses of the Iowa prairie and a passerby might take more notice. If there are children in the car, and they've heard the old superstition, they might point with a shout, grab hold of a button and put their right thumbs in the air to ward off bad luck or to make a wish.

Down two-lane highways, blacktop roads, and gravel lanes; through small towns and back out into farmland; rural cemeteries dot the landscape with headstones that sprawl across rolling hills or sit sedately in small rows beside neat country churches. Cemeteries provide a fascinating blend of humor and history, of remembrance and regret, of legends and lies. The rural cemetery may be the last great frontier of our collective consciousness, a seldom-discovered look into our creative and complex past. Touching the lichen-covered limestone erected by our ancestors, smiling over the sentimental verses that laid mom or infant or beloved husband to rest, we are entertained by a grass-covered museum, an open-air history book that visitors are welcome to enter free of charge.

THE LAND

Finding cemeteries to visit in Iowa is as easy as looking for them. Almost every small town has one. Often just driving down the roads on the edges of a town will reveal one, or follow a road to a steeple since many early cemeteries were laid out on land donated by a local family so that the community could build a church. Acres of land set aside for a church and a cemetery were often those that had been deemed unsuitable to farm because they were too hilly or because the soil wasn't good. In many cases a cemetery began with a simple family burial on private land. If the family moved on, or if more families moved to the area, the land was donated to the county or the township in order to protect the original graves. According to records, the Dumont Cemetery in Butler County, northwest of Waterloo, was started on an acre of land donated to the town in April 1890, by Dr. T. A. Dumont so that he could bury his father, Samuel B. Dumont. The cemetery was officially incorporated in May, and over the years, more land was purchased, first from Dr. Dumont and then later from other town residents who owned property bordering the original land. It is in this way that many cemeteries have grown to their current size.

Reading through public records from any Iowa town gives a clear picture of how much a part of the community cemeteries were in the early 1900s; what an integral role they played in a town's everyday life. Often local ladies' organizations would hold bazaars, ice cream socials, or bake sales to earn money so that their cemetery could be improved in some way; adding a fence or erecting a flag pole, for example. In 1920 in Albion, located on Highway 330 just northwest of Marshalltown, children who didn't participate in the annual Memorial Day celebration were threatened with not receiving their end of the year report cards. This declaration brought out a record number of students carrying fresh flowers and marching in the parade to honor the town's fallen soldiers.

Riverside Cemetery in Shell Rock is one of the largest in Butler County and the minutes of their cemetery association meetings offer further insights into the early business of starting a cemetery. In 1907, the articles of incorporation were adopted for the Riverside Cemetery, and later that year a man named Richard Hall was employed to dig graves at fifteen cents an hour. The price the association charged for this service was three dollars during the summer and five dollars during the winter. In 1909, the decision was made to purchase more land, and the association appointed a committee to offer a thousand dollars for the land lying on the southwest side of Main Street. The minutes show that, if the owner refused to accept the offer, the committee was prepared to threaten to take legal steps to force him to sell. The property was purchased on April 15.

In subsequent years the committee voted on making numerous improvements. A tank and a well were added, as well as a vault, driveways, walks, a fence, and brick pillars and a wall at the Washington Street entrance. And finally, in September 1924, the motion was made and carried that the association would refuse to bury any dogs in the cemetery, although what series of events might have led to this vote is never mentioned.

In addition to land donated to the town or purchased outright, plots lying near churches were natural sites for cemeteries. Visitors to cemeteries that were started in the 1900s may notice that Catholic churches often have cemeteries attached, or that one section of a large cemetery is set aside only for Catholic burials. This is because the concept of consecrated ground required a site entirely separate from Protestants and non-believers. Today, an individual plot may be consecrated at the time of interment, eliminating the need for separate burial grounds.

Larger cemeteries may have a separate space set aside for infants and small children. These are often marked with simple, small stones that say "Baby" or "Sister" or may just have a first name engraved. Others may include a sentimental verse or a lament mourning the loss of an innocent. These so-called baby cemeteries were often where parents chose to bury a child if they had no other family members already interred close by. A large number of infant and child deaths during the same period of time might indicate that an epidemic swept through the town, taking its weakest members along with it.

SYMBOLS AND EPITAPHS

Once a visitor locates a cemetery in which to browse around, the most obvious starting point is to examine the symbols, names, dates, and epitaphs etched into the headstones. These words and pictures represent the public declarations as well as the private assertions as to the worth and personality of the man or woman lying beneath. Some symbols are repeated over and over and a sense of how each generation looked at the whole notion of dying becomes evident. Very early graves from the mid to late 1800s may have stern admonitions to the living about the pain of death for those people who chose not to follow a righteous path during their

Fig. 7.1. *Lasers* have made it possible to put detailed images on gravestones, like this aerial view of the family farm. (Photograph by Nina Metzner.)

lifetime. In the early 1900s, the message was somewhat softened but still carried heavy religious connotations and sentimental poetry. Today's modern headstones may seem almost irreverent in comparison. As today's society pulls away from organized religion, the epitaphs and symbols deal with more worldly issues and focus on the person's life rather than their afterlife.

The most common symbols on headstones are meant to represent the eternal life to follow or point the way to heaven. On very old graves, look for clasped hands or a single hand with an extended finger pointing upward. Other popular designs include shafts of wheat, lilies, ivy, roses, willow trees, and broken or tipped urns. It is no surprise that these symbols are used by the devout and the impious alike since the notion of passing from this world to the next prevails in our society despite a persons' religious beliefs or lack thereof. Everyone eventually has to come to grips with mortality. All of these icons in some way symbolize the hope that the deceased has taken leave of mortal life but will be reborn into an eternal bliss.

The less religious symbols used to represent death, a tree stump, for example, remind us that no one is exempt from being "cut down" in life. Almost every early cemetery has at least one headstone shaped like a tree. In Dunkard Cemetery in Butler County, located south of the town of Greene on Highway 14, a very old marker made of limestone and carved in the shape of a tree stump can be found, although what may be writing on the top is no longer clear enough to be read.

Images that surround the death of a child or an infant are the most poignant since the death is seen as untimely. A lamb, representing innocence, is frequently used on older headstones. In some cases the lamb is in relief on a standard rectangular stone, but other headstones may have a lamb lying on top of the marker or may be the marker itself. In Behrends Cemetery in Butler County there are two stones in the shape of lambs. One marks the grave of Carrie A. Linn who died on December 10, 1868 at the age of six months and five days. Her epitaph reads, "Beautiful and lovely She was given, A fair bud on earth to blossom in Heaven." Not too far from that stone is the second lamb with only "Frankie" marked on it—no last name, no dates. Doves, flowers, and shepherd's crooks are also often used on children's headstones. Behrends Cemetery is a small, abandoned burial plot just one mile east of Parkersburg on Route 14. All of the graves but one (there are only seven stones left) seem to be those of children. The other is the wife of John

Fig. 7.2.   *The Cut-off Tree,* indicating a life cut short, was a common gravestone in the late nineteenth and early twentieth century. This one, of F. L. Axthelm and Theresa W. "his wife" and their children, is in Bethel Cemetery west of Wellman. (Photograph by Robert F. Sayre.)

Ford, no first name given, who died March 17, 1874 at the age of fifty-one.

Other popular symbols on Protestant graves are: an open Bible, clasped hands or a single hand with its index finger pointing to heaven, an angel, an oak leaf, an acorn, and wheat. They are meant to represent a strong faith, a belief in a heavenly hereafter, or the harvesting of the faithful. The cross was seldom used on Protestant gravestones until well into the twentieth century. In Iowa a cross on a nineteenth-century grave almost always indicates that the person was Catholic. The passions of the Reformation were still strong, and Protestants avoided using crosses because they were associated with Catholics.

A cross on a Catholic marker very often includes a circle behind the intersection of the two pieces of the cross which symbolizes an eternity with no beginning and no end. Catholic symbols also include the Sacred Heart of Jesus surrounded by a crown of thorns, or a heart pierced by a sword which represents the Virgin Mary's heart. It is not unusual to see an image of the Blessed Virgin sitting in little niches cut into the tombstone or an angel clasping a cross to her chest with one hand and pointing the way to heaven with the other.

Jewish gravesites embrace a different set of symbols. In the Jewish cemetery on Linder Road in Iowa City, the most commonly used symbol is the Star of David symbolizing the ancient state of Israel. The majority of stones are inscribed in both Hebrew and in English but even there some universal symbols are in evidence. Fanny Eva Kimmel, who died in the 1920s at age ten, has the traditional tree trunk headstone indicating a life cut short. Smiling out from the middle of the stone is a black and white photograph of the young girl, hair in curls bedecked with ribbons. Affixing pictures of the deceased onto the headstone was especially popular at the turn of the century for people of all faiths and the images were generally posed in the stiff demeanor of the Victorian era. The practice is becoming more common again with casual snapshot images that attest to the person's likeable personality.

Another headstone in the Linder Road Cemetery decries the death of an infant daughter and is etched with a bouquet of flowers and a butterfly, perhaps indicating the ephemeral nature of life. Headstones in a Jewish cemetery might have small pebbles or coins lying on top indicating that a visitor came by to pay respects. On one grave, the traditional pebbles have been replaced with shells, a starfish, and even the small plastic figure of a scuba diver which

Fig. 7.3. *The Star of David* marks this grave of a strong-minded Jewish mother and grandmother. The two stones on the ledge were left by visitors. (Photograph by Nina Metzner.)

give passersby some indication of how the deceased chose to occupy his time when he was alive.

With today's computer technology almost any symbol can be etched into stone. In the Richland Cemetery, located on the northwest side of the city of Richland, in southeast Iowa, just off Highway 78, one headstone includes a hammer and a saw over the man's name and an upright piano over his wife's name, making their earthly talents clear to cemetery visitors. Another stone has a sun with the words "He was our ray of sunshine" on top and at the bottom the University of Iowa's Herky the Hawk, indicating that he was also a sports fan.

In addition to symbols, headstones offer another useful source of information—the epitaph. On early headstones, these were often religious sentiments, many taken directly from the Bible, or romantic poetry rich in hyperbole and flights of fancy. This final word gave the deceased's surviving family a chance to vent, to preach, to grieve, and in general to lay claim to a permanent relationship with the departed. If the death was that of a child the epitaphs were often wracked with naked emotion. The loss of a spouse or a young sibling produced pledges of eternal remembrance and loyalty. The passing of an older person who had lived a long and productive life generated sober, philosophical reflection or sometimes a warning to the living. A verse that is repeated in nearly every heartland cemetery and most probably was imported

Fig. 7.4. *Modern Tombstones* often convey more than just name and dates: in this case a sentiment, nickname, parents' names, and "G.P.'s" support of the Hawkeyes. The inscription on the base also identifies his grandparents. (Photograph by Nina Metzner.)

from eighteenth-century England is a stern reminder, not meant to comfort the bereaved:

> Remember me, as you pass by.
> As you are now, so once was I.
> As I am now, so you must be.
> Prepare for death and follow me.

Used well into the twentieth century, that bleak message was gradually replaced with more gentle and sorrowful sentiments although the specter of death remains. In Lowell Cemetery near Clarksville, between Mason City and Waterloo, Nancy Dearth, wife Of Isaac, died in 1886 and was buried beneath this verse:

> Oh our loved and only Mother
> Never shall my soul forego
> Those fond ties that death has severed
> With the ruthless grasp of woe.

The notion of the deceased going to a happier place is pervasive in epitaphs. Ruann Curry who died at twenty-two years of age in 1878 has this on her headstone:

> We mourn because she's left us,
> So early thus in life
> But he who hath bereft us,
> Hath freed from sin and strife.

And likewise, on the headstone of Sarah Knight, who died in 1892 at 62 years of age, the verse reads:

> Weep not dearest children
> I have left you for a happier home.
> And in heaven I'll bid you welcome,
> For I'm only going home
> All my trials and cares are over,
> I'm numbered with the blest
> I have reached my golden city
> Where there is eternal rest.

David Van Gundy, who died in 1873 and whose headstone proclaims him to be a Civil War veteran, leaves behind an epitaph that focuses on the irreversible nature of death:

Farewell my wife and children all,
From you a father Christ doth call.
Mourn not for me, it is in vain;
To call me to your sight again.

Some sentiments are a mixture of words meant to comfort the survivors as well as a reminder of the agony of death for non-believers. The following is on Sarah Van Gundy's stone also in the Lowell Cemetery:

Farewell children,
I am sleeping in the cold and silent grave,
But my children cease to mourn me,
though I rest beneath the sod
For the gentle angels bear me
To the bosom of our God.

Children's epitaphs often combine a pledge of how wonderful the child was and a hope that he or she has gone to a better place. The epitaph for Wesley J., Sarah and David Van Gundy's son who died at the tender age of ten expresses it well:

This lovely bud,
So young and fair
Called hence by early doom
Just came to show how sweet a flower,
In paradise would bloom.

The four-month-old daughter of May and J.H. Neal, Bernice, who died in November 1884 and who is buried in the Oakhill (sometimes called Pilltown) Cemetery near Dumont in Butler County, has an epitaph that is even more poignant:

Precious one from us has gone,
A voice we loved is stilled,
A place is vacant in our home
Which never can be filled.
God in his wisdom has recalled
The boon his love has given,
And though the body moulders here,
The soul is safe in heaven.

The idea of a vacancy existing now among the living family members of the deceased is a sentiment repeated often. In the Richland Cemetery, on a stone so old the only way to read the epitaph is to trace each letter with a finger, is the following poem:

> The vacant place the empty chair
> We see them day by day
> And Oh! They fill our hearts with care
> Since our loved one went away.

Marriages produce their own kinds of symbols and epitaphs. Husbands and wives are usually buried side by side, generally under one headstone, many of which are engraved with entwined wedding rings or hearts and the date of their marriage. A fairly recent development is to list the first names of their children under the heading "the parents of." One such couple was laid to rest in Oakhill with this epitaph:

> Our Father and Mother
> United in Life
> Undivided in Death
> Rest Father and Mother
> With hand on your breast.
> Poor tired hands they
> Needed their rest.
> How we all loved you
> But God loved you best.
> For he giveth his loved Ones rest.

Christopher and Lucina Betts who died in the late 1800s and are buried in the Lowell Cemetery share a similar sentiment with passersby as well as a promise of resurrection:

> In labor and in love allied,
> In death they here sleep side by side
> Resting in peace the aged twain
> Till Christ shall raise them up again.

Not all epitaphs are serious. Some make light of the notion of death or comment in a humorous way on the person buried beneath. In a cemetery near Cranston, a small town north of Wapello, there is a stone marked simply, "King of Bavaria." One of the town residents believed he was the exiled King of Bavaria, so the townspeople had that put on his headstone. In Springdale Friends Cemetery, about fifteen miles east of Iowa City, there is a headstone with the image of a semi-truck etched on it, and the name "Bowman" cut into the side of the trailer. Springdale is also an old abolitionist town, twice visited by John Brown, and on the east side of the cemetery is another headstone that reads "Uncle Tom / Thomas W. Jenkins / Called as a Slave / Richard Lewis / Died Dec. 9, 1902 / Aged 83 Years." What a story that suggests.

HISTORY LESSONS

Cemeteries offer a fascinating glimpse into the past for visitors who take the time to consider the family ties and the dates displayed in stone. The last names alone often give a clue as to the nationality of the earliest settlers in the area. The role call also attests to the Iowa prairie's melting-pot appeal to people from all over Europe. In Richland Cemetery the names range from Watson, Adams, Hadley, and Breen; to Nordyke, Yoder, McPherson, and Shelangoski. In Lowell Cemetery, Berend M. Ooster who died in 1918 at age twenty-three has an epitaph written in his native German, *"Christus ist mein Leben, Sterben ist mein Gewinn."* (Christ is my life, Death is my Gain) No doubt his family took some comfort in using the old language to eulogize Berend so far from their own country. Likewise, the spelling of the names in a small cemetery located on County Road 38 just north of Williams Prairie, in Johnson County attests to the gradual Americanization of the Czech immigrants who settled in that area. The family names remain the same, but the spelling becomes more Anglo-American.

Still richer stories lie just a little deeper. For example, surrounding the gravestones of infants and children is a mini-history lesson of childbirth and child rearing in the mid to late 1800s. In Halls Grove Cemetery in Butler County, also known as Hesalroad or De Boises Woods Cemetery, there are two family plots, one that lists the deaths of the children of William and M. Hesalroad and the other the deaths of the children of J. A. and S. A. Armstrong. Reconstructing the time lines of these deaths presents a heartbreaking picture of two families who buried 5 and 8 children respectively.

The Hesalroads had five children: Henry Wilson, Margaret Ann, Anna Louisa, Minnie Sophia, and Mary Catherine. Margaret Ann was just three months old when she died in September 1861 and was followed in death just two months later in November by her brother Henry who was two years three months and eight days old according to the cemetery marker. Childless for five years after those two heartbreaking losses, Mrs. Hesalroad gave birth to Anna Louisa on January 14, 1867. Anna lived just fifteen days, dying on January 29. After three more years in a household without children, Mrs. Hesalroad gave birth to Minnie Sophia in December 1870. Minnie managed to hang onto life until January 1872 which made her about the age her older brother was when he died. It is very likely that Mrs. Hesalroad was already pregnant with her last daughter by this time, Mary Catherine who was born July 2, 1872 and died January 2, 1873 at the age of six months. The five small stones beneath a larger stone which lists the children's names, birth dates and dates of death, offer no clue about what might have happened to Mr. and Mrs. Hesalroad; they are not buried near their children.

The Armstrong family's children didn't fare any better. Between 1858 and 1868 they buried eight children. Five of them died in 1867. One in January, three in March, and one in April leading to the conjecture that there was an epidemic, perhaps smallpox or cholera, since one of the children, Mary J. had already turned eighteen at the time of her death.

Of course, the history offered up by a cemetery is incomplete. Did the Armstrong's have other children who lived? What happened to the parents of these unfortunate children? It is not unusual to find a series of infant graves with the children's mother dying in childbirth along with the last child, but that isn't the case here.

There are other stories to be told to passersby who pay attention. Oakhill Cemetery is divided down the center by a road. A flag pole stands on the south end of the cemetery with a stone beneath it that reads: "Dedicated to the men and women of the community of Bristow who served their country in all wars." On the north side of the cemetery is a gravestone for Douglas H. Kemp who was born July 7, 1922. The stone gives his nickname, "Doug," and announces that he enlisted November 2, 1942 and was an Instructor in the U.S. Army Air Corps. He crashed at Goodfellow Field, San Angelo, Texas during World War II and died May 3, 1945. But the reset of the story is told with the addition of his wife's marker, Kathryn Rose. She was two years younger, having been born March 29, 1924. She married Doug on November 1, 1942, the day before he enlisted. During their brief two-and-a-half year marriage they managed to spend enough time together to have a daughter, Janelle Kay. Kathryn Rose only lived to be forty-nine. Janelle's fate is unknown since she is not buried with her parents. Eventually, her own story may be spelled out on a gravestone in some other cemetery.

The Rochester Cemetery, just north of I-80 in Cedar County, is now noted as an outstanding example of a prairie-savanna. The broad limbs of ancient oaks spread out over prairie grasses and flowers. But according to old local legend it is the site of the grave of the mother of Sarah Bernhardt. She was born, legend has it, in Rochester, Iowa, and named Sarah King. Her mother died when she was five, and she ran away to join a troupe of traveling actors in Muscatine, later going to a French convent in St. Paul, Minnesota, before becoming famous in Paris. Then in 1905 a heavily veiled woman carrying a long ribbon-bound box got off a train at West Branch, hired a rig and driver from a local stable and was driven to the Rochester Cemetery. After her curious driver returned his passenger to the station, he drove back to the cemetery to find roses scattered on the grave of Mrs. King. By some accounts, Madame Bernhardt had appeared at an Iowa City theatre the previous night, although the historians of the Federal Writers Project concluded in the 1930s that "there is no record of such an appearance."[1]

MILITARY SERVICE

Lynnwood Cemetery on the west side of Clarksville, a city northwest of Waverly, dates back to the late 1800s. One of the earliest graves belongs to Daniel Tichenor, son of A.F.& E. who died April 3, 1878 at the age of fifteen years six months and seven days. But it's equally as noteable for the number of veterans buried there. From John McClain who served in the War of 1812 and Japeth Curtis who served in the Black Hawk War; to the four Viet Nam veterans, Ernest Lee Ball, Verlan Davis, Roger Hites, and Vernon F. Nordman; soldiers from every major war are represented including the Civil War, the Spanish American War, the Mexican Border Service, World War I, World War II, and the Korean War.

Most grave markers for men and women who served their country are marked with a simple block-style cross or a Star of David if the soldier was Jewish, the war in which they served, and their rank at the time of their death. In addition, many of them have small markers placed into the ground beside them with an

Fig. 7.5. *Markers on Veterans' Graves* generally name the war in which they served. Some, like this, also allude to the deceased's rank. "Sarge" must have been in her forties during World War II. (Photograph by Nina Metzner.)

olive wreath and an eagle forged out of iron. Of course, these graves are even more apparent around Memorial Day when small American flags mark their sites.

GHOST STORIES

Iowa cemeteries also have their ghosts. Whistling past a cemetery on the dark edge of town on a cool fall evening is part of every small town Iowa child's memory.

Nye Cemetery, which is located near the Old Mill in Wild Cat Den State Park just off Route 22, west of Montpelier, has the graves of many children who died in a smallpox epidemic in the early 1900s. At dusk, if you stand quietly, you can hear the children talking and playing together. In Malby Cemetery near Wapello there is a mass grave with the victims of a cholera epidemic buried together. At certain times, although local residents disagree on when exactly that is, you can hear families calling to each other trying to reunite parents with lost children. An old cemetery located on River Drive and Rockingham road in Davenport also has a mass grave that is nothing more than a grass-covered mound today. The fever that took the lives of those buried there still lingers in the moans and death rattles visitors can sometimes hear emanating from the grave just after sunset.

Although angels are generally thought to be benevolent and protecting, heavenly guides sent to lead lost souls to their eternal rest, they are also the stuff of eerie legends. This is possibly because of the imposing figures carved larger than life and placed strategically around cemeteries. In the Greenwood Cemetery in Muscatine, there is an angel near the Musser family mausoleum which turns blue in the light of a full moon. No supernatural characteristics are credited to her, but she is referred to as the Blue Angel. In Oakland Cemetery in Iowa City, there is a Black Angel that stands overlooking the Feldevert family plot. It was commissioned by Teresa Feldevert in the early 1900s to honor her husband and son who are buried there. The nine-foot angel has become a somewhat sinister figure attached to a fairly terrifying legend. Like all good legends, this one is slippery on specific details, but according to most versions, the statue was shipped to this area from overseas and began her journey as a white statue. By the time it arrived here it had inexplicably turned completely black. On some nights, the angel's face is turned skyward toward heaven, but some nights her head is bowed toward earth as though with deep sorrow. Anyone who touches the statue who is not a virgin, will die. Local high school students have added the notion that to kiss the angel at midnight will allow you to bring great disasters on your enemy provided you yourself are pure of heart. It is also believed that anyone who attempts to deface the angel will come down with an incurable disease or fatal illness. Rumor has it the black angel turns a shade blacker every Halloween.

Southeast of Ottumwa lies Mars Hill Cemetery which has purportedly been the site of numerous ghostly apparitions. Follow Route 63 south and then left onto Copperland Road. Turn right on 100th Avenue and watch for the cemetery entrance on the left side. Mars Hill Church was built around 1850 and services are occasionally still held there today. The story goes that years ago when the church was somewhat newer, a young woman had her baby baptized and then inexplicably walked to the nearby bridge that leads to the cemetery and threw the baby into the water, drowning him. Some nights you can hear a woman scream as though in terror or agony as you pass across the bridge. Visitors who take pictures in the cemetery at night often have their film "ruined" as fog-like images, ghostly apparitions, appear to manifest themselves around the headstones.

Most visitors to an Iowa cemetery will probably hear nothing more than the wind in the trees as it whips across the open fields and flat meadows. But taking along a flashlight, just in case, might not be a bad idea.

FAMILY PLOTS

A hallmark in every cemetery is the family plot marked with a headstone surrounded by smaller stones. The main stone is usually engraved with the family's last name as the small stones list the names or the relationships of each person buried there: Mother, Father, Sister, Brother; or Evelyn, John, Wayne, and Elizabeth, for example. Wealthy families sometimes surrounded the plot with a low cement wall or an ornate wrought iron fence. Sometimes the main stone is an imposing tower, attesting to the family's importance in the community.

Another history lesson is written in the way the man's wife is referred to at her final resting place in the family plot. Early markers often don't give the woman's first name but merely refer to the deceased as "Wife" or "Mother." Some go one step farther, identifying the husband on his wife's grave as though the woman had no identity of her own. In Behrends Cemetery one headstone explains that the deceased buried beneath is Ford, wife of John Ford who died March 17, 1874 at 51 years of age. In Lowell Cemetery John Armstrong is buried alongside his wife, Mrs. John. He died in 1873 but there are no dates next to his wife's name. Many times only the woman's first initial was used to identify her rather than her name. It is only well into the twentieth century that women were routinely identified with their own first and last names.

Some cemeteries are almost completely devoted to one family. Van Metre Cemetery in Benton County is a very old cemetery from the mid-1800s where the Van Metre family is buried. There is a very large headstone, perhaps ten or twelve feet tall, that lists John

E. and Josina who appear to be the parents, and their four children, Mary Josina, George, Henry C. and Hubert who were all under two years of age at the time of their deaths. The only graves other than those of the Van Metre family seem to be those of children: two Wilson infants who died in 1900 and 1901; Joe Stocker who was fourteen years old at his death in 1879; Frankie and Duggie Collins, who died at ages three and one respectively in September 1864; and Josephine Webster, who died a young wife at age 19.

During the 1990s, there were even signs of the approaching millennium hidden in the blocks of stone on family plots. It was long customary for the surviving spouse to have his or her name and birth date engraved on the headstone at the time of the other spouse's death before the stone was set. In the past, the death year was left at 19__ to be filled in at the time of the spouse's own passing. As the year 2000 neared, however, cemetery monuments began listing only the name and birth date, leaving the date of death empty in case the surviving partner lived into the next century.

DISAPPEARING CEMETERIES

Some cemeteries are most notable for having disappeared. Many early graves were marked with wooden markers which have deteriorated over time leaving some grave sites and cemeteries nothing more than a memory.

According to the Butler County Courthouse Records, between 1877 and 1896 at least twenty-two people from the Butler County Poor Farm located in Jackson Township were buried next to the housing built for the poor. Later records are missing so it's difficult to determine the exact number of people buried in the now-vanished cemetery. Because this cemetery was one which by necessity used inexpensive wooden markers to mark the graves, all that remains are the slight indentations showing the grave spots, a few wild plum trees, and some scattered wildflowers to mark the graves of these forgotten souls.

Unfortunately, cemeteries are falling into neglect for other reasons. The weather, time, and vandals are slowly destroying these valuable monuments to our past. Many limestone and sandstone markers are already unreadable or lie broken in half. At Rochester Cemetery stones are sometimes hidden in the tall prairie grass and broken by mowing machines. The local historical society is repairing them, however. In the Nye Cemetery, several of the oldest headstones have been laid flat and encased in cement to preserve

Fig. 7.6.   *Many Rural Cemeteries* in Iowa are immaculately maintained, thanks, partially, to a state law that permits townships to assess a tax for their support. (Photograph by Robert F. Sayre.)

them. Even so, the inscriptions on most of them are nearly impossible to read. The imposing angels sculpted of marble are softening around the edges and will look like little more than pillars of salt in a few more generations. Fortunately, an Iowa law called the Cemetery and Park Tax was passed in 1981 which allows townships to impose an extra tax to improve and maintain cemeteries. As more townships avail themselves of this opportunity, the condition of rural cemeteries may improve.

But as death and dying more and more become a big business and are less often left in the hands of loving family members, the face of cemeteries will continue to change. Some cemeteries have already begun imposing rigid rules regarding the size of the headstones that are acceptable, the proper placement of wreaths and other memorials at gravesites, and the dates by which old decorations must be removed. Some have even forbidden the planting of real flowers because it makes the cemetery more difficult to mow. Cremation, which was once considered taboo in many religions as an impediment to resurrection, is now encouraged due to space limitations in existing plots. Also, scattering a loved one's ashes in a meadow or over a favorite river appeals to modern society's current sensibilities more than being buried under identical rows of ground-level plaques.

TAKE ANY EXIT

Visitors passing through the state who take the time to visit these little pockets of peace and quiet while they are still intact will discover a whole new way of looking at this part of our culture. Most of us only visit our friends' and relatives' graves and never stop to consider the lives and stories of those folks lying beside them. Armed with just a little information, visitors can read the past in the symbols, epitaphs, dates, names, and headstones themselves in any cemetery they visit. Take along some sheets of paper and a soft lead pencil to produce rubbings to bring out those nearly unreadable names and epitaphs. Take a camera to capture the beautiful old monuments and sculptures before they crumble and disappear. But mostly, take along some imagination and let the gravestones tell you a story of lives lived and loved ones lost and of the surprisingly varied manifestations of the human spirit and creativity of our Iowa ancestors.

Note: A good starting place for cemeteries to visit in your own area is to check a county's website. Many counties list the cemeteries and include where they are located and the names of the people who are buried there. These sites, however, will not always provide a complete guide since it often falls to volunteers to maintain and update them.

NOTE

1. Federal Writers' Project, *Iowa: A Guide to the Hawkeye State* (The Viking Press: New York, 1938; reprinted by Iowa State University Press: Ames, 1986), p. 486.

❧ 8 ☙

"Going to Church"

Patricia Eckhardt

Everywhere you go in Iowa you see churches. Next to farmsteads and small towns, they are the most common landscape feature and one that clearly symbolizes the traditions and piety of the people. Yet they are also one of the most varied, for they come in all sizes, ages, denominations, and styles. Schools, libraries, and courthouses are, in comparison, more uniform and certainly less numerous. A small town of three thousand people will have no courthouse, unless it is a county seat, and probably will have only one school and one library. But it will likely have at least four churches.

It will have, we might expect, a large redbrick Catholic church, in a German Gothic style, with twin front towers. Across town will be an imposing, smooth-stone Methodist or Baptist church with a classical portico and a dome, built in the 1920s. Down the street will be an older, white, wooden or redbrick Congregationalist or Presbyterian church, with an austere but handsome steeple that recalls the small-town churches of New England. And in a newer part of town it will have a modern A-frame in blonde brick with a big steel cross beside it that was built by the Lutherans in the 1960s. And it will probably have more – a brand new pole-barn structure on the outskirts of town, built for a new evangelical sect; a simple Quaker meeting house; and possibly a

143

plain-fronted African Methodist Episcopal church or a Jewish syn-
agogue.

No doubt a similar conglomeration of buildings and congregations could be found in many other states. But we emphasize the
variety in Iowa because of the prejudice that Iowans are more uniform than Americans elsewhere—as supposedly all alike as their
land is supposedly all flat. Not so. "Eleven o'clock on Sunday
morning is the most segregated time in America," it has been ob-
served, and the same could be said of Iowa. Its seemingly uniform
rural culture is divided into what Dorothy Schwieder calls "rural
ethnic neighborhoods." For these groups and neighborhoods,
whether in town or country, the church is usually the gravitational
force that holds everyone together. It was in the beginning of Iowa,
is now, and probably ever shall be.

And so Iowa churches and church architecture are a fascinating, multicolored window into the diversity of Iowans and Iowa
culture. They reflect the traditions, theologically, iconographically,
and socially, of their different memberships. The differences in the
outside appearances of the churches reflect the internal differences
as well. These choices are not absolute, but Roman Catholics,
Lutherans, and some other Protestant denominations prefer the
"basilica" plan, a rectangular space with a central aisle. Presbyte-
rians, Congregationalists, and Methodists often prefer the "auditorium" plan with semicircular seating. Episcopalians prefer a series of differentiated spaces through which one progresses
physically and spiritually—from entrance to narthex to nave to
chancel. In these interior plans, each congregation generally tries
to recreate the plans of the British or European churches they de-
rive from, although there has been a move, too, to adopt current
American architectural styles.

This article focuses mainly on the churches of the countryside
and small towns, but many magnificent churches are to be found
in Iowa's major towns and cities as well. On High Street in Des
Moines, for example, one can find a Roman Catholic cathedral in
the Romanesque Revival style, a major Lutheran church in Gothic
design, and the domed Beaux-arts style First Methodist Church designed by Proudfoot and Bird at the intersection of High and Pleasant streets. The city of Dubuque possesses a stunning collection of
German-American Gothic churches with ornate towers. Most notable of all is Sacred Heart Church designed by Fridoline Heer in
1881. At 1340 Third Ave., S.E. in Cedar Rapids is St. Paul's United
Methodist Church with its great sanctuary in the form of a

banked, semicircular auditorium. It was originally designed by Louis Sullivan, although his original plans were much changed by subsequent architects. It joins two traditions: the so-called Akron plan, a late-nineteenth-century church plan that places Sunday school classrooms next to the sanctuary, and the modern American architectural "Prairie" style, which grew out of the English Arts and Crafts Movement. There is a story to every church.

The following three sections of this essay employ three different methods for exploring the meanings in Iowa's churches. The first method is based on a concept used in the study of all material culture, "period style," the concept that every human production contains elements which identify its time and place of manufacture. Churches built from 1850 to 1880 have a similar appearance because their builders, Iowa's early settlers, shared the same difficult frontier conditions. They are expressions of religion in its most simple form, or so it appears, but they are individual as well and often reveal their builder's ethnic identity and religious traditions within their simple forms. Churches built later generally have more-ornate styles because of their members' increasing wealth and changing taste.

A second method is to pick out churches that exhibit extraordinary architecture and explore what makes them special. Some congregations felt that only the best in architecture was appropriate to house their congregation and thus sought out an architect to create a unique and special building. To them the church was an expression of both their piety and their worldly success. But even these churches express cultural traditions and ethnic influences.

The third method studies a group of churches within the context of a specific architectural and cultural history. "A Pilgrimage Road" explores German Gothic architecture transplanted to America by a group of German Catholic settlers. These churches are part of the long tradition of European ecclesiastical architecture, but they are American as well. Gothic styles—and there are several versions developed in different cultures—continue as a living architectural language to be continually reused.

Before we get started, a few words of advice. A church's main reason for being is to house the sacred rituals of its congregation. No matter how beautiful a church's exterior, it is only half of the story. Churches shelter a community of people gathered for corporate worship. Go inside a church if at all possible. Some churches are much more decorated or developed as works of art inside than the exterior might suggest. Be grateful when a church is open to the public, but many churches will be locked. Please respect this. Unfortunately, there is a market for stolen religious artifacts. Most churches have to be locked or have a caretaker nearby to protect their paintings, sculptures and ritual articles from theft and their interiors from vandalism.

"LITTLE WHITE CHURCHES"

Iowa's simple one-room churches are similar to one-room schools in many respects. Both are small, with only one room and a small entryway. Both are part of our vision of a bucolic past. In pioneer times church services were often held in the schoolhouse. But the church provided more than just a cultural presence. It gave a sense of moral and spiritual continuity with people's past and perhaps very distant ancestors. In many early communities, the church was also a strong governing force. Today most of the old schoolhouses are gone, but many churches survive, even though frequently in poor repair or abandoned. They are to be treasured.

The "Little White Churches" bring to mind the hardships of those who came to America and on to Iowa where they tried to establish a home and a semblance of culture. I am surprised by the nostalgia these churches evoke in me. We all have ideas about our ancestors being settlers. My own Ohio and Virginia ancestors came to America early, and I do not usually think of them as immigrants settling in new territories, but these churches remind me that, in fact, they did.

The simplicity of these churches is another of their charms. Whatever their denomination, they give us a momentary sense of a simpler, more rugged, less complicated existence. They are symmetrical and balanced, with only a small tower or spire and sometimes an apse or a sacristy of some kind to suggest their religious purposes. Their construction is also basic, though individual. I hope you will enjoy these examples and find more. These small churches are endangered.

Norwegian Evangelical Lutheran Church, between McGregor and Guttenberg
This seems to be the perfect "Little White Church." It is located on one of the most picturesque portions of the Great River Road in Iowa, between McGregor and Guttenberg on County Road X56. You encounter it only a few miles out of McGregor, set in the eroded hills and valleys of "little Switzerland," as this part of Iowa

is called. There are two Lutheran churches near each other. You want the smaller one on the west side of the road a little to the south. This very small church, built in 1861, has a small square tower with a spire. Simple and plain, it seems tiny and struggling, as were its Norwegian and Swedish founders as they tried to farm this difficult but beautiful land. A cemetery is close behind the church. The plainness, with a suggestion of Scandinavian tradition, is quite Lutheran. The church is closed now and used only for an occasional anniversary, family reunion, or burial in the cemetery. The interior is simple and rustic, with a hand carved altar and pews (Fig. 8.1). It might hold thirty people. The caretaker told me that

Fig. 8.1. *This interior of the Norwegian Evangelical Lutheran Church* in rural McGregor illustrates the simplicity of a "Little White Church." The altar and appointments were all handmade by early members. The reproduction of "Christ Praying in the Garden of Gethsemane" over the altar is familiar to all Lutherans. (Photograph by Patricia Eckhardt.)

Fig. 8.2. *New Sharon Church* at Smithtown stands on a hill and surveys the rolling agricultural land of eastern Iowa. It displays the plain symmetrical one-room shape of the "Little White Church." (Photograph by Patricia Eckhardt.)

his grandfather made the small baptismal font, a bowl standing on legs. He said that he was baptized there himself. He expects to take his place in the cemetery with his ancestors when the time comes.

New Sharon Church and Cemetery, Smithtown
Smithtown never actually became a town, but the church and cemetery and a farmhouse stand sentinel to the efforts of its planners (Fig. 8.2). Local inhabitants know Smithtown, located near the corner of 125 St. and 120 Avenue northwest of Lost Nation, but it is not on any map of the county or the state. To reach the church you go west from Lost Nation on Highway 136, then turn right on the second paved road going north (not on the map). After

about one mile, you can see the church on your right on a hill. It was built in 1865 and was originally called New Sharon Church. This church is fairly sizable with four tall shuttered windows along each side of the nave. The entrance is through a square tower with a square second stage on which rests a small spire. From this spot you can see for miles in every direction. Look in the cemetery to discern the Anglo-Saxon surnames of this settlement.

Little Brown Church in the Vale, Nashua
Though brown, this is the most famous "Little White Church" in Iowa, immortalized in the hymn, "The Church in the Wildwood" (Fig. 8.3). Its fame also reveals the sentimental attachment people

Fig. 8.3. *The Little Brown Church* in Nashua is the church associated with the hymn "The Church in the Wildwood." It has always been painted brown and continues to be nestled in the original "wildwood." (Photograph by Patricia Eckhardt.)

have to these churches. Standing on the eastern edge of Nashua, which is at the junction of Highways 218 and 346 about halfway between Cedar Falls and Mason City, its simple form resembles the Norwegian Lutheran Church south of McGregor, but rather than the quiet sense of abandonment one feels there, one sees almost constant activity here. For the Little Brown Church is a popular wedding chapel, and men and women in wedding clothes seem to be continually getting in and out of cars and limousines. The pastor lives across the street, and facilities for dinners and other wedding related services are nearby.

There is a romantic story about the church and its association with the poem and song "The Church in the Wildwood." William Pitts, a young music teacher, was traveling by stagecoach from Wisconsin to Iowa to visit his future wife in about 1856. He had some time to walk around in Nashua and came to a "wildwood," or woods still in a natural state. He envisioned a church there, and that vision inspired a poem which he put to music and put aside. In the meantime, over the next several years, a church actually was slowly built there.

In 1862 Pitts and his wife moved to Fredericksburg to be near her elderly parents. Coming to Nashua, he was amazed to see a church in the exact location where he had envisioned one, and it was painted brown. He went home and found the song and taught it to his music class who sang it for the dedication of the church in 1864.

St Mary's, Newport

St. Mary's is a Catholic version of the "Little White Church." You can reach it on County Road F8W, north of Iowa City in Johnson County. Most Roman Catholic churches in Iowa are stone or brick, even some of the many country churches. St. Mary's is wood, but it still exhibits some distinctive Catholic characteristics. There is more elaboration of interior spaces than one usually finds in the simple one-room church of this type. The extensions on each side at the rear make room for the sacristy and office/entrance that flank the apse, making it T-shaped in plan. And there is a balcony for the organ at the rear of the sanctuary over the entry. The pedimented window cornices are a reflection of the Italianate style, a change from the usual Gothic window or simple rectangular window types. The cemetery, beside the church, is filled with interesting headstones. This church is a local landmark and the focus of preservation efforts today.

ARCHITECTURAL GEMS

After a few years of success and security, even small congregations could really "strut their stuff" in constructing a church. These showpieces were usually the second or third church built by their congregations, and great efforts were made to build the most beautiful, or traditional, or exceptional, or unique church the congregation could afford whatever its size. Some employed styles from their European or British homelands, others sought the most modern, up-to-date style possible. They hired the best architects they could and saw that every detail was good and right. They Praised God through architecture.

This does not mean that these churches turn their back on tradition and ethnic heritage. Catholic conservatism, Episcopalian anglophilia, and Lutheran modernism can still be discerned, but mixed with those cultural influences is an awareness of contemporary American architectural styles and trends. The architects certainly added their own personal style, but they did so to help the congregation realize its vision for the church. These churches are as rich in cultural messages and meaning as are more specifically traditional or ethnic types of architecture.

Saints Peter and Paul, Rural Solon—Czech Heritage
This rural church exhibits all of the style of a city church (Fig. 8.4). You can find it northeast of Solon. As you go north from Solon on Highway 1, turn east on NE 120th St. and left on Taft Road. You can see it as you approach. The European Catholic heritage of Saints Peter and Paul is evident in the twin spires, but they exhibit a peculiar American tendency to take a tradition and give it a new twist. The two towers are of different heights. The only time this happened in Europe was when there was not enough money to complete a church, and one tower was left unfinished. At Chartres Cathedral, outside Paris, for example, fires and other disasters resulted in the rebuilding of several parts over the centuries, always in the then-current style. When the north spire was finally completed in 1513, the current late Gothic style was used instead of replicating the early Gothic south tower built in 1145. Perhaps Chartres, which was much admired in late-nineteenth-century America by medievalizing Victorians like Henry Adams and traveling architects as well, inspired a sort of American non-essential imitation. Façade towers of different heights became very popular for Catholic churches in Iowa from 1900 to 1930. There are at

Fig. 8.4.   *The altar in Saints Peter and Paul* in rural Solon illustrates the so-called Roman style. Based on ancient Roman architecture, it is completely different from the more usual Gothic altar, being composed of domes, rounded arches and columns, and painted to simulate marble. The Roman arch is used consistently throughout the church, as seen here in the barrel-vaulted ceiling of the apse. (Photograph by Patricia Eckhardt.)

least 29 of them. Only one earlier church of note has this feature, Fridoline Heer's Sacred Heart in Dubuque (1881).

Saints Peter and Paul exhibits all of the trends in Catholic church construction popular in 1916. The congregation was Czechoslovakian, but the architecture is American Catholic. Mixed in with the uneven tower feature is the preference for the so-called "Roman" style, which employs round arches for windows and doors and in the interior framing. The Roman Style is a new synthesis employing the round arch as a design motif. If it has a precedent, it would probably be found in the *Rundbungenstil* or round arched style from nineteenth-century Germany. The Roman Style is an American Catholic style. I have never found it used for churches of other denominations although they might use Richardsonian Romanesque or Romanesque Revival styles.

The beautiful interior of Saints Peter and Paul illustrates further the use of the "Roman" style. The whole interior is designed with arches from the barrel-vaulted ceiling to the shape of all openings. The altar, in keeping with the style of the building is composed of arches and domes on columns rather than the usual pointed Gothic composition. Even the painted surfaces of the altars, faux marble on wood, carry out the Roman theme. The windows reveal the ethnic heritage of these Catholics, as do the Czech names on the gravestones across the road. Another clue to the Czech connection is in the inscription over the door that says in Czech, "Saints Peter and Paul Pray for Us."

The subjects of the windows illustrate the international and historic scope of the Catholic Church while focusing as a minor reference on the local Czech congregation and its agricultural environment. The standing saints, done in beautiful stained glass, are St. Wencelas, a favorite of the Czechs; St. Nicholas of Flue (Switzerland); St. Patrick; St. Jerome; St. Teresa of Avila; St. Anthony; and St. John the Baptist. In addition, there are St. Barbara, patron saint of lightning, and St. Swithum, patron saint of drought. A roundel of St. Cecelia, patron saint of music, is located in the balcony where the organ and choir are located. (Call Jean Litts at 319-644-2394 to see the interior.)

Trinity Presbyterian Church, Indianola – English Arts and Crafts
I couldn't help but laugh out loud when I first saw Trinity Presbyterian Church. Its humor, cleverly clothed in serious historic armor, made it a joy to contemplate. Trinity Church presents itself as a conservative square block of red brick, but look a little longer and this all falls apart as the subtle asymmetrical treatment becomes apparent. The use of three kinds of brick to indicate different parts of the structure is very in keeping with the Arts-and-Crafts aesthetic in an individualistic way. Paving brick forms the base with a red brick for the main body of the church and details picked out with yellow brick. Using yellow brick to suggest "quoins" around the windows and at the corners is a Beaux-Arts detail. Quoins are usually larger stones that are placed at corners and openings to take the added stresses of the roof and walls, but here, they are purely decorative. The yellow brick almost makes them look like candy corn set in the

gingerbread house of the witch in the story of Hansel and Gretel. The now lost quirky steeple, hit by lighting two times, would have added to this impression when it was first built.

Three sides are identical in design and joined by the two entrance blocks at the corners, one with a tower. The windows are very interesting in their historical references, but appear a strange mixture. Almost bizarre details become apparent. Most bizarre are the false arrow slits on either side of the rose windows. Arrow slits were for the protection of medieval castles. Was Trinity Presbyterian under attack? By the Lutherans perhaps? These obvious medievalisms relate to the Arts and Crafts Movement's championing of the Middle Ages as a time before mass production, when craftsmanship was more honored.

The church, for all of its mixture of details, is a very well designed and planned building worthy of an important architect. The Des Moines architect W. T. Proudfoot, of Proudfoot and Bird, designed it in 1901, and Indianola was Proudfoot's hometown. Proudfoot and Bird was the preeminent architectural firm in Iowa around 1900. They were academically trained architects who employed the Beaux-Arts style for most of their university buildings and courthouses. They only designed six churches in their large oeuvre of over six hundred buildings, and no two are alike.

We can see the religious-ethnic preferences of the architects in the British styles they employed for their churches. The Methodist, Presbyterian, or Episcopalian congregations who hired them knew that they would design a church which was modern, but which fulfilled each congregation's cultural expectations. Proudfoot was well aware of their preferences as a Methodist born of Scottish parents.

The interior of Trinity Presbyterian is a masterpiece of planning. Each entrance opens into a vestibule where coats can be hung and each contains stairs to the galleries, which are on three sides. These vestibules enter into the two aisles, which radiate from the centrally placed altar and pulpit. The church is an example of the auditorium plan with a semicircular arrangement of pews. The windows, which on the exterior seem so capricious, exhibit their function on the interior. The "rose" windows light the galleries and the row of arched windows light the main floor. The windows employ the preferred green, gold, and mauve colors and employ the stylized leaves and flowers favored in Arts and Crafts designs.

There is a modern addition in the rear, which does not obstruct the public view of this historic church, but through which you might gain entry.

St. Joseph's, Elkader—by a Master Stonecutter
The wonderfully scenic county seat town of Elkader lies in the center of the great hills of northeast Iowa, and from a distance, the rusticated stone church at the edge of town with the bluff behind it makes a very traditional, almost conventional picture. But as you move closer, you begin to notice unusual details (Fig. 8.5). You notice the wonderful, textured stone and the interesting windows with a definite plan in their fenestration. Lower windows have more simple designs for their mullion and lancet divisions than do those in the tower. Windows higher on the tower are

Fig. 8.5. *St. Joseph's Catholic Church* in Elkader exhibits the architect Guido Beck's skill in the use of stone. The delicacy of the tracery of the windows contrasts with the rough stone surfaces of the building. The elaborate, lace-like window over the entrance leads the eye up to the carved Sacred Lamb of God above it in the pediment. (Photograph by Patricia Eckhardt.)

more complicated than those located below. The whole plan is to direct the eye to the entrance and to the tower above. Over the door the tympanum (triangular transom) windows have very elaborate mullions making a distinctive pattern. The mullions seem almost vine-like, and the shapes of the lights are like flowers or leaves. They point up to the Sacred Lamb of God sculpted within the gable above.

But there is more to be discovered after observing the complex and artful windows. The architect has used color as well as form and texture in his composition. As you look at the windows of the nave you realize that the vousoirs or wedge-shaped stones around the tops of the arched parts of the windows and entrance are a different color than the stone on the rest of the church. The effect is subtle, but it is definitely there. Around the door mustard-colored stone is carved in a smooth curve as it spreads out from the tympanum window to the front plane of the entrance. This leads your eye upward to the carved lamb high above. One more elaboration awaits the careful observer: the straightness of the corners and edges on the rough masonry walls has been subtly enhanced by the pecking out of a shallow vertical groove in from the corners about one inch.

Who could be responsible for such a masterful handling of the stone? The answer can be found in the person of Guido Beck, a German émigré architect. Beck, a German university professor's son, was trained in Germany in architecture and stonemasonry before immigrating to America. He made his home in Dubuque and designed many important churches in Iowa and surrounding states. Stone was his favorite material, and his churches are usually in rough textured stone as at St. Joseph's.

When Beck first came to America he worked at the National Arsenal in Rock Island, Illinois as a stonecutter. There he must have met Mr. Green, owner of the Stone City Quarry who provided much of the stone for the arsenal. Beck used Stone City stone here in Elkader and for many other projects. He designed the Catholic Church in Stone City as well.

St. Paul's Episcopal Church, Harlan – The "Anything But Vernacular" Wooden Church

Harlan is the county seat of Shelby County in west-central Iowa. You can get there from Interstate 80 by driving north on Highway 59. Located in a residential neighborhood, St. Paul's Episcopal Church at first appears as a large house, and like a house it is painted in gold and rust colors, but that notion is soon dispelled as you contemplate the unusual design (Fig. 8.6). We see here again the work of Proudfoot and Bird, who designed Trinity Presbyterian Church in Indianola, and they again chose an individualistic, high style. Constructed in 1900, St. Paul's reflects the English country church in the Gothic Revival style. The Gothic Revival was extremely popular in the early nineteenth century, but by 1900 was only popular for churches. Gothic never seems to go out of style for churches.

Fig. 8.6. *St. Paul's Episcopal Church* in Harlan joins the traditions of the English Gothic Revival with the artistic individuality of the architects, Proudfoot and Bird. The picturesque tradition is evident in the varied colors, textures, and shapes of the church. In this side view the main entrance is the one on the left partly hidden by the tree. The outline of the roof also reveals the progression of interior spaces thought appropriate by the Episcopalian denomination. (Photograph by Patricia Eckhardt.)

St. Paul's is an intricate work. The front has no door. Rather, we see the side of a low chapel. From the street one's eye moves up a progression of shapes and details. Above the chapel is a rose window in the gable end of the nave and the square tower with a spire over the crossing above that. The entrances are at either end of one side, in the tradition of English Gothic churches.

The church is clad in a variety of materials, reflecting the late-nineteenth-century picturesque aesthetic's fondness for many textures, as well as many details and a balanced asymmetry. There is a high brick base with clapboard and shingle walls above. The windows do not have simple Gothic arches, but multiple lobes or points. The main entrance is also elaborated with columns and a glass tympanum above the double doors with simple Gothic tracery. Although this church is clearly influenced by Anglican traditions, one cannot imagine an English church with such an intentionally daring combination of materials and decorative elements.

The interior plan is equally unusual. After entering the chapel area, one turns to enter the nave, which is perpendicular to the chapel. A dark, powerful-looking open beam ceiling of the English Gothic type dominates the nave. It contains the lantern tower. Beyond it is the broad, elevated chancel. Added to the dark richness of the interior are stained glass windows in deep rich colors. The basilica format of the interior maintains the English preference for a series of processional differentiated spaces. We again see Proudfoot and Bird adapting English traditions to please an Anglo-American congregation, yet doing it with a originality.

Holy Angels, Roselle—Preparing for the Millennium
Roselle is a tiny village in the west-central part of the state. You can see it from the junction of U.S. 71 and E46, south of Carroll. Dominating the town is this large brick church with an impressive central tower of the German Hall Church type, discussed below under Holy Trinity in Luxemburg. The congregation that built it must have wanted to see it from all of their farms and fields and be able to spiritually fly to it at any time. The design is balanced, the building solidly constructed.

As the name suggests, the theme of this church is angels (Fig. 8.7). There are angel statues at the heads of the aisles; there are angels in the windows; angels everywhere, as if everyone were awaiting the millennium. Yet there is no sense of fury or haste. This church retains more of its original painted and stenciled interior than any church I have visited in Iowa. In addition to the paintings and carvings of angels, there are interesting 1890s stained glass windows portraying standing saints. The builders of this church had wealth, respect for careful workmanship, and a great faith in the permanence of their farms and little town. It is a peaceful spot at which to contemplate the changes in the Iowa countryside, and to invoke a guardian angel.

A PILGRIMAGE ROAD

When I think of a Pilgrimage road I always think first of the famous medieval pilgrimage road from Tours (or Vezelay), France,

Fig. 8.7. *The interior of Holy Angels Catholic Church* in Roselle retains most of the original decorative painting that most churches have lost over the years. Here can be seen the total effect of the combined arts, sculpture, painting, and architecture as it was originally intended. (Photograph by Patricia Eckhardt.)

to Santiago De Compostella in Spain. But pilgrimages are not only a quaint activity of the past. Devout Moslems continue to make a "once-in-a-lifetime" visit to Mecca, and the road to Compostella is still used today by a few pilgrims and many tourists enjoying the beautiful countryside and the spectacular chain of churches and monasteries which line the path about one day's walk apart.

Our pilgrimage is from McGregor to Dyersville in northeast Iowa to see a series of spectacular German Catholic churches and enter the world of the German immigrants who built them. It may be religious, or simply a refreshing tour for those interested in architecture, history, and scenery, but who are unaware of these places. Our goal is the great Basilica of St. Francis Xavier, but there is much to be seen on the way.

We are entering the world of German Catholic piety. The German settlers in this region desired to recreate in the new environment of Iowa an economically secure, moral world similar to the one left behind in Germany. They were not so interested in "getting ahead" as they were interested in creating a permanent settlement and maintaining their traditions. The New World was different, of course, and they wanted to own their own land, but they wanted to continue the cultural and spiritual environment they had known. They did not think of themselves as isolated settlers, but rather as a community that continued its traditions and religion. The church was an integral part of their communities and an important focus and place of comfort for their lives. All of life's important events, from baptism, to marriage, and death were honored in the church. They put great effort into building the finest churches they could, and the architecture of these churches is German in every detail.

But we can also, if we want, glimpse the world of religious and ethnic politics in late-nineteenth-century Iowa. However politically incorrect to say today, individual ethnic and religious groups did try to found homogeneous communities. But this did not shield them from conflict. The Catholic immigrants to Iowa faced conflicts with the old Protestant "Yankees" among other Protestants, and more friction among the various ethnic communities within the Catholic church itself. Nevertheless, in all but the smallest communities, such as New Vienna or Petersburg, there was always more than one religious denomination living reasonably peacefully in close proximity – in keeping with American traditions of religious freedom and tolerance.

McGregor—St. Mary's Church
We begin our trip in McGregor where Main Street meets the Mississippi River. You might have spent the night in one of the charming historic inns on Main Street such as the American House or Little Switzerland Inn near the river. Now, as you begin your drive up Main Street nestled in the "notch" between the bluffs, you see the impressive St. Mary's Church at the head of the street.

Placed so prominently, St. Mary's seems huge as framed by the view up Main Street. This historic stone church designed by the German émigré architect Guido Beck is actually small. McGregor was not a predominantly German Catholic town. Enter this church if it is open, collect your thoughts in the quiet, and prepare yourself for the pilgrimage to come. Notice the Gothic architecture and the devices the architect used to make the church conform to its difficult, but dramatic site. Notice the use of all of the arts together: architecture, painting, sculpture, and stained glass. Great artistic effort has been used to create an environment which enhances spiritual reality, an effort you will meet again and again this day.

We met architect Beck earlier when describing his masterpiece of stonemasonry, St. Joseph's in Elkader. His personality was so strong that it seeps through usually colorless historical documents. They tell us, for example, that he was known for his temper and knew how to "chew-out" a contractor. The emotional but generous Beck was a temperamental perfectionist.

Leave McGregor on Highway 340, a portion of the Great River Road, and head up the bluff. You will soon pass the entrance to Pike's Peak State Park, with its five-hundred-foot bluffs overlooking the Mississippi, but we are headed for even higher ground. Continue south on X56 and you will pass the Norwegian Lutheran Church you learned about in "Little White Churches." Continue on and enjoy a wonderful ever-changing scene of fields, hills, and valleys until you come to the big hill down to Guttenberg. From this point you have a grand view of the Mississippi Valley. Follow the River Road down and into the heart of the town. You will have no trouble spotting the twin towers of St. Mary's.

Guttenberg—St. Mary's Church
This twin-towered church is the first of several we will encounter on this pilgrimage trail. It is a specifically European medieval variant of Gothic architecture, not the American Gothic Revival style, and it is the preferred style for Catholic churches in this region

when there was enough wealth to construct it. Although we know that German immigrant architects designed this and other churches, the form was probably the one desired by the German settlers and their church officials as well, at a time when they were moving into Guttenberg (originally called Prairie La Porte) in great numbers.

St. Mary's is constructed in red brick with stone accents. In keeping with the German Gothic style, the square brick towers are elaborated with many decorative horizontal bands. It has tall spires with crosses at the tips, a characteristic of German Catholic churches in Iowa and the Midwest. It was constructed with the standard Gothic plan and structure, which employs a gabled roof over the nave and separate shed roofs over the side aisles. The clerestory windows, a medieval device introduced to allow more light into the middle of the church, are placed in the wall above the arcade which divides the side aisle from the nave. The interior is elaborate, but somewhat modernized. The original interior statues, altars, and decorative wall painting have been replaced with those of more modern design.

Continue south on U.S. 52 to Luxemberg, and enjoy another interesting scenic stretch of road. You will drive up the bluffs between outcroppings of stone, drop down again at Mill Ville, and return up to the cap of gently rolling farmland. As you approach Luxemburg, you will see a great towered church looming in the distance. It stands on a hill top 1,180 feet high, marking the achievement of the German settlers who came to this area in the 1840s and '50s when it had the undignified name of "Flea Hill."

Luxemburg—Holy Trinity Church
A plaque over the entrance tells you in German that this rather stark and angular church was constructed in 1876. It was designed by one of Iowa's most important early architects, Fridoline Heer. It is an early work, and lacks the polish of his later works such as the Dubuque County Courthouse and Sacred Heart Church in Dubuque and the Basilica in Dyersville toward which we are progressing. The façade with its single centrally placed tower consists of simple surfaces and shapes. Heer makes the tower relatively tall and the spire it supports almost the same measurement again. The proportions are not easily analyzed and seem as awkward as they are distinctive. The spire almost looks like a pointed nun's cap. The base of the cap sits on the nest of crosses on the tower gables. The small circular windows on the upper side façades appear like snowflakes on the broad redbrick façade.

The light-colored interior provides a respite and place for contemplation (Fig. 8.8). Holy Trinity is a prime example of the German Hall Church type. This is a late medieval Gothic development. The architect, Fridoline Heer, was certainly familiar with this variant of the Gothic style. It was a major architectural form in southern Germany where he trained as an architect and stonecutter. This format is used by Heer and by Guido Beck for numerous churches in eastern Iowa. In this version of late Gothic (fourteenth and fifteenth centuries), the aisles are divided from the nave by a tall screen of thin columns supporting arches, but there is no

Fig. 8.8. *Holy Trinity Catholic Church* in Luxemburg is émigré architect Fridoline Heer's earliest church in Iowa. This view reveals the basic German Hall Church pattern with tall windows in the aisle walls providing all of the light for the interior. The aisles are separated from the nave proper by a colonnade of tall, slender columns. The original interior painting scheme has been painted over, but the original carved wooden altars remain. (Photograph by Patricia Eckhardt.)

clerestory wall or windows above that. The entire church has a single gabled roof covering nave and aisles alike. Light streams into the church from the tall windows along the outer wall. One might expect that the nave would be dark without the added light from clerestory windows, but the interior of Holy Trinity is surprisingly light and airy in contrast with its stark exterior.

For the most part the interior has escaped modernization. Some of the original interior ceiling painting remains, but much has been modernized or painted over. The original altars with their ornate details and multiple statues remain. The abstract geometric and floral windows are from the 1870s and do not have the figures and scenes that later windows will contain. A beautiful organ inhabits the balcony at the rear of the church.

Continue south on Iowa Highway 136 to the little town of New Vienna, only four miles south. Here we again see a tall spire growing ever taller as we approach. This is St. Boniface.

New Vienna—St. Boniface
The church of St. Boniface, built between 1883 and 1887, sits in the company of a former convent, an interesting nineteenth-century rectory, a school, and a stone water tower. Next to the church is the cemetery with an unusual monument or mausoleum at its center. In the upper story one can see a large statue of Christ crucified through the glass windows, but as we drive by we cannot see his head. The statue was planned to be viewed from below in the cemetery, so be sure to walk through it.

The spectacular spire topping the single limestone tower dominates the town and commands our attention, as do medieval churches in Europe. Its spire reveals its European inspiration with its ribs, dormers, and stringcourses of various types as well as polychrome slate shingles. The mysterious Martin Heer might be the architect. It is not known whether he was related to Fridoline Heer, but sources suggest that they might have been brothers. Others suggest he was a priest. He worked for Heer for a time and later worked with Guido Beck. Martin Heer came from Germany and returned to Germany before his death. He is credited with designing this church and Saints Peter and Paul in Petersburg as well. His work seems more European than either Fridoline Heer's or Beck's.

The interior has the wide-open space of the German Hall Church model although it is not strictly a Hall Church. It has very large windows along the exterior walls, and tall arcade arches, but there is a narrow clerestory with lunette windows. The altars are original, and the carver is known to have been local. He wrote his name, Edward Hackner, inside the back of the main altar. He probably carved altars in other churches nearby. The altars here are very much like those at Holy Trinity at Luxemburg and even those at Dyersville. The church houses the famous Schulke Tracker Organ made in 1891.

Although it takes us off our direct path to Dyersville, it is well worth seeing Saints Peter and Paul in Petersburg, only four miles to the west. Take County Road C64 west. It is not marked, but turn west where it says "post office." You will come to a "T" intersection. Turn right or north and go until the next paved road to the left or west (less than 1 mile) and proceed to Petersburg. You will see the church from quite a distance.

Petersburg—Saints Peter and Paul
Rising like a specter, the three spires of Saints Peter and Paul grow as we approach (Fig. 8.9). The church is constructed of stone with a tall central tower and two lower towers. It is said that the central tower was from the previous church, but this is probably not true. The present tower seems of a piece with the rest of the church and the stonework appears identical. It was probably constructed on the earlier tower foundation. The other towers are unusual in that they are placed angling outward at forty-five degrees. All three towers have tall, pointed spires. The only other church I have found that has three towers on the façade is the famous St. Louis Cathedral in New Orleans, and Saints Peter and Paul does have a similar appearance from a distance.

The interior of this church is imposing, with its broad open space and large expanses of stained glass. The windows are simply extraordinary and worth the visit. The window on the right nave wall nearest the entrance portrays St. Boniface, and was a gift from St. Boniface church in New Vienna. The variety of green and reds in this window are stunning. This church is "consecrated," a designation indicating that it was paid for before it was opened for use, and that it must be maintained.

Retrace your steps to New Vienna and proceed south to Dyersville on 136. It is only four miles. It seems impossible that there could be so many great churches within such a small area. As you approach Dyersville you will see the twin towers of the church across town on the west. You will also see the sign at the edge of town pointing the way to the Field of Dreams, the baseball diamond made famous by Joe Kinsella's novel and the movie. On this

Fig. 8.9. *The distinctive triple spires* and imposing mass of Saints Peter and Paul dominate the small town of Petersburg and the countryside around it, as did medieval churches in Europe. (Photograph by Patricia Eckhardt.)

pilgrimage we are going on to a different "Field of Dreams," the Basilica of St. Francis Xavier. Make your way to it by driving toward the extraordinary towers.

Dyersville—The Basilica of St. Francis Xavier
One sees the large and elaborate basilica across town, but the balanced composition of its exterior seems to deny its immense size (Fig. 8.10). Were it not for its three large entrances and its eight bay length, it could be another fine brick Catholic church in northeast Iowa. But the detail and refinement of the façade begins to take effect as you look. The architect, Fridoline Heer, once a student sculptor, designed the towers using only abstract elements—

stringcourses, moldings, dormers, and other architectural accents. The towers have four stages or floors, each more elaborate than the next, culminating in the fourth story with its small gables in the center of each side. Above this rise the complex spires with many little dormer windows and horizontal bands topped by crosses.

Some statistics are in order here. The original cost of the church in 1888 was $100,000.00. The towers are 212 feet tall and 20 feet square, the gold leafed crosses are 14 feet tall, and the clock faces are 6 feet in diameter. The exterior dimensions are 70 feet by 175 feet, and the main roof of the nave is 76 feet tall. Still, the exterior presents such a balanced appearance that you do not think it unusual.

Fig. 8.10. *The Basilica of St. Francis Xavier* rises high above the town of Dyersville. Its twin-towered form reveals the European and German roots of its architect and congregation. (Photograph by Patricia Eckhardt.)

The Basilica of St. Francis Xavier, constructed in 1888, is the masterwork of the Swiss-born architect Fridoline Heer. Heer designed many churches in northeast Iowa as well as many other buildings including the Dubuque County Courthouse. Heer, born in Wallenstadt, St. Gall province in 1834, followed in the footsteps of his master builder father. He was trained in Switzerland and Germany in architecture and stonemasonry, and in addition, studied sculpture at the School of Fine Arts in Munich, Germany. He came to the United States in 1868 and worked in various towns and cities, including Chicago. He settled in Dubuque in 1870 and opened for business as an architect. After that he designed over two hundred buildings in Iowa and surrounding states.

The interior of the basilica is a match for the powerful and detailed exterior. It is overwhelming in its beauty and detail. The church seats twelve hundred people. The height of the main altar is fifty-two feet. There are sixty-four stained glass windows. There are wall paintings, ceiling paintings, altars, statues, beautiful stained glass, carved columns, and refined details everywhere. Every detail is finely rendered, even the beautiful carpentry of the old confessionals. But, in spite of all of this detail, the architect has managed to create a harmonious environment, which is both awesome and elevating.

There is another presence here as well, that of the Pope. This church is a minor basilica, one of the Pope's own churches, and his papal pavilion, an umbrella-like structure in red and yellow, stands partly opened in the sanctuary on the right side. Pope Pius XII raised St. Xavier to basilica rank in 1956. There are thirty-three minor basilicas in the United States, but the Basilica of Saint Francis Xavier is the only one in a rural setting. There are only five major basilicas in the world, all in Rome. Because the church has the rank of basilica, it is given its own coat of arms which stands on a pole to the left of the sanctuary. This is the heraldic shield of the Dyersville community surmounted by the papal canopy.

The side altars are as large as the main altars of Holy Trinity in Luxemberg and St. Boniface in New Vienna and just as ornate, covered with architectural columns and arches filled with a multitude of carved statues. The main altar is elaborate, but rather than a rear piece similar to the other altars, it has an elaborately carved baldachin or canopy, a sign of the elevated status of the church and another reference to the Pope.

As you take in all of the painted scenes, the carved wood, the statues, the soaring space of the nave, you can think of the pilgrimage you have made this day. This is a fitting conclusion to a wonderful journey devoted to architecture as an expression of the religious spirit and the history and natural beauty of northeast Iowa.

Note: There are very few books on American ecclesiastical architecture, the study of religious architecture in America having been ignored or avoided until recently. This article has been based almost entirely on primary sources. *America's Religious Architecture* by Marilyn Chiat, is a recent book on the subject, but there are only four examples from Iowa. Peter Williams' *Houses of God,* is good as far as it goes. His analysis of colonial and Anglican churches in the eastern United States is excellent, but he thinks there is nothing of interest in the Midwest and the rest of America's religious architecture is treated only anecdotally.

❧ Part III. ❧

Nature's Places

⤐ 9 ⤏

Iowa's Countryside

Carl Kurtz

Fig. 9.1. *Central Iowa Farmstead,* with traditional barn, in eastern Story Co., central Iowa. (Photograph by Carl Kurtz.)

Fig. 9.2. *Winter Dawn on the Iowa River,* in Marshall Co., central Iowa. (Photograph by Carl Kurtz.)

Fig. 9.3. *Jonquils, Tulips, and Service Berry,* Polk Co., spring. (Photograph by Carl Kurtz.)

Fig. 9.4. *Juvenile Least Bittern Chicks*, Errington Marsh, Polk Co. (Photograph by Carl Kurtz.)

Fig. 9.5. *Waterfall at Falling Springs*, Fayette Co., northeast Iowa. (Photograph by Carl Kurtz.)

Fig. 9.6. *White Water-lily in Anderson Lake*, a prairie pothole marsh, spring, Hamilton Co. (Photograph by Carl Kurtz.)

Fig. 9.7. *Summer Thunderstorm and Rainbow* over an Iowa cornfield in western Marshall Co. (Photograph by Carl Kurtz.)

Fig. 9.8. *Aerial View of Strip-Cropping* on the Dick Witt farm in western Marshall Co. (Photograph by Carl Kurtz.)

Fig. 9.9. *Showy Tick-trefoil* in a six-year-old reconstructed tallgrass prairie at Prairie Creek Wildlife Refuge, Marshall Co. (Photograph by Carl Kurtz.)

Fig. 9.10.   *Country Road* and late afternoon shadows in western Marshall Co. (Photograph by Carl Kurtz.)

Fig. 9.11. *Mature Red Oak Forest* at Dow's State Preserve, Linn Co. (Photograph by Carl Kurtz.)

Fig. 9.12. *Late Summer Sunrise* over backwaters of the Mississippi, near Harpers Ferry, Allamakee Co. (Photograph by Carl Kurtz.)

Fig. 9.13. *Autumn Morning* and a Sugar Maple at Mormon Ridge, Marshall Co. (Photograph by Carl Kurtz.)

Fig. 9.14. *Indian Grass* on an autumn prairie in late afternoon light on Stevenson Family Preserve, Broken Kettle Grassland (Nature Conservancy), Plymouth Co., northwest Iowa. (Photograph by Carl Kurtz.)

Fig. 9.15. *Colo Grain Elevator* and afternoon thunderstorm, eastern Story Co. (Photograph by Carl Kurtz.)

Fig. 9.16. *Cumulonimbus Cloud* at sunset over autumn tallgrass prairie at Prairie Creek Wildlife Refuge, Marshall Co. (Photograph by Carl Kurtz.)

Fig. 9.17. *Early Morning Light*, with steam rising over the Des Moines River, Boone Co. (Photograph by Carl Kurtz.)

Fig. 9.18. *Dusk and New Moon,* over a farm in Union Co., southwest Iowa. (Photograph by Carl Kurtz.)

Fig. 9.19. *Old Motor Mill in Autumn,* along Turkey River, Clayton Co., northeast Iowa. (Photograph by Carl Kurtz.)

Fig. 9.20. *Old Log Barn chinked with limestone,* Winneshiek Co., northeast Iowa. (Photograph by Carl Kurtz.)

❧ 10 ❧

Snow Geese, Eagles, Swans, and Pelicans— A Wild Bird's-eye View of Iowa

James J. Dinsmore

Many people, Iowans and visitors alike, think of Iowa as entirely covered with agriculture and devoid of meaningful wildlife. But the fabulous fertility of the Iowa soil produces food and shelter for wildlife as well as people, as is proven, unfortunately, by the numerous road-killed deer, raccoons, pheasants, and skunks that are scattered along the edges of our roads at various times of the year.

The variety and profusion of wildlife in Iowa is historic too. A few years ago, I discussed the history of Iowa's wildlife in a book titled *A Country so Full of Game*. The title came from the words of Joseph Street, an Indian agent who joined a group surveying land in northeastern Iowa in 1833. He wrote, "I had never rode through a country so full of game. The hunter who accompanied me, though living most of his time in the woods, expressed his astonishment at the abundance of all kinds of game except buffalo."

At that time, just prior to settlement by Europeans, White-tailed Deer, elk, Black Bear, wolves, bobcats, waterfowl, prairie-chickens, Wild Turkeys, and numerous other species were all found in Iowa, in some cases in great numbers. By the end of the century, it is true, Iowa was essentially completely settled and those species and numerous others were greatly reduced in number or, in some cases, were no longer found in the state. The combination of habitat change along with hunting and trapping by early settlers had had a terrible impact on many of Iowa's wildlife species.

Moreover, since 1900, there have been further assaults on the natural habitats of Iowa as prairies have been plowed, wetlands drained, and woodlands cut down. As a result, the landscape of Iowa has been greatly altered, perhaps more so than that of any other state. Nevertheless, despite these changes and losses, Iowa still supports a surprising variety of wildlife species. Granted— some of the more spectacular species of mammals like wolves, mountain lions, elk, and even bison have disappeared. But Iowa still has populations of about seventy species of mammals, according to a recent study by J. B. Bowles and other mammalogists, and some, like deer, even thrive under the conditions of agriculture and suburbanization. There is an even greater variety of birds. About four hundred bird species have been reported in the state including about three hundred that appear every year, as T. H. Kent reports in his "Checklist of Iowa Birds." Of these, about 150 species nest in the state virtually every year. As with mammals, a few species no longer occur in Iowa, including the Carolina Parakeet and Passenger Pigeon, which are now extinct. Others that have not been seen in Iowa for years include the nearly extinct Eskimo Curlew.

Despite these losses, there also have been some spectacular gains in the wildlife found in Iowa. Most Iowans know that White-tailed Deer are now found statewide and, in some places, are even considered pests. Canada Geese and Wild Turkeys, species that were common in pioneer times and then disappeared from the state, have been restocked and now are found statewide. In addition, a number of other less-recognized species have also returned to Iowa and, in some places, can be found if one just takes the time to get off the main roads at the right time of year and do a little exploring. In the pages that follow, I will describe a few of these special places where, at the right time of year, Iowans can find some reminders of the great abundance of wildlife that is Iowa's heritage.

SNOW GEESE

Casual travelers driving along Interstate 29 in western Iowa near the town of Missouri Valley in November are probably aware that something is going on when they see flocks of thousands of geese in the air and in harvested fields along the highway. But they may not know that one of the great concentrations of waterfowl in

North America is found just a few miles away at DeSoto National Wildlife Refuge. The refuge entrance is on Highway 30, just an eight-mile drive west from the Missouri Valley exit. Although a nominal fee is charged to enter the refuge, it is well worth it for the opportunity to see the thousands of geese and other birds, as well as the very good informational displays in the refuge center. From roughly mid November until early December, DeSoto National Wildlife Refuge hosts one of the largest concentrations of geese to be seen anywhere in North America.

The annual migration of Snow Geese through western Iowa every fall is an amazing spectacle. Snow Geese, which have two color phases, one largely white with black wingtips and the other a mixture of bluish-gray and white (commonly called the Blue Goose), nest on the tundra of northern Canada, Alaska, and eastern Siberia. Every fall, these geese, which currently have a breeding population of an estimated five million birds, move south to their wintering grounds. Most of the birds that nest around the Hudson Bay and northern Canada move south through central North America, eventually reaching their wintering grounds which are concentrated near the Gulf Coast from Louisiana to Mexico. This migration, which begins in September, starts out at a rather leisurely pace as the birds move south onto the wheat fields of southern Canada and North Dakota where they feed on waste grain left after the harvest. They remain there until the first spell of cold weather or a heavy snow cover forces them to move farther south. Typically that occurs in late October or early November, and then tens of thousands of geese stream southward into the Missouri River Valley. From their lofty point of view, the wildlife refuges along the Missouri offer essential food, shelter, and rest. Some of these refuges are traditional sites where they stop every year, and DeSoto National Wildlife Refuge is a major stopping place after they leave eastern North and South Dakota.

The geese are attracted to DeSoto for several reasons. Probably the two most important are that it provides a safe place where they can roost at night, and it provides access to considerable food on the corn fields that stretch out for miles to the north and south of the refuge.

The arrival and departure of the geese are subject to the vagaries of weather, food availability (which in turn is subject to current agricultural policies among other things), and disturbance. In most years, a few geese arrive in October but the big buildup is not until early or mid November. In some years, the buildup is gradual

Fig. 10.1. *A Snow Goose in Its Dark Phase,* photographed in February 1995, in Johnston. In this phase it is also known as a Blue Goose. (Photograph by Stephen J. Dinsmore.)

as flocks continue to move south from farther north and then linger at DeSoto. In those years, the birds may remain well into December before moving farther south. To anticipate the arrival, experienced goose watchers keep an eye on the weather forecasts and look for the first severe storm with low temperatures and heavy snow to sweep across the northern Great Plains. Such weather will force the geese to leave southern Canada and the Dakotas and move south to DeSoto. The snow cover is particularly important since it buries the waste grain in the fields and prevents the geese from finding food. At that point it is time for the geese to continue their migration south toward DeSoto. Once they reach DeSoto, the same weather factors affect their stay here. A severe storm with heavy snow will push them farther south into southwestern Iowa, Missouri, and eventually, the Gulf Coast.

Another factor determining when the geese will arrive in Iowa is the availability of waste grain in the fields. Modern corn harvesting equipment, despite its efficiency in harvesting huge fields, still leaves considerable grain on the ground. Researchers at Iowa State University estimated that an average of four hundred pounds of corn per acre was left on the ground after harvest (see Frederick et al. 1984). The flat Missouri River floodplain that stretches north and south from DeSoto refuge is intensively farmed with thousands of acres of corn planted there every year. Daily, the geese leave the refuge and fly out to these fields to feed. At first they concentrate on the fields closest to the refuge and with the most waste grain. As the food on these closest fields gets eaten, the flocks move farther to find food (Frederick et al. 1987). Eventually, as the food is consumed, some flocks move south to find additional food even before bad weather forces them to move.

DESOTO NATIONAL WILDLIFE REFUGE

DeSoto National Wildlife Refuge, established in 1959, covers about seventy-eight hundred acres of lowland along the Missouri River west of Missouri Valley, Iowa. Most of the refuge is in Iowa, but it also includes an isolated island of land in Nebraska that was cut off by an old oxbow of the river. The refuge is flat and most of the land is covered with agricultural crops, grasslands, or floodplain forest. The showpiece of the refuge is a modern visitors center that overlooks an oxbow lake. Expansive viewing windows give the visitor a broad view of the lake and the geese that commonly rest there when they are not feeding in surrounding fields. The visitors center has marvelous displays describing the interactions between early European settlement on the plains and the wildlife that inhabited that region. As well as a flyway for birds, the Missouri River was a highway for the riverboats that carried supplies upstream to trappers, miners, and settlers. Many of those boats sank in the treacherous waters of the river, and the remains of a number of those boats have been discovered. The most spectacular find was the remains of the Bertrand, a supply boat destined for the mining camps of western Montana that sank in 1865. Thousands of relics from that boat, ranging from mining shovels to felt hats to pickled cherries, have been recovered, and many of those items are on display at the visitors center.

As you enter the refuge, you will receive a map along with information on what parts are open to visitors. At the center, you can obtain further information on current conditions, how many geese are present, and get oriented to the layout of the refuge. For most visitors, viewing from the center and driving the auto tour road provide a good view of the wildlife.

One wing of the visitors center juts out toward the oxbow lake. At the end of the hallway, tall windows on the sides and even overhead provide a great vista of the nearby lake and woods and the wildlife that use those areas. Usually the most obvious are the Snow Geese. During migration, at least a few are on the lake almost any time of day and typically most of the geese spend the night resting on the water of the oxbow lake. However, even when thousands of geese are using the refuge, additional thousands will be away for much of the daylight hours. The exit of these flocks near sunrise every morning is spectacular. Tens of thousands of geese rise up off the lake, filling the air and making a noise that rivals the sounds of a large crowd at a football game. The birds then stream off to surrounding fields to feed.

By late morning or early afternoon, flocks start returning to the refuge with the major buildup usually occurring late in the afternoon near sunset. Again the noise is deafening, as the number of birds on the lake grows until they seem to fill every square foot of water and extend on around the oxbow and out of sight of the visitors center. As they return, watch them descend toward the water. Snow Geese often turn on their sides and drop like a rock for some distance, rolling out of the descent just as they approach the water. This behavior, called side slipping, is an interesting part of the mass of activity. The combination of the thousands of geese filling the air and the clamor of their calls is a spectacular experience, and there is no better place to enjoy that experience than at DeSoto.

Although the Snow Geese usually dominate viewers' attention from the visitors center, a number of other waterfowl also stop at DeSoto during migration. The two that usually are most evident are Canada Geese (they have the familiar black neck and

Fig. 10.2. *Snow Geese at DeSoto National Wildlife Refuge,* December 1, 1990. Such spectacular flocks are more common in the fall than the spring. The geese glean corn from neighboring fields during the day and return to the refuge in the evening. (Photograph by Stephen J. Dinsmore.)

head with the white cheek patch) and Mallards (the green head that most Iowans recognize). Hundreds or thousands of both move through DeSoto and usually are seen in front of the visitors center. Other species of ducks, cormorants, grebes, and various other waterbirds are often there too. The Missouri River Valley is also a flyway for Bald Eagles, and usually a few eagles can be found perched in the tall cottonwoods that line the banks of the oxbow. Although all of them may not have the white head and tail of the adult plumage, their large bulky profile is easy to pick out as they wait for the opportunity to feed on a dead fish or a sick or injured duck or goose.

Another species of wildlife that is common at DeSoto is the coyote, which often preys on injured geese. If you notice a flock of geese appearing nervous and swimming away from the shoreline, or a sudden flight of them taking off from along the edge of one of the large flocks, check to see if a coyote is responsible. The geese generally spot a coyote before you do. Coyotes skulk along the edge of the flocks and then make a sudden charge, trying to surprise the birds and catch one that is slow to take flight.

The other way to view the refuge is from your vehicle. Every fall, to accommodate the huge crowds of people who visit the refuge, the refuge staff set out an auto tour route. This route usually includes roads through the interior of the oxbow island where flocks of geese, unseen from the refuge headquarters, may be resting and where White-tailed Deer, hawks, and other birds and mammals can be seen. The usual rule for the auto tour is that, to prevent disturbance to the geese, you must remain in your vehicle. Actually, a car is a great blind and typically allows people to approach wildlife closer than they could if they got out of the car. Often the auto tour includes a few stops where you can get out and walk on established nature trails. Note that besides geese, DeSoto refuge is also famous for its poison ivy, which may grow into large vines hanging from the trees. A good way to avoid the poison ivy is to use the large elevated wooden blind that overlooks the oxbow lake. It is a favorite place to watch the geese as they come in to roost in the evening and a great place for photographing the birds.

Snow Geese also migrate through Iowa, especially western Iowa, in the spring. However, the spring flocks tend to be somewhat smaller (more birds move through central Nebraska in spring) and less dependable in when they arrive and depart. Typically, the first Snow Geese arrive in February as soon as most of the snow disappears and the majority have moved through the state by the end of March. However, DeSoto National Wildlife Refuge does not attract large flocks of Snow Geese in spring. Wait until fall and enjoy a real wildlife treat.

BALD EAGLES

Bald Eagles are one of the largest and most spectacular birds of prey found in Iowa. Although many people are aware that eagles are found in the state, most don't realize that they are actually fairly easy to find, especially during winter. Bald Eagles were prob-

Fig. 10.3. *Snow Geese at Waco Basin Wildlife Management Area.* Spring migrations are best seen in Nebraska, where this picture was taken, March 1, 1995. (Photograph by Stephen J. Dinsmore.)

ably fairly common nesting birds along Iowa's rivers and lakes when Europeans first reached the state. However, those birds were greatly persecuted and, by the early 1900s, nesting eagles had disappeared from Iowa. By the 1960s, eagles were in trouble across most of North America, especially because of problems related to pesticides that were found in their food. With the banning of the use of DDT in the 1970s, eagle numbers started to increase and in 1977, a single Bald Eagle nest was found in northeastern Iowa. For the next decade, the nesting population of eagles in Iowa remained low and as recently as 1990, only eight active nests were known to exist in the state. However, in the next few years, the number of nests increased greatly and in 1998, an amazing eighty-four Bald Eagle nests were known to be active in Iowa, according to B. L.

Fig. 10.4. *Bald Eagles* are now a common sight in Iowa in January and February, fishing in the open water of the larger rivers. This one was photographed at Lake Manawa in Council Bluffs. (Photograph by Cheryl Elswick.)

Ehresman. Encouragingly, all signs point to a continued increase in their numbers in the near future.

Even before Bald Eagles started nesting again in Iowa, there were other signs of recovery of their populations, such as the rapid increase in the number seen migrating through and wintering in Iowa. During fall and spring migrations, hundreds of Bald Eagles were seen passing through the state and, in recent years, more than a thousand eagles spent the winter. Most of these wintering birds are found near water, especially below dams or other places where some water remains unfrozen throughout the winter. Wintering birds usually arrive in November or December, as soon as the lakes and rivers start to freeze over. Along the Mississippi River, their wintering grounds depend on the severity of the winter. In the rare mild winters when the river stays mostly open, eagles may winter all along Iowa's eastern border. More commonly, most eagles move to around Davenport and points south where at least some water remains unfrozen throughout all but the coldest winters. There the eagles spend much of the day perched in large trees along the river-bank and feed on fish, waterfowl, or other prey. Open pools below dams, where many fish may be injured as they pass through the outlet of the dam, are favorite eagle feeding areas and reliable places to find Bald Eagles most winters.

Bald Eagles on the Mississippi River
One of the most reliable places to find eagles in Iowa is below lock and dam 19 in Keokuk. The lock and dam are located near down-town Keokuk off of State Highway 136. Parking is available

Fig. 10.5. *While Bald Eagles* favor perches in tall trees, they also some-times put down in shallow water and on the ice. (Photograph by Cheryl Elswick.)

nearby and there is a walkway across the lock to a sidewalk that overlooks the tailwaters of the dam. During winter, eagles are nearly always perched in the large trees that line the bank or are on the ice and sandbars in the river. You may also want to drive south along the riverfront to Hubinger Landing where they gather along the river. Another good place to find eagles is along County Road X28 (the Great River Road) north from Keokuk to Montrose. Although this road does not always provide an open view of the river, eagles can usually be seen perched in trees nearby. Bald Eagles can also be seen below the lock and dams at Davenport (lock and dam 15), Le Claire (lock and dam 14), Clinton (lock and dam 13), and Bellevue (lock and dam 12). Several of these cities (notably Keokuk and Davenport) have held Bald Eagle days every winter, usually in January. These festivals often include films and lectures, and spotting scopes are set up to give people better views.

Bald Eagles at Red Rock
In central Iowa, probably the most reliable place to find Bald Eagles in winter is at Red Rock Reservoir. This 19,000-acre reservoir, formed by a dam on the Des Moines River near Pella, annually plays host to two hundred or more Bald Eagles. Most of them roost in trees along the riverbank just downstream from the dam. Although a few usually can be seen in those trees throughout the daytime, the best time to see large numbers of eagles is in the morning or evening when they are leaving or entering the roosting area. During the daytime, eagles feed along the Des Moines River downstream from the dam, along the reservoir itself, and in the surrounding countryside. One of the better places to observe them is from an observation deck near the Army Corps of Engineers visitors center. The center is usually closed during the winter when eagles are present, but you can get access to the viewing deck throughout the year. Maps to various places at the reservoir are usually posted at the visitors center. To reach this site, take the Washington Street exit (exit 40) from Highway 163 west of Pella. Proceed west 0.7 miles and turn south onto County Road T15. Follow that road three miles to the visitors center on the south side of the dam. The observation deck is behind the visitors center and overlooks the main pool of Red Rock Reservoir. During the day, scan the trees that line the banks of the lake and also look for large dark blobs on the ice. Bald Eagles not only roost in the trees along the lake but perch on the ice itself. Because of their large size, they are easy to find although viewing may be difficult if they are far

away. At sunrise, many of the eagles that have spent the night in trees below the dam fly up over the dam and proceed out onto the lake where they will feed during the day. These birds generally move singly, their labored, lumbering flight making them easy to pick out as they pass in front of you. In the evening, the flight is in the opposite direction as they move from the lake to the riverbank trees where they spend the night.

Directly across the highway from the entrance drive to the visitors center is a road that proceeds to the south tailwaters area. The road ends in a parking lot overlooking the tailwater below the dam. This is a good place to look for Bald Eagles perched in the large trees along the riverbank downstream from the dam. Also check the map at the visitors center for directions to the large recreation area across the river from you (north of the tailwaters area). Several roads through that area provide greater access to the riverbank and the potential to see more eagles.

SWANS IN NORTHEASTERN IOWA

Another large spectacular bird that migrates through Iowa is the Tundra Swan, a species that some of the older bird field guides still label as the Whistling Swan. This is the most abundant of the swans found in North America. As the name suggests, Tundra Swans nest on the arctic tundra of northern Alaska and Canada. In fall, most of the Alaskan birds move south to winter in the large interior valleys of California. Of more interest to Iowans are some of the Alaskan birds and those that nest in arctic Canada. Most of these move southeast across North America, eventually ending up along the Atlantic Coast from Chesapeake Bay south to North Carolina where they spend the winter. Although most of these birds move through Minnesota, Wisconsin, and other states to the east of Iowa, every fall a number of them regularly stop on the Mississippi River from La Crosse, Wisconsin, south into northeastern Iowa.

The best place in Iowa to observe these birds is at the pool formed by lock and dam no. 9 near Harper's Ferry in northeastern Iowa. There, every year, several hundred swans stop during their southward migration. Some years as many as a thousand swans may gather there for a few days or weeks before continuing to the southeast. They usually don't allow one to get very close, but their loud whistling calls make their presence obvious. In addition, a large white bird is pretty obvious on the water. The adults are essentially all white while the young birds from that year's breeding season are more grayish. Often the birds are still in family groups—the parents and the one, two, or rarely more young that they raised that year. Their large size, white coloration, and graceful movements make them a delight to watch.

Viewing these swans can be a bit challenging, especially if there has been recent rain. In Harper's Ferry, follow County Road X52 (the Great River Road) north out of town. After about 2.6 miles, the road bends to the left, taking you away from the river. At this bend, leave the county road and turn onto Red Oak Road, a gravel road on your right that continues to follow the river. The first half mile of this road is fairly smooth and may give you some glimpses of the swans. Road conditions allowing, continue on another 0.2 miles from the end of the gravel to a point where you can see much of pool 9 on your right. If the swans are present, you should be able to see them from here. Red Oak Road does continue on for about another mile along the river and then turns inland, eventually rejoining X52. However, be warned that it is often very rough and deeply rutted and after rain may be impassable. Use appropriate precautions. Another viewing point is at Heytman's Landing. This can be reached by turning east from X52 about seven miles north of Harper's Ferry and proceeding to the river.

The best time to see Tundra Swans in Iowa is in November. The dates can vary from year to year, depending on when the river freezes over. Some birds may arrive as early as late October and a few may linger on well into December, especially in mild winters.

PELICANS IN CENTRAL IOWA

Although many of the alterations that humans have made to Iowa's landscapes have been harmful to wildlife, some have been beneficial, at least to some species. One example of the latter is the damming of several of Iowa's large interior rivers and the resultant large reservoirs that have formed behind those dams. Two of the largest are the Red Rock and Saylorville, on the Des Moines River southeast and northwest of Des Moines. The reservoirs behind these dams attract thousands of waterbirds, especially during migration. Perhaps the most spectacular are the large flocks of American White Pelicans that migrate through central Iowa, especially in fall. White Pelicans have been visiting Iowa for centuries as they move between their wintering grounds along the Gulf Coast and their nesting colonies on the northern Great Plains of the United States and north into southern Canada. Prior to the damming of the Des Moines River, these flocks were found mainly in western Iowa and tended to move through the state quite rapidly in late summer and early fall. With the large reservoirs now present above these two dams, thousands of pelicans routinely gather on them each fall. These flocks are most evident on the upper ends of the reservoirs where the birds commonly roost on a number of small islands. These islands, formed by deposits of Iowa's rich soil that have washed off the farmlands upstream, in turn, remind us of some of the bad effects of poor stewardship of the land and the steady buildup of silt that eventually will reduce the value of these reservoirs for boating and the storage of floodwaters. Meanwhile, however, the islands attract the pelicans.

Typically, the first groups arrive in early August. Their numbers rapidly build up so that by the end of August and into September, thousands of pelicans can be seen. By the end of September, the southward exodus resumes, and by mid October all but a few stragglers have moved on. In between, though, these birds provide a spectacular scene. They gather in large, densely packed flocks on islands or mudbars where they rest during much of the day. Periodically, groups will leave, laboriously taking flight and moving to feeding areas. With their huge eight-foot wingspans, they are like nature's cargo planes. If the bird is on the water when it begins its flight, it runs along the water's surface, beating its wings until it finally clears the water, and then pulls its legs and feet back in tight to the body. Once airborne, the birds usually circle a few times, typically in a group, as they gradually gain altitude. Their lumbering wingbeats are slow but powerful. If the birds are not going to move far, they usually stay low over the water and fly to their feeding site where they land and begin feeding. If they are going to fly some distance, they may rise to a height of several hundred feet, usually circling in a flock with other pelicans. Rather than beating their wings constantly, however, pelicans are famous for using rising columns of warm air (called thermals) that form over water on warm sunny days. Pelicans cleverly ride these thermals and use them to help gain altitude. Thus their flight consists of several slow, deep wingbeats, followed by a glide. Slowly but steadily the birds circle, taking several minutes, until they have reached their desired altitude, and then glide off toward their destination.

These flights are most spectacular against a blue sky, when the white flocks are perfectly illuminated. But as the birds continue their circular flight pattern, they eventually turn to an angle where they are no longer at a broadside to the viewer. Amazingly, at this point, they suddenly vanish from view, as if by magic they were suddenly removed from the sky. In a few seconds, as their circular path continues, just as suddenly they reappear. I have watched this numerous times and always am amazed at how such a huge bird can vanish and then reappear in the open against a clear blue sky.

On the water, feeding flocks of pelicans often put on a good show. Unlike their close relative, the Brown Pelican that is found along the coastlines of the southern United States, White Pelicans do not dive from the air to capture their food. Rather, they feed by using their large bill and the pouch suspended from it as a large fishing net. They dip the bill into the water and take in a large quantity of water and whatever fish or other food it may contain. They then tip their head and bill down, allowing the water to drain out of their pouch and retaining the fish that they then swallow. Since most fish can easily swim away from a single feeding pelican, White Pelicans improve their chances by foraging in groups. They form a line swimming side-by-side in shallow water, driving fish in front of them. As the fish are concentrated in front of the pelicans, the birds then dip their bills and pouches into the water, often in unison, scooping up the prey in front of them. Sometimes these lines of pelicans are semicircular in shape, again driving the fish in front of them until they are herded into a small area. Once the prey is concentrated, the pelicans feed rapidly to take advantage of the easy pickings. Such cooperative feeding, which is somewhat rare in birds, enhances the pelicans' ability to fuel their large bodies and to provide for their young.

Two of the best places to observe pelicans are a small observation deck along State Highway 316, north of the town of Swan that overlooks the upper reaches of Red Rock Reservoir southeast of Des Moines, and at Jester Park, a county park on the west shore of Saylorville Reservoir near Polk City in northern Polk County. A third place is from the Highway 17 bridge across the upper end of Saylorville Reservoir near the Polk–Dallas county line. The Jester Park site is especially good because the islands the birds roost on are fairly close offshore and you have several miles of the reservoir spread out in front of you, allowing you a view of both the roosting birds and their flights to nearby feeding areas.

These are just a few of the best examples of some of the wildlife that awaits you if you take the time to visit some of Iowa's special places. For the most part, the views are free and you just need to be in the right place at the right time of year. Remember that these are wild animals and that their schedule is their own. With a little planning and foresight, however, you will be able to enjoy some of the best spectacles Iowa has available for you.

REFERENCES

Bowles, John B., Daryl L. Howell, Richard P. Lampe, and Howard P. Whidden. "Mammals of Iowa: Holocene to the end of the 20th century." *Journal of the Iowa Academy of Science* 105:123–132, 1998.

Dinsmore, James J. *A Country So Full of Game.* Iowa City: University of Iowa Press, 1994.

Dinsmore, Stephen J., Laura S. Jackson, Bruce L. Ehresman, and James J. Dinsmore. *Iowa Wildlife Viewing Guide.* Helena, MT: Falcon Press, 1995.

Ehresman, Bruce L. "The recovery of the Bald Eagle as an Iowa nesting species." *Iowa Bird Life* 69:1-12, 1999.

Frederick, Robert B., William R. Clark, and Erwin E. Klaas. *Behavior, Energetics, and Management of Refuging Waterfowl: A Simulation Model.* Wildlife Monographs no. 96, 1987.

Frederick, Robert B., Erwin E. Klaas, Guy A. Baldassarre, and Kenneth J. Reinecke. "A method for sampling waste corn." *Journal of Wildlife Management* 48:298-304, 1984.

Kent, Thomas H. "Checklist of Iowa birds—1998 edition." *Iowa Bird Life* 68:73-84, 1998.

❧ 11 ❧

Iowa's Lost Lakes

Robert F. Sayre

"Land of Ten Lakes." Thus did *Des Moines Register* columnist Donald Kaul and one of his readers characterize Iowa some years ago. Such self-mockery is modern Iowa humor. Iowa cannot rival Minnesota's extravagant boast that it has "10,000 Lakes," so we try to laugh about it.

But Iowa was not always so deprived. Although few people know it, between ten and twenty percent of Iowa was once wetland.

North-central Iowa was once so covered by lakes and marshes that travelers from the eastern United States could not cross it except in winter. Ioway Indians had crossed it only by following glacial eskers, the ridges of sand and gravel deposited by streams of glacial meltwater. Pioneer farmers in Pocahontas County joked that to farm there you needed a boat. Just to the south, in Calhoun County, people could once ice skate from Lake City to Rockwell City, about fifteen miles. The towns of Plover, Mallard, and Curlew in Pocahontas and Palo Alto Counties were named by Charles Whitehead, president of the Des Moines and Fort Dodge Railroad for the waterfowl he and his employees and passengers shot along the route. In addition, along the Mississippi and Missouri and other major rivers were many bounded bends and ox-bows.

Fig. 11.1. *"Ponding" After a Heavy Rain* is a sure sign of the location of a former wetland. Crops on such land are chancy, being stunted or washed out and difficult to cultivate and harvest, so that the land is a good candidate for the Wetlands Reserve Program. (Photograph by Robert F. Sayre.)

What changed this immense and wide-spread "wetlandscape" was the digging of drainage ditches and wells, beginning in the late-nineteenth century and continuing until the 1950s, which drained the water from these millions of acres of lakes and marshes and converted them into fertile and (usually) dry cropland. Only the plowing up of the prairie had a greater impact on the landscape of Iowa and surrounding states. By destroying aquatic plants, eliminating the habitat for millions of birds and fish, and contributing to later flooding, drainage may have had an even greater impact than plowing, although it is hard to say for sure because the two went on together and affected each other. Land that was drained was then plowed. Land that had been plowed led to the deterioration of neighboring wetland and the increased desire of its owners to drain it.

To carefully read the Iowa landscape, therefore, requires looking not just at land but at *water*—including the water that is no longer here but has nevertheless left its traces. The flat fields that you drive by may once have been lake bottoms, marshland, or the floodplains of rivers. The straight "streams" through fields or along their edges are probably drainage ditches. Their depth and "fall" are precisely engineered, and if you look closely you can see

Fig. 11.2. *Owl Lake Ditch* in Humboldt County was once proudly known as Iowa's deepest drainage ditch. Though little seen today, its size is still impressive, as seen in this picture, taken in July 1998. The great ditch also suggests how much water once flowed out of the lake it emptied. Such ditches, large and small, are common sights in north-central Iowa. (Photograph by Robert F. Sayre.)

the pipes or "tile lines" feeding into them to carry off water from rain and snow. More traces of water, past and present, can be seen in the bare spots in fields, where water has settled and the ground has been too wet for crops. Once upon a time these were probably marshes. In some places you can even see the surviving shorelines of the drained lakes, with the roads that were built to skirt their edges.

Growing appreciation of the value of wetlands adds to our interest in these lost lakes and marshes. They not only provided habitat for ducks, geese, cranes, beavers, muskrats, otters, fish, turtles, frogs, and many other birds and insects; they purified water, reduced the dangers and the severity of floods, restored aquifers, and preserved water during periods of drought. By slowing down and holding back water, they also reduced soil erosion—another illustration of how the health of land and water are connected. Take care of water, as the conservationist knows, and you take care of soil; take care of the soil, and you take care of water. Management of land and water are integrally related.

Yet discovering Iowa's lost lakes requires looking at more than the land. Drainage, ditching, terracing, road building, and the effects of a century of farming have radically altered both the cover and the contour of the land. Not even the closest observer can always be sure of what once was here. Moreover, the Iowa lakes were for the most part prairie lakes where the borders between a lake, its surrounding marsh, and the upland beyond were constantly in flux. In wet periods the lake rose and expanded out into the marsh and the marsh into the prairie. In dry periods it contracted into little more than a marsh itself. This quality of prairie lakes also confused and distressed the settlers from New York, New England, and Europe. These lakes seldom had fixed shorelines with sandy beaches. They had no surrounding pines and birches. Some did have neighboring oaks, but these too may now be gone, cut for firewood or to make way for corn. So by now the marshy shoreline may have become a cornfield, and the lake just a small marsh or merely the low point in a field.

Since these changes in the land have happened over what is now four, five, or six generations, human memories are not reliable either. Swan Lake in Pocahontas County, northwest of the town of Laurens was drained in 1911, and no one now living ever saw it. Stories of lakes like Swan Lake are passed down from one generation to the next, but the stories from two or more generations back fade away. As they do, people erroneously assume that the landscape they knew as children, or that their parents or grandparents knew, was the original landscape, even the primordial one seen by Indians and the first settlers.

There are other ways of locating the old lakes of Iowa, however. The surveyors who surveyed the state between the 1830s and 1870s were required by the Federal Land Office to take notes describing the land they crossed. These notes have been preserved and reprinted and can be seen at the State Historical Society and the State Geologist's office. Jim Giglierano at the State Geologist's office has even entered them into a computer, superimposed them on a state map, and thereby produced a remarkable colored map of "1832–1859 Vegetation of Iowa." Lakes and wetlands, described variously as bogs, marshes, swamps, meadows, ponds, pools, slues, bays, and drains, all appear in blue and can be located township by township. Old maps are also very helpful. A. T. Andreas's *Illustrated Historical Atlas of the State of Iowa* (1875) has large county maps that show the lakes. The township maps in old county plat books are even more detailed. Another aid are the soil maps prepared by the U.S. Department of Agriculture, which can be seen at every county extension office. The soil types on former lakes and marshes are much more consistent than on drier land, so that on soil maps the lake beds appear as large areas of uniform soil, and are actually identified as old marsh bottoms and lake beds. Additional sources of information are the county histories that were published in the late nineteenth and early twentieth centuries and the old annual reports of the Iowa Geological Survey which, from the 1890s on, published volumes on the geology of nearly every one of Iowa's ninety-nine counties.

But the most convenient and compact guide is *Iowa Lakes and Lake Beds,* which was prepared by the State Highway Commission in 1916. You may wonder why the highway commissioners were surveying lakes. The answer is that people were already touring and vacationing with cars, and in 1915 the legislature had directed the commission to divide the lakes of Iowa into three classes: (1) "Lakes that should be preserved, with an estimate of the cost of improvement"; (2) "Lakes that should be drained, the state retaining title to the land ..."; and (3) "Lakes that should be drained and the land sold." So the commission, with help from geologists, biologists, geographers, and other experts spent two busy years visiting, mapping, and evaluating the condition of sixty-seven surviving lakes around the state. A list of them by county follows, along with very brief summaries of the comments and

recommendations in the report, followed by their current condition and use. One can see that even when the commission recom-
mended retaining a lake it has not necessarily survived, or has survived only as a marsh. Notes on the current condition are based on
descriptions in the *Iowa Sportsman's Atlas* (1994) and *Okoboji
Wetlands,* by Michael J. Lannoo.

Table 11.1

County Lakes	Area, Acres	Condition, Use, Recommendation, 1916	Condition & use at present
Allamakee			
Big Lake 1	200	Retain	Renamed New Albion Big Lake
Kains Lake	200	Retain	Mississippi Flood Plain
Big Lake 2	679	Retain	Now Lansing Big Lake
Mud Hen Lake	164	Retain	Hunting area
Buena Vista			
Storm Lake	3,080	Improve, "natural playground"	Popular resort
Pickerel Lake	171	Build dam to raise 2 feet	Marsh, Hunting area
Calhoun			
Tow Head	151	Drain	195 acre drained lake bed for Hunting
North Twin Lake	509	Retain	State Park, 574 acres
South Twin Lake	596	Retain	Shallow preserve & refuge
Cerro Gordo			
Clear Lake	3,643	Keep, buy land for state park	Major vacation area
Clay			
Trumbull Lake	1,190	Retain, good for sportsmen	Hunting area
Round Lake	450	Retain, good for sportsmen	Hunting; waterfowl refuge
Dan Green's Slough	285	Good hunting reserve	Hunting area
Elk Lake	261	Leave as is, "very attractive"	Hunting, includes Wapiti Marsh
Delaware			
Silver Lake	32	Retain, add land for a park	40 ac lake w/ 53 ac camp grnd
Dickinson			
Spirit Lake	5,660	Connect w/ E. Okoboji, buy land for state park	Popular resort
East Okoboji Lake	1,875	Keep, add park	Popular for hunting & fishing
West Okoboji Lake	3,788	Deepest, most popular	Major resort
Center Lake	264	Retain, add park	Shallow lake, w/ timber borders
Silver Lake	1,096	Maintain water level, add park	Park, hunting, fishing

Lake			
Diamond Lake	111	Beautiful, reserve for park	Shallow, ringed by park
Welch Lake	57	Retain	Game fish nursery
Hottes &	312	"parts of Spirit Lake,"	Shallow, "experience
Marble Lakes	175	open a channel to it; possible fish hatchery	hypoxia during droughts" (Lannoo, 8)
Little Spirit Lake	214	Add culvert & park; on MN border	Hunting, waterfowl
Swan Lake	298	Retain	Shallow lake-marsh. Now Little Swan Lake
Prairie Lake	105	Retain, raise level 2 feet	Hypoxic in droughts
Pleasant Lake	82	Keep as is	private
Jefferson Slough	80	Plan to drain	Jemmerson? "bullfrogs" (Lanno 143)

Emmet

Lake			
Four Mile Lake	185	Keep for game birds	Marsh, hunting
Grass Lake	152	Drain	Drained lake bed
Birge Lake	140	Drain; obstructs road to Lutheran church	Drained lake bed; hunting
Tuttle Lake	981	Damaged by drainage of lakes in MN	Park and wildlife area
Iowa Lake	832	Beautiful; keep, add park	Shallow; wildlife area
West Swan Lake	1038	Drainage avoided; preserve	Shallow; wildlife area
Mud Lake	363	Hunting spot, don't drain	Part of Wolden Rec. Area
High Lake	451	Hunting spot, retain	Part of Wolden Rec. Area
Twelve Mile Lake	211	Build dam to maintain level	Shallow; wildlife area

Greene

Lake			
Goose Lake	411	Dries up in droughts; drain	Shallow marsh; hunting

Hamilton

Lake			
Little Wall Lake	230	Popular for hunting; deepen	Park, boating & fishing

Hancock

Lake			
Eagle Lake	837	Birding, hunting; improve	Shallow lake-marsh; hunting
Wood Lake	42	Combine with Eagle Lake	Woodland area; hunting
East Twin Lake	184	Keep for hunting, fishing	Shallow lake-marsh
West Twin Lake	109	Keep, add local park	Used for fishing, picnics

Harrison

Lake			
Noble's Lake	160	Keep; protect from MO River	Shallow marsh; wildlife area
Round Lake	327	Believed sold as swamp land	Marsh, hunting reserve

Johnson

Lake			
Swan Lake	37	Drain	Shallow lake, abuts Hawkeye Wildlife Area
Babcock Lake	58	Sell	Part of Hawkeye W. Area

Table 11.1   continued

County Lakes	Area, Acres	Condition, Use, Recommendation, 1916	Condition & use at present
Kossuth			
Goose Lake	103	Retain	Shallow lake-marsh
Swag Lake	46	Part in MN. Buy park land	Burt Lake – campground
Lee			
Green Bay Lake	271	Made part of drainage district along Miss. R.	Access point to Miss. R.
Monona			
Blue Lake	918	Missouri R. bend. Improve	Shallow lake-marsh
Osceola			
Rush Lake	317	Keep & improve; good hunting	Shallow lake-marsh
Iowa Lake	242	Preserve as is	Fishing & hunting site
Palo Alto			
Medium Lake	991	Keep, assist local people in improving	Now Five Isl. Lake, from Emmetsburg north
Silver Lake	667	Keep, add park	Hunting site
Rush Lake	460	Keep, raise level	Marsh
Lost Island Lake	1,076	Very pretty; add dam & park	Marsh
Virgin Lake	200	Beautiful; add park	Shallow; hunting
Pocahontas			
Clear Lake	165	Overgrown; dredge, add park	Now Little Clear Lake Rec. & Wildlife Area
Lizard Lake	251	Pretty but little used; improve	Lake-marsh; hunting
Sac			
Wall Lake	923	Popular resort; improve	Renamed Black Hawk Lake; State Park added
Winnebago			
Duck Lake	77	Shallow; hunting & trapping; raise & improve	Now Harmon Lake; marsh & prairie; hunting
Woodbury			
Brown's Lake	840	Cut off Missouri R. bend; pop. fishing & swimming resort	Lake-marsh; hunting
Worth			
Silver Lake	310	Attractive; hunting, fishing, Picnicking; keep	Enlarged recreation & hunting area

Wright

Cornelia Lake	262	Camping, fishing, picnics; keep	Beside Lake C. Park; fishing, boating, camping
Elm Lake	429	Pretty; dredge; add park	Marsh; hunting, trapping
Wall Lake	935	Shallow; fishing & hunting; dredge; add park	Now Big Wall Lake; shallow lake & marsh; hunting
Twin Sisters Lake	100	Shallow; fishing, hunting; add park	Now Morse Lake; hunting, fishing

The conclusion of the highway commissioners in 1916 was that Iowa's lakes were in bad shape. Because of cultivation of adjacent fields, they were silting in and filling up with cattails and marsh grasses. Many were surrounded by private land and thus inaccessible to the public. Owners and vandals had often removed sand, gravel, and rock from their shores. As the lakes deteriorated, pressures grew to drain them, with people also complaining of their mosquitoes and even blaming the lakes for the rudeness of hunters and fishermen who used them. Farmers complained that they attracted huge flocks of blackbirds which stole seeds from their fields and later broke into the tips of the ears of ripening corn. (The report devotes twenty-seven pages to an examination of this, concluding that the damage was not as great as believed.) Photographs in the book show eroded outlets, broken dams, and muddy shores.

The commissioners feared that Iowa was losing a valuable esthetic and recreational resource. As further documentation of this danger, they included another list of the lakes they could not report on—the ones that had already been drained, sold to private owners, turned over to counties, or otherwise disposed of. This list is not so long, and there are, obviously, no descriptions. But these thirty-seven lakes, in twenty counties must be mentioned too. Today some have been partially restored and survive as marshes and wildlife and hunting areas. Others are the subject of restoration efforts. But as a group they are, you could say, Iowa's most lost or longest-lost lakes. Looking for traces of them is a challenge to careful observation.

Calhoun: Pond Grove
Clay: Mud Lake
Clinton: Goose Lake

Dickinson: Lily Lake, Pratt Lake, Sylvan Lake
Emmet: Cheevers Lake, Ryan Lake, Swan Lake (East)
Fremont: Wabonsie Lake
Hamilton: Cairo Lake, Island Lake, Iowa Lake
Harrison: Minnewashta or Soldier Lake, Round Lake, Dry
    Lake
Humboldt: Bass Lake, Impassable Marsh, Owl Lake
Kossuth: Bancroft Lake, Eagle Lake
Louisa: Muscatine Slough, Wapello Lake
Muscatine: Odessa and Keokuk Lakes
Palo Alto: Elbow Lake
Pocahontas: Swan and Rat Lakes
Pottawattamie: Big Lake, Boyer Lake, Carr Lake, Honey
    Creek Lake
Sac: Lard Lake, Rush Lake
Webster: Bass Lake No. 2
Woodbury: Sand Hill Lake
Worth and Winnebago: Rice Lake
Worth: Brights Lake

As Table 11.1 reveals, most of the natural lakes of Iowa are and were small and shallow. Even the four biggest, two in Dickinson and one each in Cerro Gordo and Buena Vista counties, that were on the edge of the last glacier, are only 3,080 to 5,660 acres. Such small lakes are less attractive to tourists and vacationers than the larger lakes in Wisconsin, Michigan, and Minnesota. People with big sailboats and motorboats, people going on summer vacations, and people looking for second homes do not go to lakes of only a couple of hundred acres. Therefore many Iowa lakes have been almost ignored. Also, the small and shallow lakes of Iowa were relatively easy to drain and convert to farmland.

Lakes are not just for vacations and boating, however. Even in the nineteenth century, long before people linked lakes with water purification, flood control, or the recharging of aquifers, the lakes of Iowa were very important to local identities.

One telling sign is the names of the townships that the lakes are, or were, in. In contrast to most Iowa townships, which bear the names of old nineteenth-century national worthies—Webster, Clay, Calhoun, Douglas, Cass, Colfax, and so on—townships with lakes tended to be named for them. The surveyors, developers, and county supervisors obviously recognized the value that land buyers would put on a lake or any "clear sheet of water," as they

Fig. 11.3. *A Popular Resort, ca. 1910,* Lakewood was a park on the north shore of Wall Lake, near Lake View, Sac County. To avoid confusion with other Wall Lakes in Iowa and to honor the Sac leader, the name was changed in the 1930s to Black Hawk Lake. Black Hawk State Park was established in 1935. (State Historical Society of Iowa Photograph.)

called it. Thus they temporarily put aside their allegiances to some grandiloquent senator or general and literally went to the lake, giving the town a name like Crystal Lake, Twin Lakes, Lake Creek, Swan Lake, Silver Lake, Lost Island, Rush Lake, Wall Lake, or Clear Lake. Or they honored the nearby water-loving animals and amphibians by naming the town Beaver, Coon, Lizard, etc. By the same principle, towns, churches, and even cemeteries were named for the water they were near. Such names not only signal the way early residents identified with the old lakes and ponds, "a landscape's most beautiful and expressive feature," as Thoreau said, they also can help today's seekers of Iowa's lost lakes, as they travel over the state, a figurative divining rod in hand, with their lips parched and their eyes aching for a spot of blue, to locate the most likely places.

Sometimes, however, one finds that the lake is gone and that the name is now deceiving, a sort of Iowa mirage. At the corner of two country roads in Humboldt County is a wooden sign pointing to "Lake Lutheran Church." The lake from which the church took its name was Owl Lake, which was described by the great Iowa geologist Thomas H. Macbride in 1898 as having been "a beautiful and permanent sheet of water, covering several hundred acres, ten or fifteen feet deep, bordered by beautiful groves of native trees." Although this was no small or shallow lake, it was drained around 1895. What one sees today is a cornfield, with a grove of oaks still on the southeast "bank" and a very deep drainage ditch, once said

Fig. 11.4. *Wetland Airstrip:* This small grass landing strip can be seen on the south edge of the town of Wall Lake. It is on part of a former wetland called "the Goose Pond" that extended a mile to the south and five to six miles east and west. The elevation of the road on the left is an indicator of the former height of the water. (Photograph by Robert F. Sayre.)

to be the deepest in the state, leading down to what was once Impassable Marsh to the south.

The town of Wall Lake in Sac County is no longer on a lake. Its lake (which should not be confused with the nearby old Wall Lake now Black Hawk Lake, or Big Wall Lake in Wright County, or Little Wall Lake in Hamilton County) is now a small airport! To the north, in Palo Alto County, in Rush Lake Township, along County Road N38 just south of Curlew, is the attractive and well-kept Rush Lake Cemetery. But Rush Lake was actually to the west in Booth Township, and it is currently described in the *Iowa Sportsman's Atlas* as a marsh, no longer a lake. Rush Lake and its rushy marshes were part of the "vast tracts of land" that, according to the *History of Palo Alto County* (1910), were "practically given away which are now being drained and reclaimed and made the most fertile farming land in the country."

Even more of a mirage is Lake City in Calhoun County. It is a pleasing, well-appointed town of about 1850 people with a good medical center and a remarkable manufacturer of wooden pipe organs, but on signs marking the edge of town is its motto, "Lake City, Everything but a Lake." The motto grew out of an incident around 1940, says Vivian Campbell, the town historian, when a man and woman from Des Moines came through wanting to buy lakeshore property. They were about forty years too late. There had been many lakes in and around town, but they all had been drained, including the largest, Pond Grove, which had been just to the east. The real estate salesman who talked to the couple tried, with the pathetic ingenuity of a booster, to turn an absence into an advantage, coining a motto which seems intended simultaneously to attract curious visitors and to undeceive them.

Curiosity about Iowa's lakes is old. *The History of Wright County* says that in the 1860s Horace Greeley of the *New York Tribune* became so interested in Big Wall Lake that he sent a reporter to examine it. The border of rocks along the southern end of the lake appeared to be so finely constructed that people believed it really was "a wall of masonry constructed by some prehistoric race of people." The reporter accepted the story, and it attracted great attention. However, the *History* continues, the "Hon. Charles Aldrich and others, interested in keeping Iowa history straight, got geologists after the theory, and after they had visited and made a report, made it plain . . . that the 'wall' . . . could be accounted for [by] the heaving of ice bringing up the stone from the lake's bed, as it usually froze to the very bottom in severe

Fig. 11.5. *Lake City, Calhoun County* did once have a lake, Pond Grove, a little east of town, but by 1915 it had already been drained, along with the surrounding wetlands. (Photograph by Robert F. Sayre.)

winters." (p. 50) This explanation probably isn't right either. The "walls" of this and other "Wall" lakes were made by the glacier. But today it is hard to find the rocks that caused such a controversy. Perhaps they were hauled away to become the foundations of houses and barns. When I asked two men who were rebuilding a cabin along Big Wall Lake whether they had heard of the old story, they said they had not. Yet one of them said he had hunted on the lake for fifty years and knew every part of it. It has not been dammed, dredged, or heavily developed, like Lake Cornelia eleven miles to the north, and is suggestive of what the larger, shallow lakes of Iowa may once have looked like.

Identification with a lake can be stronger and more lasting᾿ than any other identification people make with a place. As an island provides relief and safety from the ocean, a lake is relief from the dryness and monotony of land. It is like an oasis—a very wet oasis—in the endless prairie. Psychologically, rivers represent change and the passage of time, but lakes represent permanence, a reflection of both the present and the eternal. They rise and fall. Their surfaces change with the weather and the light, as they also change with the seasons. But the cycle goes around, and the lake is still there, a mirror of what encircles it and whoever looks into it. To quote Thoreau again—and he is the great philosopher of lakes—"It is the earth's eye; looking into which the beholder measures the depth of his own nature."

The drainage of Iowa's lakes, therefore, has seemed to many people like a terrible devastation: a destruction of places of both public pleasure and private devotion, an offense against nature and human nature, a gouging out of the eyes. Some of the fiercest and longest legal battles in early Iowa were fought over lakes. Landowners, who had generally acquired them at low cost, as unsold public land, wanted to drain them in order to gain their much greater value as farmland. They argued that they had that right and that the lakes caused disease and were small and worthless. Lake-lovers countered that the lakes were small only because of drought or degradation and that they had given great public benefit for fishing, hunting, and recreation, and should be public property. The lawsuits over Lost Island Lake and Mud Lake in Palo Alto County, West Twin Lake in Hancock County, Owl Lake in Humboldt County, and Goose Lake in Greene County were particularly bitter, the last two ultimately reaching the U.S. Supreme Court. Lakes were also the object of numerous acts of the legislature and reports of the attorney general. The lakes of Iowa are not as tranquil as they look—or used to look.

Similar battles have been fought over their restoration. Following the Supreme Court decision, Goose Lake was drained in 1920. But contrary to expectation, it did not make very good farmland, and in 1954 the drainage system was changed and it was, according to a sign on its shore, "allowed to refill with water making it a nesting area for waterfowl again." But it was not allowed to fully refill. The bend in the county road along its east side shows that its level was once four or five feet higher. A drain keeps it a marsh, not a lake.

In the case of other lakes, committees have been formed, people have done research on their histories, and lengthy proposals have been written on the engineering, costs, and benefits of their

Fig. 11.6.   *This Cage Guards the Drainage Outlet* of the former Goose Lake in Greene County, north of Jefferson, Iowa. Though still called a lake, the outlet keeps it a shallow marsh. The lake was drained in 1920 after a lengthy lawsuit.

restoration. One such effort was started in the late 1980s and early 1990s in Pocahontas County to restore Swan Lake.

Swan Lake's profound hold on people is suggested in a quotation from the February 9, 1905 *Pocahontas County Sun* with which the backers of the 1991 restoration project began their proposal:

> Swan Lake used to be one of the most beautiful lakes in Northern Iowa and also one of the best lakes for fishing. People used to come to this lake from as far as Eagle Grove. On its banks, under the shade of the trees, the school children had picnics. Businessmen and farmers

alike took their families there for a quiet Sunday after-noon's rest, and fifty years from now they will still be doing so, if we save Swan Lake.

The original writer had been fighting the move to drain the lake in 1905, a move which had started because it had already de-teriorated. Like other lakes, it had silted in. A drought in 1894 had nearly dried it up. A dam had then been built to try to raise it, but the dam was poorly situated and badly designed, and seepage and flooding ensued. Still, people loved it. There was even a little steamboat that made excursions around the lake and to an island near one shore. So petitions were drawn up, and people went to Des Moines to testify against drainage. But they lost, and Swan Lake was drained in 1911.

In the interim numerous people have dreamed of restoring it. The site acquired additional fascination when, in February 1945, a Japanese balloon bearing an incendiary bomb descended onto one of the farms on the site of old Swan Lake. It was one of the paper balloons which the Japanese sent up toward the end of World War II, hoping to ignite forest and range fires. Crowds came to see it before it was taken away by U.S. Army intelligence offi-cers. Records were kept secret, and the story was not printed until 1976. That the balloon landed on the old Swan Lake was purely accidental, and fortunately it started no fires. Of course, had Swan Lake still been full and not a farm, a fire would have had no chance.

I first heard about Swan Lake in October 1991, from Ron Harms of Laurens, one of the people working for its restoration. In the summer of 1998 I went back to talk to two other Swan Lake advocates, or lovers, Don Beneke and Don Winkler. We met in Winkler's law office, where he was looking at his collection of Indian arrowheads, potshards, drills, and hide scrapers, most of which he had found on the former Lake's island. Since these arti-facts represented many cultures, from as far away as the Rockies, and many centuries, recent and long past, Winkler felt sure that the lake, with its once huge populations of ducks and geese, and the island, because of its natural safety, had for centuries been at-tractions to Indians. Restoration would help more people to ap-preciate this, in addition to all the other benefits. In fact, he was so determined to restore at least a part of the lake that he had bought land at one end of it, where he planned to build a small dam. That would be a beginning. Later Don Beneke took me out in his van to show me the old shoreline and the best vantage points. One old farmstead, now just a corncrib and the remains of a barn, had a sign, "Lakeside Farm." But all of Swan Lake, as well as its neighbor Muskrat or Rat Lake, was now filled with corn, five to six feet tall, and soybeans, one-and-a-half to two feet tall. Compensating the farmers for the loss of such productive fields would be very expensive, and the old laws that once facilitated the drainage of wetlands gave special authority to the landowners who favored drainage. On the other hand, Beneke pointed out, farming such land did have risks. "Come look after a good five-inch rain," he said, "and you'll have no trouble telling where those old lake beds are."

There is an added incentive now for restoring some of the lakes of Iowa: the need to close agricultural drainage wells. These "ag wells" or ADWs, began to be dug in the 1890s as a means of draining lakes and marshes directly down into the underlying aquifers rather than into streams and rivers. By the 1950s, when laws were passed to prohibit any new ADWs, hundreds had already been dug. As Thomas Macbride wrote in his 1899 report on the geology of Humboldt County, where many of these early wells were dug, farmers had noted that some "lakelets" or kettle-holes naturally drained down into the aquifers, and "taking their cue from the natural state of affairs, have begun boring holes in the bottoms of the marshes or lakes not having such outlets by nature." If a well could take water out of the ground, it could also be used to pour water down into the ground. The danger, as Macbride foresaw, was that contamination went in too.

> Soil, sand, clay, and detritus of all sorts seem to be received with impunity. The propriety of sending the discharge of unfiltered surface waters into the water couches that must supply at the same time the wells and springs of the county, is, perhaps, a matter that will one day merit consideration at the hands of the sanitary engineer.

Macbride's prophecy came true in the 1970s and '80s, when it was discovered that poisonous agricultural chemicals—residues from fertilizers and pesticides—were getting into the groundwater. This led to passage of the Groundwater Protection Act in 1988 and a bill in 1997 to encourage the closing of ADWs. With the building of huge hog confinement operations, with correspondingly large manure lagoons, alarm has also spread that manure spills will enter groundwater through the ADWs. In fact, one such hog operation could drain into old Owl Lake and so pollute groundwater and/or the Boone River.

Closing ADWs and allowing natural lakes and marshes to revive has thus taken on another justification. In addition to the other benefits—recreation, habitat, flood prevention, and soil preservation—lakes and marshes that fill up over the sites of closed ADWs can save us from being poisoned.

And yet restoring an Iowa lake or marsh takes time, in fact, decades. Take the example of Beed's Lake in Franklin County. It is not actually a natural lake, but the curious successor to a mill pond that was built in the late 1850s by a Campbellite preacher. The preacher, named T.K. Hansberry, dammed Spring Creek at a point between limestone bluffs and built a saw mill which he used to cut the lumber to build a flour mill. Wheat was the area's main crop in those days, and the mill met a great local need. William Beed bought it in 1864 and for forty years made improvements to the mill and enlarged the dam until the pond above it became a favorite local gathering place for picnics, boating, and hunting. But as corn gradually replaced wheat, there was less and less need for the mill, and in 1904 it closed. Floods soon washed out the dike around the dam, the pond dropped, and picnicking and fishing declined. In 1917 a farmer named Henry Paullus bought it, drained what was left of the pond, and planted forty acres of corn, encouraged, probably, by the high prices during World War I. But the people in nearby Hampton missed the pond, and in 1926 a newly formed Izaak Walton League chapter made plans for a new dam that would impound a larger pond, a lake, to be paid for with a forty-five-thousand-dollar tax levy. Voters from elsewhere in the county, however, felt that the lake would do them no good, and the levy was defeated. In 1933, a revived Izaak Walton League tried again. Henry Paullus and other landowners agreed to sell a total of 254 acres, the city of Hampton would issue eight thousand dollars in bonds, and more money would be raised by selling sixty-three building lots on the north shore of the lake. The lake itself would be turned over to the state conservation commission.

This proposal succeeded. Then in 1934 the Civilian Conservation Corps (CCC) entered the picture, providing for a still larger dam, 170 feet long and 34 feet high, which could not only impound a larger lake but handle the floods that might back up behind the new dam. The CCC worked for four-and-a-half years, and when Beed's Lake was finally opened, it had a boat dock, swimming beach, bathhouse, parking lot, picnic area, three-mile

footpath, and a game refuge. Today, Beed's Lake State Park has
319 acres, including the 99-acre lake. On a summer weekend there
are hundreds of campers and picnickers, and you can see many
boats out on the lake.

A more recent restoration, which also has taken many years
of planning, is Burrow's Pond, to the west of the little town of
Nemaha in Sac County. It is on land that used to belong to the Rutledge family, and for years the Rutledge men and boys and their
friends hunted there. In 1893 W. A. Rutledge formed the Farmers
Mutual Hail Insurance Company. It became a very successful en-
terprise, and later W. A. Rutledge drained the pond. Like many
other landowners then, he thought that he was helping "improve
the country." But in 1939 he wrote, "Time has revealed that I was
a destroyer of natural resources." So in 1993, as a way of marking
the centennial of the founding of the company, Perry and Foster
Rutledge, two of his sons, began an effort to acquire the land from
the four current owners and restore the pond and its marsh. As
seems clear from a plaque unveiled at the re-opening ceremony in
May 1998, it was work that required the funds and expertise of
many people and organizations. Considering that good farmland
in that area sells for between 2500 and 2700 dollars per acre, the
land alone, around 290 acres, is worth over 700,000 dollars. As
Dave Holstad, a DNR employee, explained to me, the restoration
also involved breaking the tile lines that once led down to and
under the marsh, so that water would no longer by-pass it. Then
lines leading to the marsh had to be raised so that they would flow
into it. This would supply the marsh but still prevent surface erosion on the surrounding fields, which would otherwise soon fill the
marsh with silt. In addition, the nearby county road had to be
raised and rerouted. A small parking lot and walking trails were
built, signs were put up, and prairie seed was planted.

Was it worth so much effort and money? Burrow's Pond is
only a marsh, so shallow that the Department of Natural Resources does not even plan to stock it with fish. It is the kind of
marsh that, not only W. A. Rutledge, but thousands of other
landowners in Iowa and surrounding states were once eager to get
rid of. And there are still thousands of people who have no appreciation for such places. On a hot summer day in Kanawha, for instance, when I asked a woman at a convenience store for directions
to East and West Twin lakes, two small lakes along the southern
edge of Hancock County, her first answer was contemptuous.
"You want to go to the lakes? With all those mosquitoes? People

Fig. 11.7. *A Lost Lake Found,* Burrow's Pond in Sac County was restored in 1998, after being drained many years ago by W. A. Rutledge, who had hunted there as a boy. By 1939 he regretted his mistake, writing "Time has revealed that I was a destroyer of natural resources." Its recovery will be exciting to observe. (Photograph by Robert F. Sayre.)

don't generally go there now." She was partially right, too. When we arrived at West Twin Lake, the mosquitoes weren't bad, but there were only three other people, two men and a woman sitting on a little dock fishing. At East Twin Lake there was nobody.

One answer to such indifference is that places like Burrow's Pond and East Twin Lake (a marsh that had also been drained once) are not preserved or restored just for people. They are for the ducks and geese, the muskrats and beavers, the turtles and frogs, and milkweed and butterflies. Those creatures don't just come on Sundays to picnic. They live there (and love the mosquitoes). But, of course, they don't vote or pay taxes or send checks to conservation groups.

So people must also appreciate the lakes and marshes of Iowa, and there are clear signs that this appreciation is growing. In 1985 the federal government established the Wetlands Reserve Program (WRP), which provides landowners with financial incentives to restore wetlands, and as of 1998 Iowa was leading the nation in the number of easements enrolled in the WRP and its counterpart, the Emergency Wetlands Reserve Program (EWRP). A total of 72,155 acres were enrolled, the second highest in the nation, behind Louisiana. That is just a fraction (less than one percent) of the 7,563,500 acres that once were lakes and swamps and marshes in Iowa, but the high national rank of these enrollments suggests that Iowa is more concerned about wetlands than nearly any other state in the country.

As this concern grows, the chances are good that people will also better appreciate the beauty of Iowa's lakes and marshes. The 1916 highway commissioners did a great thing by exposing the bad condition of them. They rescued them from oblivion. But the commissioners' primary interest was in lakes, not marshes, because lakes could be sites for picnics, parks, and vacations. Large lakes were therefore better than small lakes, and lakes with beaches and shade trees better than prairie lakes. They had a sort of New Hampshire idea of what a lake should look like. Marshes they valued as hunting places, and it is good that they did; but they showed no anticipation of such modern values as water purification, groundwater recharge, flood prevention, and wildlife habitat.

Some of those old attitudes are still very strong. Michael Lannoo, in an excellent book, *Okoboji Wetlands: A Lesson in Natural History*, writes of our need to get over an "aquarium ethic"—the idea that lakes should be managed just to produce game fish. We need, he says, to develop a "wetland ethic," a key part of which is appreciation of the amphibians who breed in sloughs and marshes, are an index of wetland health, and attract the waterfowl (pp. 142-43). Marshes, in turn, are essential to the health of lakes. Without them, he writes, "our recreational lakes become dumping grounds for all the grunge in rainwater runoff. Wetlands serve as sinks for chemicals. Fertilizers that ordinarily wash into wetlands to produce cattails, without wetlands wash into our lakes to produce algal blooms. Farm chemicals and roadside runoff that would be biodegraded in wetlands, without wetlands go directly through culverts into lakes and contaminate our fish" (p. 113). So if you love lakes, you better love marshes; and if you like big lakes, you better like little lakes, too.

Actually, over the years, Iowa has had a number of famous lake lovers. Native son Aldo Leopold returned to Iowa when he was doing game surveys in the early 1930s, and in October 1931 wrote a report recommending the restoration of South Twin Lake in Calhoun County. Ding Darling, the nationally famous cartoonist for the *Des Moines Register,* used his cartoons to fight drainage, opposing it not just from the sportsman's point of view but also from that of the birds and animals. Paul Errington, who grew up beside glacial marshes in east-central South Dakota and later taught zoology at Iowa State University, wrote *Of Men and Marshes* (1957), a major work in the movement to restore wetlands. All these men were initially hunters. Errington, in fact, called himself not just a "sportsman" but a duck "predator." For months at a stretch, when he was a boy, his family practically lived on ducks. Ducks were their favorite food. All kinds of ducks. "Ducks, ducks, ducks," he wrote. Such delight transferred into a delight in the whole ritual of duck hunting, duck viewing, and marsh stalking. Sometimes the watching was so engrossing that he "botched the hunting." And as he grew older he became a careful observer of all of the life around marshes, from the "big-river oxbows" of Iowa, south to Georgia and Florida and north to Canada.

Perhaps it is wrong to call Iowa a landlocked state and make jokes about its "ten lakes." There once were many more, and once many people who loved them. It would be more correct to call it, at least once upon a time, a waterlogged state; a spongy, boggy, squishy land of lakes, marshes, and wet prairies, where water was as great a natural resource as soil. Even the so-called "dry prairies" of the Loess Hills and other high ground were "dry" only because the water ran off, or into, the soil rapidly. It was these lakes and marshes, along with the rivers and river bottomland, that made Iowa a "land so full of game," as James Dinsmore has shown.

"Iowa, The Waterlogged State." The name will never appear on license plates! But it should be kept in mind by everyone seriously observing the landscape. The phrase may also come to mind when we have three, four, or five inches of rain in twenty-four hours and the TV weather forecasters warn us to beware of flash floods—floods that would never have become so fast or so destructive if the lakes and marshes had not been drained. Were we truly waterlogged and were all that water absorbed by the soil and held in lakes and marshes, we would not be flooded.

Why drain our lakes to make more farms when we are already suffering from over-production? (1923).

Fig. 11.8.   *Des Moines Register Cartoonist Ding Darling* was an outdoorsman and relentless opponent of agricultural drainage. But this cartoon from 1923, though prophetic, had little effect on state and national policy.

But these calculations are for the hydrologists. The lake lover can only say that the lost lakes of Iowa have not vanished as completely as some people think. Their traces are there, in the landscape and in our records. And in every rainstorm, in every drought, in every flight of waterfowl and melancholy grumble of a frog, their ghosts haunt us.

FOR FURTHER READING

Andreas, A.T. *Illustrated Historical Atlas of the State of Iowa.* Andreas Atlas Co.: Chicago, 1875.

Birdsell, B. P., ed. *History of Wright County, Iowa.* B. F. Bowen & Co.: Indianapolis, 1915.

Dinsmore, James J. *A Country So Full of Game: The Story of Wildlife in Iowa.* University of Iowa Press: Iowa City, 1994.

Errington, Paul L. *Of Men and Marshes.* Macmillan Co.: New York, 1957.

Foster, Lance. *"Tanji Na Che:* Recovering the Landscape of the Ioway," in *Recovering the Prairie,* ed. Robert F. Sayre. University of Wisconsin Press: Madison, 1999.

Foster, Mrs. J. E. *Franklin County History, 1852–1970.* Franklin County [Iowa] Historical Society, n.d.

Iowa Sportsman's Atlas. Sportsman's Atlas Co.: Lytton, IA, 1994.

Iowa State Highway Commission, *Report ... on the Iowa Lakes and Lake Beds.* State of Iowa: Des Moines, 1917.

Lannoo, Michael J. *Okoboji Wetlands: A Lesson in Natural History.* University of Iowa Press: Iowa City, 1996.

Leopold, Aldo. "Iowa Conservation Plan: Lake or Marshland Project." Files of Iowa Dept. of Natural Resources, Black Hawk District Office, Lake View, IA.

Macbride, T. H. "Geology of Humboldt County," in *Iowa Geological Survey,* vol. 9 (Annual Report, 1898). Iowa Geological Survey: Des Moines, 1899.

Madson, John. *Where the Sky Began: Land of the Tallgrass Prairie.* Sierra Club Books: San Francisco, 1982.

McCarthy, Dwight G. *History of Palo Alto County, Iowa.* The Torch Press: Cedar Rapids, IA, 1910.

McCorvie, Mary R. and Christopher L. Lant, "Drainage District Formation and the Loss of Midwestern Wetlands, 1850–1930," *Agricultural History,* vol. 67 (Fall, 1993), 13–39.

Pioneer History of Pocahontas County, Iowa. The Times Print: Fonda, IA, 1904.

Prince, Hugh. *Wetlands of the American Midwest: A Historical Geography of Changing Attitudes.* University of Chicago Press: Chicago, 1997.

"Shall Swan Lake Be Saved," *Pocahontas County Sun.* Laurens, IA (February 9, 1905).

Stuart, I. L., ed. *History of Franklin County, Iowa.* S.J. Clarke: Chicago, 1914.

United States Department of Agriculture. "Better Wetlands." USDA Natural Resources Conservation Service: Des Moines, 1995.

United States Department of Agriculture. "Wetlands Reserve Program—1996 Farm Bill Conservation Program." USDA Natural Resources Conservation Service: Des Moines, 1996.

Vileisis, Ann. *Discovering the Unknown Landscape: A History of America's Wetlands.* Island Press: Washington, D.C., 1997.

❧ 12 ❧

Iowa's High Points

Jean Cutler Prior

Maps are remarkable pieces of paper. They are small flat representations of distant physical places. The street map in a phone book or the pages of a road atlas can take us across town or across the country without leaving our chair. There are few maps, however, as intriguing as those depicting elevation and terrain, especially the colorful sheets published by the U.S. Geological Survey (USGS). They catch our eye and imagination with green woodland tracts, blue meandering rivers, and curving brown contours that portray the shapes and elevations of a piece of the earth's surface.

It may surprise some people that Iowa's landscape would even come under the scrutiny of those whose mandate is to map differences in elevation, in such a seemingly "topographically challenged" state. However, Iowa's heights and breadths have been completely mapped and committed to paper at a scale of 1:24,000, the popular 7.5-minute quadrangle series, so called because each map spans that area of latitude and longitude. The effort fills 1,083 rectangular sheets with accurate information about elevation, location, and shape of Iowa's land surface. This mapping was many years in progress, beginning in the 1890s and completed in 1985. The on-going pursuit of increasingly accurate maps of the earth's surface is both historically and scientifically fascinating, and it is likely that advancing technology will bring further refinements in the future. The information that derives from this map-making process also can take some unusual and non-technical directions. As it turned out, one of the most unexpected pieces of information to emerge from the 7.5-minute series mapping of Iowa concerned the location of the state's highest point above sea level. While Iowans awaited a final clarification of the matter, these trustworthy maps of our ground's basic measurements also became a source of drama, controversy, humor, reverie, and insight into human nature. At the same time, we came to appreciate further that Iowa's "high points" are not necessarily a matter of elevation.

For years anyone who consulted an authoritative reference on each state's high point found the listing for Iowa given as: "Ocheyedan Mound, Osceola County, 1,675 feet." Generations of Iowa school children absorbed this uncontested fact in studies about their home state. Pronounced "O-chee-dan," the French explorer Jean Nicollet explained its meaning as, "a name derived from a small hill, the literal meaning of which is 'the spot where they cry,' alluding to the custom of the Indians to repair to elevated situations to weep over their dead relatives."[1] The word *"Ocheyedan"* in the Dakota Sioux language means a "mourning ground" or "place of mourning." Ceremonial crying was traditional among the Dakota Sioux and other native peoples of this region.

Geologically, Ocheyedan Mound speaks to an even more distant past. Its physical origins lie in the final advance of glacial ice pushing southward into Iowa, even as the glacial climate began to warm. This advance of the northern Laurentide Ice Sheet, just fifteen thousand to fourteen thousand years ago, covered only the north-central part of the state, a region known today as the Des Moines Lobe. Iowa's capital city sits at the southern limit of the glacier's flow. The ice actually moved into Iowa as a series of surges; each carried abundant dirt and rock material within its grasp, then stagnated and slowly melted across the north-central counties. By twelve thousand or eleven thousand years ago, most of the ice had disappeared. The effects of these events are seen today as distinctive landscape features and deposits that took shape in direct contact with the ice and its waning phases of melting and disintegration. Meltwater washed stony debris into tunnels that opened through the decaying ice mass; streams poured out from the glacier margins, and catastrophic floods periodically burst forth as temporary ice dams gave way.

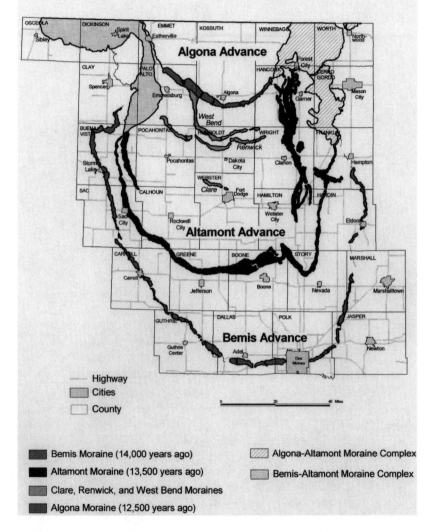

Fig. 12.1. *Glacial Moraines* loop across the north-central Iowa landscape, marking the extent of various surges of the Des Moines Lobe ice sheet into Iowa between fifteen thousand and twelve thousand years ago. (Iowa Dept. of Natural Resources, Geological Survey Bureau.)

Of the many fascinating names given to topographic features of such freshly glaciated terrain, the word "kame" applies to Ocheyedan Mound. It was first used by Scottish geologists to designate "a steep mound or hill of glacial origin." Ocheyedan Mound is a classic among glacial kames. Its conical form composed of sand and gravel rises abruptly from a lower surrounding plain. The sand and gravel were sorted and carried by meltwater flowing across the glaciers' surface and then were washed down a large hole, or "moulin," scoured by swirling meltwaters. After the surrounding ice was gone, the sand and gravel filling was left as a mound on the landscape. Early Iowa naturalist Thomas Macbride, in the "Geology of Osceola and Dickinson Counties," described these hills in 1899 as having beautiful prairies on their lower gentler slopes, and on "their crowns are often beds of gravel capped with bowlders and reefs of driven sand."[2] In addition, kames usually show abrupt changes in size and sorting of their internal deposits, and Iowa's kames contain significant amounts of other earth materials that result from mud and other wastage debris sliding haphazardly into the moulins.

The geological and ecological heritage of Ocheyedan Mound was recognized on October 10, 1984, when twenty-four acres were officially dedicated as a "State Preserve." These special sites are recognized and protected by Iowa law as the best remaining examples of our state's natural and cultural heritage. The mound was a twenty-four-acre gift presented by William Shuttleworth of Cedar Rapids, a descendant of the family that purchased the 160-acre farm with its mound in 1909. Joined by state legislators and political candidates, some three hundred people climbed the mound's grassy slopes on a windy, overcast afternoon for the dedication ceremony. They listened to the remarks of various speakers and witnessed Governor Branstad sign the document that established the State Preserve. Also participating were members of the State Preserves Board, the state geologist, Donald Koch, members of the Iowa Natural Heritage Foundation, the Osceola County Board of Supervisors, and the Osceola County Conservation Board, who manages the preserve today. The dedication ceremony concluded with Ocheyedan Boy Scout Troop 174 raising the United States and Iowa flags and the playing of the National Anthem by the Ocheyedan Community School band. The event was recorded by the local press and by Iowa Public Television cameras.

The first indication that the mound's ground was not as solid as it appeared occurred in July 1970, in the form of a memo to a

Fig. 12.2. *Ocheyedan Mound* rises abruptly from its surroundings and is a prominent northwest Iowa landmark. The isolated hill, composed largely of sand and gravel, is an outstanding example of a glacial kame. It formed as glacial meltwaters poured sediment into an opening in the stagnant ice sheet about thirteen thousand years ago. In 1984 this site was dedicated as a State Preserve in recognition of its geologic history and native prairie ecology. (Photo by Tim Kemmis.)

USGS district engineer describing the results of certain elevation traverses to Ocheyedan Mound while mapping for the new Lake Park NW 7.5-minute quadrangle. The survey crew obtained an elevation of 1,612.5 feet, which was so different from the 1,675 feet on the record books that a second, more precise, closed alidade traverse was run from a known benchmark to the top of Ocheyedan Mound. The average of the two surveys was 1,613.5 feet. The memo went on to speculate that the highest point in Iowa could be in an area north of Sibley, on the Iowa–Minnesota state line. The unmapped area was proposed for field work, but the project was not yet authorized.

Eight months later, on March 29, 1971, state geologist Samuel Tuthill, was officially notified via a U.S. Department of Interior letter that this field survey "caused a change to be made in the location of the highest point in Iowa. It was determined that the mean elevation of 1,613.4 feet is now considered to be the correct elevation of Ocheyedan Mound." The letter went on to say that pending more detailed mapping of the area, the new highest point in Iowa was to be located 0.6 miles southeast of Bigelow, Minnesota, at the T-intersection of a gravel road to the south from the State Line Road. The new high point elevation given was 1,654 feet above sea level.

Shortly afterward, on Sunday, April 4th, the *Des Moines Register* ran a story by science writer Otto Knauth pointing out that the U.S. Geological Survey had picked a new high point without making a specific search for it. "This seemingly haphazard method of determining something as vital to Iowa's welfare as its highest point" brought comment from the chief of the special research unit of the Map Information Office in Washington, D.C. He said the selection was made under pressure from statistically minded almanac and map makers who "were on our backs to give them a new high point." He went on to point out that the State Line Road was also regraded two years earlier, and he didn't know what effect that activity might have on the site's elevation. "Who knows," he wrote, "maybe there is a hump out there someplace that is higher than the T-intersection. If there is, we don't know about it."

This brewing controversy over the state's high point revealed that northwest Iowa, and in fact much of the rest of Iowa, was deficient in accurate maps of the land surface. The USGS official conceded that, "nobody will know for sure just where the new high point is until the area has been mapped. Under the present schedule, that won't be for several years." A follow-up map along with surveying notations was sent. The state geologist filed this information under "Iowa Highpoint Crisis," and wrote Governor Robert Ray's administrative assistant that he would take it up with the director of the U.S. Geological Survey.

Having gotten wind of a revised elevation for Ocheyedan Mound, an editorial published in the *Worthington Minnesota Globe* on March 11, 1971, suggested that, "Ocheyedan Mound, the 'hill of mourning,' has again become something of a mourning ground with the allegation that the famed Mound is not the highest point in the state of Iowa." The writer laments, "The times are like that. Everything we had ever believed to be true is proved false." Then, as though writing to the innocent youngster "Virginia," whose little friends were telling her there was no Santa Claus, the author points out that grownups place great worth on facts. "They have no romance in their hearts, no sentiment, no imagination. . . . Well now, Virginia, they say the Mound is not the highest point in Iowa. Don't listen to them. The Mound is as high as you will have it, Virginia." This opinion, perhaps tongue-in-cheek considering the state of origin, was filed and annotated by the state geologist as "Other Topographic Myths."

In April 1971, Governor Ray received a letter from Mrs. Ellen Stopsack, "The Mound Lady" as she came to be known after forty-three years of living in its shadow and keeping a scrapbook of its considerable human history. "So you have another high point in Iowa. How come; who goofed?" she wrote. In an attempt to dispel some of the confusion related to the matter, assistant state geologist, Orville Van Eck, replied that the early elevation estimates were furnished by railroad surveys. At that time, elevations were determined by barometric altimeter, which relied on the fact that as elevation increases, atmospheric pressure decreases. Because atmospheric pressure is a constantly changing phenomenon, the method requires that many corrections be made during the measuring process. In addition, a rapid means of transportation between measuring points is vital, and this certainly was lacking during the early surveys. It is understandable that the results were not precise. He pointed out that the 1971 survey to determine the elevation of Ocheyedan Mound must be accepted as having a much higher degree of accuracy than anything done earlier. He concluded diplomatically, "Nevertheless, the fact that the Mound may not be the highest point in the state in relation to mean sea level does not detract in the least from its distinction of being the most conspicuous topographic feature in that part of Iowa. The history associated with the Mound is widely recognized and undoubtedly it will continue to attract people from many areas."

State Geologist Tuthill met with the U.S. Geological Survey in Washington, D.C. on April 6, 1971, and a few days later received a letter from Acting USGS Director Radlinski regretting the "embarrassment and unfortunate publicity concerning the highest elevation in your State of Iowa." He went on to say, "We have asked our Central Region Engineer to send survey parties into the area as soon as possible in an attempt to determine the point of highest elevation. We will notify you immediately of our findings."

Interim correspondence indicates that delays ensued because so much of Iowa was not mapped and that the mapping program was poorly funded. Then after nearly three years, on January 19, 1974, Dr. Tuthill received a letter from A. C. McCutchen, Chief, USGS Mid-Continent Mapping Center in Rolla, Missouri, "enclosing as promised, an advance print of the Sibley NW quadrangle showing what is to date considered the highest elevation in the State and the method used to determine it." Enclosed with this letter was a July 20, 1971, memo from the Field Surveys Branch and an attached preliminary map diagramming the contours and elevations for two traverses to determine the highest elevation on the so-called "Sibley Project." It relates, "The results of the two independent alidade traverses indicate that the point in Mr. Sterler's feed lot, T. 100 N., R. 41 W., N.E. ¼ Sec. 29, with an average elevation 1,669.85 is 1.5 feet higher than any other point on the Sibley Project. We have no absolute assurance that this is the highest point in Iowa although this is the highest point we have encountered to date. Until such time as the State is completely mapped, we cannot be certain."

The mapping held, however, and Merrill and Donna Sterler became the keepers of the state's high point, a mound of earth that is 1,669.85 feet above sea level and about four miles northeast of Sibley, the Osceola County seat. At the time, the site was indeed occupied by a cattle feedlot on the Sterler farm, and the decision was made not to place a formal benchmark monument there.

As the U.S. Geological Survey pointed out in their July 1971 memo accompanying the preliminary field sheets, there were four locations within about three miles of each other that were candidates for the highest point. These sites all occur along the same topographic ridge, generally trending north to south, and bowed slightly to the west. This high ground is the outermost ridge of what geologically speaking are the Bemis and Altamont moraines, the accumulations of glacial deposits along the western margins of two separate but overlapping surges of the Des Moines Lobe ice. This geologic combination produced the widespread landscapes of irregularly scattered hills and undrained basins, known to geologists as "knob and kettle terrain." These features are particularly prominent in Osceola and Dickinson counties along the western margin of the lobe, as well as in Hancock and Cerro Gordo counties along its eastern flank.

Local stream courses also reveal an intriguing chapter of this glacial history. The headwaters of the Little Ocheyedan River rise on this moraine, about a mile east of the Sterler farm. The sluggish stream first heads east and south, joining the waters of the Ocheyedan and Little Sioux rivers. They set off as if bound for the Mississippi on Iowa's far eastern border. In fact, that was their ancestral destination before the Des Moines Lobe ice advanced into the northern Iowa counties. The ice front blocked the rivers' drainage and rearranged the landscape so those eastward flowing tributaries became part of a large glacial lake that took shape to the southeast in the Spencer area. The rising waters finally burst through a narrow divide to the west, sweeping past what is now Gillett Grove, Sioux Rapids, Linn Grove, and Peterson and quickly carved a deep narrow valley through which they flowed to the Missouri River, as they do today. This drainage diversion nearly doubled the size of the Little Sioux River basin. The water that once left this area as part of the Mississippi watershed had become part of the Missouri River watershed, and the "M and M Divide" in Iowa was permanently altered.

Donna Sterler was raised on the high point farm, and she always knew it was high ground. She reflected to *Register* writer Otto Knauth in June 1977, on the feeling of being up high, of seeing a long distance, and observing the way the ground fell away. On a clear day you could see the grain elevator in the town of Ocheyedan, about ten miles to the southeast. She recalled that it was not unusual for a long freight train to stall on the nearby Chicago and Northwestern tracks, unable to make the grade. Though no official plaque or sign marked the state's new natural summit, the Sterlers did have a personalized license plate on their pick-up truck that read "HIGH PT."

The Sterlers were, and continue to be, gracious and patient hosts to "peak-seekers," those travelers who strive to reach the nation's topographic summits. Among them have been members of the national High Pointers club, whose goal is to ascend the highest points of all the states, and whose vacation itineraries are planned with this objective in mind. This group did not regard Iowa's high point as one of the more difficult peaks. "The only problem was to find it," said one member from Ontario, Canada, who remembers Iowa as one of the more beautiful high points— "a very nice pastoral scene." Some visitors on the Sterler property will walk several yards in each direction to ensure the high point isn't missed. Others ask for a rock or pebble as a souvenir of their quest. One peak bagger from New York told the Sterlers this was his second time around the state's high points. The first time he collected a stone from the top of Ocheyedan Mound, and now he wanted a stone from the Sterler's property. Another visitor offered to buy them a membership in the Iowa Mountaineers, an Iowa City–based climbing club. Merrill Sterler himself suggested that the *Des Moines Register*'s Annual Great Bicycle Ride Across Iowa (RAGBRAI) start at his farm and end at the state's low point at Keokuk where the Des Moines and Mississippi rivers join. "It would be downhill all the way," he said.

Disgruntled Iowans were still expressing opinions about the new high point in 1984, as Ocheyedan Mound was about to receive the State Preserve designation mentioned earlier. A *Des Moines Register* editorial on February 11th, commented that

> Ocheyedan Mound should once again become Iowa's highest point. It held that distinction for decades, until some spoilsport found that a spot where Iowa slopes up toward Minnesota is fifty-six-and-a-half feet higher. He could have kept it to himself, but he didn't. . . . The high points in forty-four of the fifty states are named "mountain" or "peak," or at least "dome" or "hill" or "knob." Only in Iowa and flat Florida are the highs reduced to the indignity of an abstractor's description [Section 29 of Township 100 North, Range 41 West, Fifth Principal Meridian, Iowa]. A state that can go to the trouble of naming an official state flower, bird, tree and rock, should name Ocheyedan Mound the official state high point. Damn the altimeters. Full speed ahead.

In a 1990 letter to the editor of the *Ocheyedan Press-Melvin News,* Mr. Gerhardt Van Drie, a retired engineer living in El Segundo, California, offered that he had detected this elevational dilemma some thirty-five years earlier. While scanning the horizon with a level from the top of Ocheyedan Mound, he had noted the higher landscape to the northwest. He had grown up within two miles of the mound, and had hiked, skied, and tobogganed on it. He did not report it at the time, he said, so that "the community of Ocheyedan [would] not lose its bragging rights to being the highest point in the State." While on vacation in Iowa in 1988, he did some further measurements, and thus proposed that a "twin peaks" situation existed. One site was on private land in a farm feedlot, where erosion and deposition were ongoing processes, while the other site was inside the gate of the Wilson Township Cemetery, on less frequently disturbed township property. He suggested, "a twin peaks high point would be better public relations for Iowa," and that "the maintenance level in the township cemetery might also improve." In 1996, he wrote to Governor Branstad, suggesting that steps be taken to recognize a "Twin Peaks" high point for the state of Iowa. The outcome of this query is unknown, but elevational data doesn't lend itself to arbitration or gubernatorial fiat; only one site measures up as Iowa's highest elevation.

Actually, the Wilson Township Cemetery location was identified and measured during the 1971 U.S. Geological Survey field mapping. In fact, their field sheet identified four points within about three miles of each other, showing a total elevational difference of only 3.1 feet. The third highest point shown is the cemetery, less than a mile southeast of the Sterler farm. These four points all occur along the same topographic ridge, the same glacial moraine, the same heap of earth and stony debris that accumulated along the western margin of the ice front fourteen thousand to thirteen thousand years ago. As a quiet, restful place to contemplate high points, the township cemetery has definite appeal. And there could be some benefit from a local initiative that focused attention on the township cemetery as a runner-up high point.

In 1998, the Iowa General Assembly passed House Joint Resolution 2004, officially naming the state's high point at the Sterler farm as "Hawkeye Point." The resolution states that,

> Iowa is regarded as one of only four states in the nation which has not designated, by name, an official highest elevation in the state. The designation would be of educational value to the school children and citizens of the State of Iowa, create additional tourism potential, be of historical significance, promote consistency with officially designated state symbols, provide a readily understandable alternate designation to the public land survey system description, and constitute a source of state pride.

In reporting this event, *The Ocheyedan Press-Melvin News* says that the name was selected by the Sterlers, a fact confirmed in a recent conversation with Donna Sterler.[3] They chose "Hawkeye Point," she said, because it represented all of Iowa, which is known as the "Hawkeye State." She also said that the former feedlot is now a meadow of grass; the fences are down, and the

Fig. 12.3. *Beautiful Open Fields* surround the Sterlers' former feedlot. (Photo by Vid Johnson.)

spot is marked by one of their old "HIGH PT" license plates nailed to one end of the original feed bunk. A covered metal box contains a registration book for visitors to sign, and they continue to come at a rate of two to three hundred per year. The state has erected signs along the neighboring roadsides that identify "Hawkeye Point."

Perhaps the greatest irony in this topographic tempest, is found as a footnote in the *Iowa Geological Survey Annual Report for 1899* (Volume 10, published in 1900) on page 197. Here Thomas Macbride, again writing his report, the "Geology of Osceola and Dickinson Counties," states that Ocheyedan Mound's "only rival [is] the summit of the moraine in Wilson township northwest of Allendorf." His footnote states, "It would be inter-

Fig. 12.4.   *Merrill and Donna Sterler,* holding a registry signed by hundreds of visitors to their land, have been gracious hosts to those wanting to set foot on Iowa's highest point. Their farm is northeast of Sibley in Osceola County. In 1998, the Iowa Legislature passed a Resolution officially naming the site "Hawkeye Point."

Fig. 12.5. *One of the Sterlers'* personalized license plates nailed to the roof of a feed bunk in their former cattle feedlot marks the spot. (Photos by Vid Johnson.)

esting once [and] for all to settle this question of altitude, but the [Iowa Geological] Survey was not in possession of the requisite instruments. From such data as are at hand, the present writer concludes that the highest point in Osceola county, and this means the

Fig. 12.6. *This Road Sign* pointing to the Merrill and Donna Sterler farm on Iowa Highway 60 northeast of Sibley is seen by the hundreds of visitors who come here every year. Many are "peak seekers" who seek to stand on the highest point in each of the fifty states. (Photo by Vid Johnson.)

highest point in Iowa, is near the center of Wilson township, and has an altitude not far from 1,670 feet." Right on Mr. Macbride!

It is remarkable how involved, officially and unofficially, people became with the high point issue. It tugged at matters of pride, science, history, symbolism, tourism, and just simple curiosity. What is it about this particular aspect of our surroundings—the highest elevation above sea level—that draws our attention?

First, there is the "everybody-else-has-one" attitude. Elevation is one of those vital statistics recorded for a place, be it a city, state, or nation. It helps to define our physical surroundings. Elevation is a focal point of map makers, preparers of almanacs and encyclopedias, as well as geographers. The connection between humankind and the land is a basic one and is of long standing. Part of that connection is the need to describe and classify our physical world. It helps us know where we are.

At the same time, high points are anomalies, set apart from the surrounding environment, so we naturally pay attention to them. They literally rise above the commonplace. This elevation difference is what motivates the peak-seekers, who continually add trophies of sorts to their list of "bagged" high points. The altitudinal check-off can provide a purpose for those who just enjoy seeing the countryside. At the other end of the spectrum are those willing to endure months of training to ascend mountain summits for the bragging rights that accrue. There is a sense of arrival and achievement; they have earned the view that awaits them. In any case, there is satisfaction with the effort to set foot on a special place, set apart from the rest of the landscape. For their effort, the peak-seekers are also set apart from the rest of humanity.

Taking the physical aspect of elevation still further, a climb against gravity is said to renew the human spirit, whether to the summit of Mt. Ranier, the top of Ocheyedan Mound, or the long rise to the Sterler farm on the Bemis-Altamont Moraine. We are absorbed by our immediate surroundings and can think in solitude with the ascending landscape. One's focus narrows to the personal effort and the terrain underfoot. The path is imposed by the topography and exposed to the sun, clouds, and wind. The reward is the big picture, a view of the landscape below, and maybe a point-of-view that puts life and time into a fresher perspective. Summits can be places to clarify our thoughts, and life resumed in the lower elevations is affected by the high-ground experience.

There are other metaphysical aspects to high places. American Indians, for example, certainly found sacred ground in elevated landscapes. Natural elements of the terrain such as caves, springs, unusual rock formations, and certainly high points of land were powerful places with strong spiritual connections. We are intrigued today by prehistoric petroglyphs and rock paintings in red ochre that depict handprints, animals, and human figures on bare rock faces across North America. These places are points of direct physical contact between prehistoric people and the land. We can jour-

Fig. 12.7. *The Trail* to the top of Ocheyedan Mound and back allows visitors to see some of the sand and gravel of which it is made and also its native flowers and grasses. (Photo by Vid Johnson.)

ney to them today, perhaps also moved by the physical character of the place, and by the knowledge that ancient people, human like us, stood, touched, and perhaps contemplated the same ground. A hike up one of the steep paths to the Effigy Mounds in Allamakee

County, or to any of Iowa's other remaining Indian mound groups that overlook the broad expanse of the Mississippi Valley, can produce the same realizations.

Even though the Sterler's "Hawkeye Point" sits atop Iowa's altitude charts, there are many other places, like Ocheyedan Mound, technically lower in elevation but distinct in form and vistas, that can bring a "peak" sense of beauty, refreshment, and reflection to the visitor. The following examples come to mind: Balltown Ridge, along a prominent geological feature known as the Silurian Escarpment, in Clayton County; Murray Hill in the heart of the deep loess country of western Harrison County; Goecken Park overlooking the Turkey River Valley community of Eldorado in Fayette County; Pilot Knob, another prominent glacial kame nearer the eastern margins of the Des Moines Lobe in Hancock County; Mt. Hosmer overlooking the Mississippi Valley in Allamakee County; Pikes Peak in Clayton County, a historic threshold for seventeenth-century explorers Marquette and Joliet; and The Backbone, a high narrow spine of durable dolomite in Delaware County. These places do literally rise above the commonplace, and the names themselves are enough to pique one's topographic curiosity.

However, Iowa's "high points" also include its tucked-in, secluded lower places. The colorful cross-bedded sandstone "shut-ins" at Wildcat Den in Muscatine County, the cavernous dolomite outcrops at Maquoketa Caves in Jackson County, the soggy verdant Hanging Bog in Linn County, and the cool groundwater spilling from vertical rock crevices at Dunnings Spring, Coldwater Spring, and Melanaphy Spring in Winneshiek County. White Pine Hollow in Dubuque County, Woodman Hollow and the Ledges in Webster County, Lacey-Keosauqua in Van Buren County and Starrs Cave in Des Moines County all enclose visitors in valleys of wooded seclusion.

Even deeply buried "high points" in Iowa can challenge us. Consider Kalsow Prairie State Preserve set in one of Iowa's more undistinguished landscapes in terms of elevation differences. This native prairie remnant in Pocahontas County is almost directly centered over one of the most anomalous features of Iowa's bedrock geology and one of the most destructive natural events ever to affect Iowa's terrain—a meteor impact crater. The Manson Impact Structure, as it is known, is twenty-four miles in diameter and seventy-four million years old, yet no evidence of the massive geological disruption below shows in the equanimity of the mod-

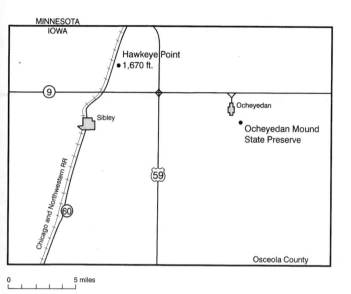

Fig. 12.8. *Osceola County* contains both Iowa's highest elevation, "Hawkeye Point," 1,670 feet above sea level, and what was formerly thought to be the highest point, Ocheyedan Mound.

ern landscape. The geological covers drawn across the feature by the later glacial arrivals and departures added over 150 feet of elevation to this now-hidden landscape. Discovered by well drillers reporting abnormally soft water, this buried feature is a definite "high point" in a tour of our state's geologic history.

Iowans, we find, do not need to be overcome by breathtaking beauty in their landscapes. They have learned to fine-tune their eyes to appreciate subtle differences in terrain. Those Iowans who farm the land for a living and pass over its contours again and again can tell you in minute detail about elevations and relief, about wet and dry, and about rocks, sand, and clay. Iowans who photograph the landscape find abundant beauty. Ask Carl Kurtz, Don Poggensee, Ty Smedes, Ken Formanek, Roger Hill, Bill Witt, or Larry Stone about our state's contours and elevations. They know where to find them, and how to see them and share them with the rest of us.

Paul Johnson, who became director of the Iowa Department of Natural Resources in 1999, points out that Iowa's land is "working land." Border to border, the human connection with it is as direct and intense as anywhere in the country. Perhaps, it is the fact that we have so extensively altered Iowa's land to human purposes and design that we focus more intently on our natural "high points," elevational and otherwise. The prairie, once a common "neighborhood landscape" in Iowa has become scarce; it is safeguarded in revered, remnant prairie preserves. So it is with our state's natural "high points." We seek and appreciate them in particular because they are so refreshingly different from our agricultural "working land" neighborhoods.

All of Iowa's high points have something to tell us of our natural and cultural roots. These places make us think more broadly and deeply about the earth, its land and water resources, its plants and animals, the people who lived here before us, and ourselves. Visiting Iowa's high points can help restore our perspective. Just find a map.

NOTES

1. Macbride, T.H., 1900, "Geology of Osceola and Dickinson Counties," *Iowa Geological Survey Annual Report,* vol. 10 (for 1899), p.195.
2. Ibid.
3. Donna Sterler, personal communication, July 16, 1999.

Part IV.

Tourism, Commerce, and the Landscape

❧ 13 ❦

Drive-Thru History: Theme Towns in Iowa

Mira Engler

"A Little Piece of Denmark", "a taste of Germany," "a touch of Holland," "a Czech village," "a Swedish capital," "an antique city," "a quilt city," "a frontier village," "a journey into the past," "a country relics little village." Is this Disneyland? No, it's Iowa.

Small-town Iowa is catering to tourists. These communities are eager to draw people to alleviate the pain of desertion by youngsters, by industry, and by retailers; to repopulate the empty stores on Main Street; to overcome a sense of placelessness and geographical anonymity; and to regain a sense of worth and pride. The idea of drawing people for jobs is imaginary. The hope of attracting customers for high culture and entertainment is far from reality. The possibility of enticing travelers on Intestates 80 and 35 to tourist attractions in nearby towns shows more promise. The Danish Windmill in Elk Horn, for example, attracts eighty thousand visitors every year, most of them travelers on the Interstate. Along Iowa's stretch of Interstate 80 alone, more than thirty towns newly styled with fresh slogans, refurbished storefronts, or redefined identities beckon the traveler; five ethnic towns, four historic villages, sixteen historical museums, four pioneer museums, four antique centers, and four collections of miniature farm or train artifacts.

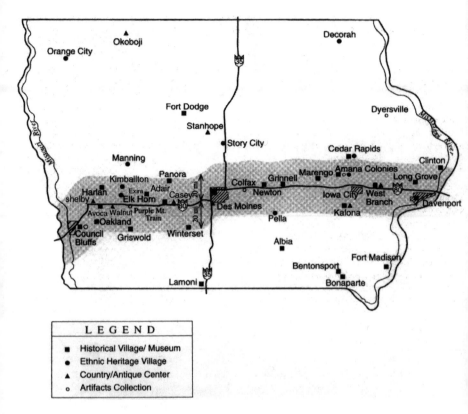

Fig. 13.1.   *Theme Towns* have sprung up mainly along Interstate 80, but can be found in all parts of Iowa. Some attractions, like the Purple Martin Railroad Museum, have closed, proving that not all themes succeed. (Map by Mira Engler.)

During the 1980s, landscape theming became an unparalleled force in Iowa, reshaping both the landscape and the lifestyle of small communities. Theming, based on consumer-society marketing concepts, continues to transform communities into commodities. The search for a theme—a unified image, an experience with a central character—is openly, loudly pursued at many town meetings. Without a theme for your town, claim the proponents, you have nothing that pulls the community together, no identity, certainly no guide to future development, let alone the fact that you simply cannot market yourself.

The success of some Iowa towns in "commoditizing" tourism leads other communities to follow suit. For some towns, developing a theme requires amplifying an existing rudimentary theme. For others, it requires reincarnating a past entity, physical or cultural; and for towns with neither existing nor past resources, developing an image entails the imposition of a foreign reality. For all towns, promoting a theme involves a desire to make the imaginary real, to embody an image visually and physically in the landscape. Town images, either connected to, or detached from, reality, are encroaching on the Iowa landscape and the Iowa mind.

PRECURSORS

In spite of the spread of the American theme town phenomenon and its arrival in the agricultural heartland, we have little information about the history, dispersion, and scope of thematic physical development. The theme town has its origins in both theme parks (amusement parks with a central theme) and in urban theme districts. Among the first theme parks were trade shows and world's fairs such as the World's Colombian Exposition at Chicago in 1893 and the 1939 New York World's Fair. According to the researcher Edward Ball, both types of fairs have nurtured the "world of tomorrow." These government- and industry-sponsored environments displayed ideal model homes, new communications systems, and the latest technology. Simultaneously, in the late 1920s, staged settings of the "world of the past" were introduced as outdoor museums. In his book *America by Design,* Spiro Kostof asserts that the restoration of Colonial Williamsburg to replicate the appearance and the life of pre-industrial America was the first preservation of an entire setting. Williamsburg and its offspring— Old Sturbridge Village, Massachusetts, and Greenfield Village in Dearborn, Michigan—were the fantasies and creations of elite groups of wealthy businessmen and collectors, who erected them as "monuments" to their forefathers' way of life and to the cradle of Americanism. When it opened in 1955, Disneyland blended themes of the past with those of the future and with . . . you name it! Today, Disneyland has come to epitomize theme parks throughout the Euro-American world. But, as Ball points out, in the 1950s theming overflowed the borders of fairs, outdoor museums, and the Disney parks and entered the world of urban planning and real estate speculation.

The second source of theme towns, the urban theme district (a district consciously planned to convey a specific image), is a trend of the past three decades. Before mid-century, districts or neighborhoods with a distinct, unified character—retail or ethnic—were not created as a marketing strategy, but rather, evolved unconsciously. According to scholar Alan Lew, the development of a collection of businesses into a unified retail district, such as seafood stores and restaurants in a waterfront area, resulted from geographic location or the presence of an important industry nearby rather than an agreed-upon idea or theme. Similarly, ethnic urban districts that helped to acculturate new immigrants, such as Chinatowns, were created primarily by social forces, and only secondarily were they intentionally planned places.

One of the earliest examples of a planned urban theme district is the French Quarter of New Orleans. Although in the late 1930s the Louisiana Constitution was amended to protect and preserve the character of the Quarter, only during the 1960s did theming become linked to economics. As Grady Clay points out in *Close Up: How to Read the American Landscape,*

It became apparent to mayors, chambers of commerce, and local development promoters during the 1960s that local identity is capable of being converted into a money-maker in the new age of universal mobility. As a result, *epitome districts* of a special sort [districts representing non-resident cultures] have become a gimmick whereby old identities may be refurbished and new ones fabricated as a device to promote the migration of industry and select population groups, especially tourists. (Italics added.)

Only recently have these fairs and expositions, outdoor museums, theme parks, and theme districts been joined by the grassroots development of theme towns. Although Charleston, South Carolina, passed zoning ordinances that preserved the city's southern plantation character as early as 1931, initiatives to boost design themes are relatively new to small towns. Alan Lew's study of Washington, Oregon, and northern California communities that adopted themes for older retail districts documents an increase from only five such districts in 1960 to more than fifty by 1983. Lew identified four themes used by these towns; waterfront-wharf, Wild West, ethnic, and historic.

In the late 1970s small towns in the Midwest caught up with this trend. In large midwestern towns, themes have usually materialized as enclaves, isolated from the rest of the town; but in small towns, adoption of a theme often entails the transformation of the whole community. Generally, small-town theming in Iowa has been instigated by an individual or a civic group and is then realized by the entire community in an effort to regain identity and economic stability.

IN THE IOWA LANDSCAPE

Whereas Iowa's primary economic base is still agriculture and its related industries, with manufacturing coming in second, tourism is the state's third leading industry. Traditional attractions have been geographical and natural features (e.g., Effigy Mounds National Monument in Marquette, and the Loess Hills in western Iowa) or unusual features or events or cultural landmarks, like the Grotto of Redemption at West Bend, the farm site at Dyersville where the movie *Field of Dreams* was filmed, and Grant Wood's *American Gothic* house at Eldon. But although these experiences have been well-packaged for tourists, they have not necessitated the alteration of the landscape or lifestyle of the community. The key differences in the new tourism are that its manufactured images alter our relationship to the past, by making reality inferior to its image and making our longing for reassurance from an imagined past greater than our desire to shape the future.

In this world of theme tourism, the Iowa past has four attractions: Old World, Frontier America, Old Town, and Agrarian America. Each has become a packaged tourist experience that has tangible physical and cultural repercussions. The Old World roots of different Iowans are encapsulated in the "ethnic-heritage" experience, while Frontier America's early settlements, forts, and battlefields make up the "frontier-pioneer" experience. The Old Town's prosperous Main Street businesses and the public life of the 1920s are captured in the "good-old-town" experience, and Agrarian America's pre-industrial farms and countryside are manifested in the "country-charm" experience. Towns often combine two or more experiences in order to amplify the overall adventure.

Guided by the state's economic development department, towns follow detailed marketing programs in which promotional brochures and ads play a major role. Titled, *Experience That Kalona Country Charm,* a brochure for the town of Kalona offers combined tourist experiences.

> The *pioneer heritage* of Kalona is richly displayed, not only in its well-presented Historical Village and Museum of antique collections, but in its living link with the past,

through the *visible authentic lifestyle* of the Amish. Both horse-drawn buggies and the latest model automobile share the same road in this *charming country town* located just 18 miles south of Iowa City. (Italics added.)

THE ETHNIC-HERITAGE EXPERIENCE

Reminiscent of the homelands of the state's European immigrants, the Old World represents Iowa's most vivid ancestral memory, and the ethnic heritage theme attempts to reconnect to European roots. Urban ethnic districts such as Little Italy in New York have attracted outsiders for decades. These neighborhoods, inhabited by ethnic populations and characterized by ethnic foods and visual emblems, were established as, and remained, ethnic ghettos, enclaves within the city. In Iowa's rural towns, large groups of people of similar descent have generally not created distinct enclaves. Although many traditions—rituals, festivals, and names—have been partially maintained, these were inconspicuous in the physical environment.

Today, traditions that were once carried on internally by communities are being promoted and commoditized as consumer goods. The ethnic theme is displayed in the landscape and fastened to building façades. Communities create heritage villages, import structures from the "Old Country," remodel Main Street storefronts, sell ethnic foods and imported gifts, and establish ethnic festivals. The Iowa state tourism brochure prepares travelers for an extravaganza of ethnic heritages. "*Celebrate Iowa's contrasts. . . . Iowa changes to suit you.* Salute Iowa's heritage at one of 600 colorful festivals. Climb inside an authentic Danish windmill or kick up your heels in wooden shoes in Iowa's Dutch-style cities. Sample Norwegian lefse, Irish mulligan stew, German sauerbraten and other Iowa ethnic specialties, served with Iowan [sic] hospitality." Welcome signs in foreign languages greet the arrivals to town. *Wilkommen, Velkommen,* and *Bitte Kommen Wieder* (please come again) in a departure sign put the visitor in the right mood.

The Dutch heritage of Pella and the Norwegian heritage of Decorah have been well known and celebrated for decades, but only recently have the two towns packaged and compacted their heritages into small theme parks that display small-scale, "authentic" ethnic structures and rituals. The town of Pella began restoring Dutch immigrant residences on Franklin Street to preserve the community heritage as early as 1966, but it wasn't until 1980 that the concept of commercialized tourism materialized in new Dutch buildings surrounded by a tall wire fence. In addition to daily tours and seasonal festivals, local and regional gatherings are now held in the village, and weddings are celebrated in its small church.

In order to make a desired image a reality, city ordinances oblige downtown store façades to dress up in foreign clothes. During the 1980s the town of Manning, long renowned for its German heritage and festivals, established design codes and, using incentives from the federal urban renewal program, remodeled some of its original, intricate Victorian brick façades in a German-Bavarian style that is uncharacteristic of the regional architecture. The German Mall is the town's most recent project. A hybrid of faux-Bavarian and American-mall styles, it contains a visitors' center, an optometrist's office, a video store, and a crafts store.

European architecture and artifacts—both replicas and imports—constitute the central attractions of these ethnic heritage experiences. In Pella, miniature windmills mark every town entrance and are scattered throughout the town center. The Vogel Mill, a replica of a Dutch mill, graces the industrial park of Story City. But the most vivid example of an imported attraction is the sixty-foot-tall Danish windmill in Elk Horn. This working grain mill was dismantled and shipped from Denmark to Elk Horn, where in 1976 it was reconstructed and furnished with displays and a gift shop.

The windmill began as one individual's dream and was made a reality by the whole community, which helped to raise funds and erect the structure through volunteer labor. Since its success as a tourist attraction in the late 1980s, a new Danish-American immigrant museum has been constructed adjacent to it. The windmill, the region's most celebrated community icon and economic stimulus, is not alone; a fiberglass statue of the Little Mermaid, erected to honor the Danish author Hans Christian Andersen, sits in the park in the nearby Danish town of Kimballton. Every winter when the statue is taken down "to keep it warm," baffled visitors wander futilely through the park looking for the lost mermaid. Such town icons as the windmill and the Little Mermaid represent the dissipation of stable relations with the physical and cultural geography. No longer connected with a common place, the emblems have been detached from their original function and emptied of content, or given new representational burdens.

Nevertheless, Manning, the Danish towns' northern neighbor,

Fig. 13.2. *The Danish Windmill* in Elk Horn, brought from Denmark and reconstructed in 1976, attracts 80,000 visitors a year. It has now been joined by a Danish-American immigrant museum. (Photograph by Mira Engler.)

Fig. 13.3. *Kimballton's Little Mermaid* adds to the "Danish Experience." Unlike the Copenhagen Mermaid, however, she goes indoors in the wintertime, "to keep warm." (Photograph by Mira Engler.)

is now augmenting its reconstructed downtown with a *Hausbarn* from Germany to be a focal point for their tourist industry. Although a group of non-Germans in the community opposed making the necessary financial commitment, the Manning Heritage Foundation has already imported the *Hausbarn* and acquired an old farm at the edge of town. Reconstruction and refurbishing of the new ethnic center are proceeding.

Festivals are another important element of the ethnic heritage experience. These have a long-standing tradition in many Iowa towns, but recently have increased in number. Six years ago, the summer *Kinderfest* in Manning, the children's festival, which has been celebrated there for more than a hundred years, was joined by the winter *Weihnachtfest,* a German Christmas festival centered

Fig. 13.4. *Manning's Main Street* today features redecorated buildings and a "German Mall," developed to emphasize a German ethnic heritage. (Photograph by Mira Engler.)

on a Christmas tree, lights, and nutcrackers. The festivals' parades, contests, exhibits, and entertainments incorporate German customs and costumes, and are intended to attract both townspeople and visitors, to restore public life to the empty downtown, to encourage family reunions, to channel money to local businesses, and to market tourism.

THE FRONTIER-PIONEER EXPERIENCE

The second face of Iowa's past is Frontier America. The frontier-pioneer experience commemorates the European-American conquerors and founding fathers of Iowa. It recalls forts and battlefields and the brave and hardy pioneers who broke the fertile Iowa sod. Iowa's four reconstructed forts, dozens of pioneer villages, and hundreds of log cabins are monuments to the era that ended with the arrival of the railroad in the 1870s.

At the forts—groups of log structures surrounded by twelve-foot-tall wooden walls and blockhouses—visitors can hear the cannons' roar and the crack of flintlock muskets in reenacted battle scenes. The Fort Museum in Fort Dodge is a replica of Fort Williams, which was actually located one hundred miles north of Fort Dodge. It was thought that the original Fort Dodge did not have the image needed to recreate a frontier-fort experience. Established in 1850 on a high plateau overlooking the Des Moines River, old Fort Dodge comprised parade grounds and a street lined by sixteen individual wooden buildings. It was not surrounded by walls and towers. Eventually its last two original log

Fig. 13.5. *Historic Manning Main Street.* Main Street today makes an interesting contrast to the Manning Main St. of the 1920s, shown in this historic picture. (Historic photograph courtesy of Bill Ohde.)

houses were moved to the museum's replica of Fort Williams constructed near Highway 20 as a tangible symbol of the city of Fort Dodge. Today the only visible remnant of Fort Dodge at its original site is a stone foundation wall below a modern warehouse. Local identity was lost to "mass" commercial identity, to the "national" image. Fort Dodge's slogan, "Frontier of the Future," was rationalized in a promotional brochure: "with the past as its prologue, Fort Dodge's pioneer spirit lives on in the closing years of the Twentieth Century."

Adjacent to the fort museum is a "pioneer village" fabricated of new and relocated old buildings along a street bordered by wooden sidewalks. According to the museum brochure, the strolling visitor "can experience the sights and sounds of a village in the 1800s. The ringing of the bell from the one-room school, the taste of stick candy from a real general store, the smell of coal smoke from the Blacksmith Shop and the quiet solitude of the log chapel."

Such pioneer villages are found in dozens of Iowa towns. Some are composed of only a log cabin or a country school, while others are fashioned as a whole street. The town of Bentonsport created an elaborate version of a pioneer village in its historic dis-

Fig. 13.6.   *The Fort at Fort Dodge* is not the original one, which was simply a group of buildings and a parade ground, as in the engraving. (Engraving, "Fort Dodge in 1854," from *The Centennial History of Webster County, Its Towns and Townships.*)

Fig. 13.7. *Fort Williams,* a Civil War militia fort that had been built and manned by Fort Dodge residents in 1862, originally stood on Iowa Lake, about seventy miles north, near the Minnesota border. The townspeople of Fort Dodge constructed a replica of the fort because they wanted a more marketable image for the Fort Museum. (Photograph from Fort Museum brochure, Fort Dodge Historical Foundation.)

trict on the Des Moines River. The community revived its steamboat era district, where nearly fifteen hundred people lived in the mid-nineteenth century. The picturesque atmosphere and low property prices have attracted young craftspeople and artists who have bought, restored, and transformed several old buildings into studios and tourist shops. The potter and the blacksmith, who met and married in the town, recently had two daughters, thereby increasing the town's population by seven percent. In small towns like Bentonsport the "historical gentrification" takes over the entire community and creates an environment where the residents' livelihoods depend solely on their ability to satisfy tourists.

THE GOOD-OLD-TOWN EXPERIENCE

A third popular theme is the Good-Old-Town of the 1920s. A strong sense of romanticism and nostalgia for this era promotes a very specific history—one that is susceptible to an appetite for relics of the railroad era. Many small Iowa communities are reassembling their former selves in new historical "institutions." But here, history stopped seventy years ago and, again, a selected past is frozen and framed.

The urban historical preservation movement of the 1960s reached Iowa towns in the mid-1970s. Since then, many museums have opened, and many town squares, streets, and buildings have been restored and placed on the National Historic Register. The town of Albia chose historic restoration as its theme and has held a Restoration Days celebration every summer since 1983. It has renovated the four blocks surrounding the town square, and some residents have returned to the apartments above the stores. Bonaparte, West Branch, and Walnut are renovating façades, theaters, and depots to bring back businesses and public life to their downtowns. Nevertheless, local residents continue to flee to malls near the Interstate, and communities are recognizing that renovation alone cannot enliven empty downtowns and that their potential clients are the fleeting tourists on the Interstate.

To attract these casual tourists, town residents collect and restore remnants and relics of past lives and "dead" traditions in museums housed in former depots, Victorian buildings, and empty stores. In Oakland, retired citizens founded the Nishna Heritage Museum in a reclaimed store space. The museum began to expand until it has consumed the country store, the hardware store, the variety store, the beauty shop, and the antique store. While the hopeful slogan, "100 Years of History Coming to Life," is inscribed on a display window, except for a drugstore and a few offices, the other stores on Main Street are empty.

While historic sites (such as the Herbert Hoover National Historic site at West Branch or the place near Adair where Jesse James was caught) have been included on tourist maps for many years, in the 1980s two new historical designatons were added to the guidebooks: the historic district and the historical village. A designated historic district, where architecturally and symbolically significant buildings have been preserved, offers the visitor a non-staged setting in Burlington, Fort Dodge, and Ames. In contrast, small towns without restorable historic districts have overcome this by fabricating historical villages. There, the tourist typically encounters a turn-of-the-century street, including a general store, a blacksmith shop, a pottery shop, a livery, a doctor's clinic, a chapel, and a city hall, often of reduced scale. These "villages" are set apart in a world unlike the everyday life of the community. Their designs express the idea of pure "imageability," the same calculus as that used in advertising. They do not serve the community's real needs or its traditions; neither do they satisfy the tourist's desire for a genuine experience of place. As Edward Ball states, "The kernel of theming lies in the priority of the image over the lived, phenomenological experiences of space."

Antiques, the consumer goods of the good-old-town days, ensure small towns a return on their investment. The overwhelming success of Walnut, Iowa, two miles south of Interstate 80, exemplifies the potential of such conversion. What began in 1983 as a single new antique store amid many empty stores on Main Street, today boasts more than ninety antique dealerships in eighteen antique stores and six antique malls. The antique seed was planted in Walnut when the Ranney family moved from West Des Moines, bringing their collectibles. They became regular visitors at the daily "Kaffee Klatch" and articulated their vision for a renewed Walnut to the townspeople and the local newspaper. After some resistance from long-time residents, who still lived in the hope that the five-and-dime and the hardware store would return, enthusiasm proved infectious. A community club came up with "Walnut—Iowa's Antique City" as a slogan, which acquired the governor's official approval and is now on bumper stickers sported by every vehicle in town. Walnut became a model for other towns seeking economic direction. Today these towns—Lamoni, West Branch, West Des Moines, Vinton, McGregor, and Kalona—are barely distinguishable from one another. Thus, the contemporary rural small town joins the world of chain stores and roofless shopping malls. Here, as in the ubiquitous American mall, people are welcome as long as they participate in the circle of consumption.

From the perspective of the local people, theming favors the tourist over the resident. In Walnut, filled with antiques from one edge of Main Street to the other, residents have to drive fifteen miles to buy groceries. Nearby farmers, who cannot afford to buy

Fig. 13.8.   *Walnut, "The Antique City,"* is just south of I-80, about forty-five miles from the Nebraska border. The old buildings on its broad main street have nearly all been converted to antique stores and malls—an exciting discovery for tourists but no longer very useful to residents of the surrounding area. (Photograph by Mira Engler.)

expensive antiques anyway, are becoming estranged from town. What was once a service and trade center for farmers has become an exclusive business district. Theming reduces the environment into a single homogenous entity; it inhibits diversity. When Dutch elm disease struck in the 1930s, it denuded entire towns. When the antique stores go, "antiqued" Walnut will not survive. It will have to find a new slogan, identity, and dress. Tourism's fashions cannot be trusted over time.

Remnants of railroading also become the commodities of Old Town. Uprooted and relocated to new sites with convenient access to the highway, or preferably, the freeway, transplanted wooden depots, steam engines, and cabooses have no relationship to original transportation networks. Locomotive steam from the Purple Martin Train Museum a few miles from Atlantic at Exit 60 on I-80 called the traveler from afar. No depot or railroad was nearby, but the logic of this whistle-stop for the automotive tourist was clear. Five train cars and a caboose contained exhibits of railroading in the 1930s and 1950s, and railroad artifacts, gifts, food, and tours were for sale. The Purple Martin Train Museum opened in 1992 and lasted for only four years. This tendency to make attractions convenient and visible to the traveler and to isolate them far from the nearby community, however, continues and is another indication that theming is primarily focused on satisfying the tourist rather than on supporting and enriching the lives of the local residents.

THE COUNTRY-CHARM EXPERIENCE

The fourth theme, "Country Charm," embodies lifestyles and settings from a pastoral ideal to which most Americans cling. The endangered status of the American family farm further perpetuates this reverence for rural life. In "Beyond Landscape Guilt," Robert Thayer claims that our generation has become increasingly passionate in maintaining and reconstructing our ideal images of places other than the automobile strip developments and shopping centers, in which we have invested little of our psychic idealism. Thus the country experience, which embodies a rural ideal devoid of conspicuous technology, eschews electric wires and power plants, offers rustic scenes of green hills and crop fields dotted with barns, farm animals, and country inns, and is complemented by handmade country crafts and homemade food. To reestablish an old country "look" and atmosphere, small towns transform their downtowns and larger towns build enclosed theme parks.

The old Amish culture, symbolizing the agrarian way of life, has always been a tourist attraction in Iowa. The dispersed, isolated Amish farms, stores, and churches in Davis and Buchanan counties have been visited continually by outsiders but have remained true to their character and appearance. However, traveling for miles on dusty roads to encounter an Amish farm has become a slow and tiresome experience that can now be exchanged for a brief stop at a new staged setting of old lifestyles just off the interstate. Living History Farms in Des Moines has reconstructed pioneer farms complete with period-costumed people who perform bygone workaday roles. And the Amana Colonies—seven small villages established by a self-sufficient, religious commune that was formally disbanded in 1932—have revived their former communal image to become the number-one tourist attraction in Iowa. The Amanas market their homemade German–American food, handmade crafts, slow-paced life, and serene countryside. Family-owned and -operated restaurants, gift shops, and bed-and-breakfasts make up this Country-Charm factory. Homes have been converted into souvenir shops, barns into restaurants, and both old-fashioned workplaces and modern factories have been opened to visitors. The Amana Society, a profit-sharing corporation that now manages and markets most of these businesses and lands, is aware of the sterility of modern life and invites tourists to enjoy "the sound of the hammer and chisel crafting hardwood furniture, the smell of hickory smoke around the meat shops, the clickety-clack of loom shuttles and the chewy texture of freshly baked · breads."

Several new institutions are becoming essential parts of the country experience establishment, among them are the old countrystore and the country inn. The country store, an obvious consumer destination, is filled with handmade crafts that capture images from the farmyard (carved pigs, cows, and weather vanes) or accouterments and smells of the family home and kitchen (quilts, lace, potpourri, and homemade candles). An increasing number of country inns and bed-and-breakfasts offer accommodations to lengthen the tourist's opportunity to consume. The number of bed-and-breakfasts in Iowa has grown from about forty in the early 1980s to more than two hundred in the 1990s. With homemade food and a home-like atmosphere, the inns seek to make an overnight stay a part of the total experience. The Mason House Inn in Bentonsport, built in 1846 on the Des Moines River as a steamboat inn, was revived in 1989 by Sheral and Bill McDermet, newcomers to the town. Guests sleep in antique bed frames but on new mattresses. They will also find a cookie jar in each room. During the hearty breakfast, Mr. McDermet, a tall charming man, pours juice into a glass without looking. A gift shop is located on the first floor, and there are guided tours with detailed stories about every antique treasure in the inn.

Recycled and transplanted vernacular farm buildings are another essential element of the Country-Charm experience. Barns and farm structures are converted into stylish restaurants, shops, or malls easily accessible to tourists. In particular, dairy barns from abandoned farms are being relocated. In Okoboji, Iowa's northern lake district, developers have transplanted three dairy barns and converted them into a complex of craft shops.

Giant specimens of crops and farm animals such as Albert, "the world's biggest bull," in the town of Audubon and the eight-foot-tall rotating cornstalk at the entry to the town of Coon Rapids leave memorable images. Collections of miniature farm structures and equipment such as the "largest known collection of farm miniatures in America created by one man" in South Amana or its competitor "the farm toy capital of the world" at Dyersville round out the Country-Charm package.

But the prototype that best encapsulates the experience is a farm near the town of Stanhope. "There's magic in Stanhope, Iowa," says the promotional brochure. The miniature village, named "Country Relics Little Village & Homestead," began in Varlen and Fern Carlson's backyard as a playhouse for their grand-children. It now features six "antique" buildings of one-half to two-thirds scale. The barn, general store, post office, school, bak-ery, livery, blacksmith, and church are all filled with turn-of-the-century sales samples, small-scale collectibles, and children's toys. Small plastic horses and cows embellish the barnyard, providing "rides" for small children. "A population of 102 'Dummies' makes each scene throughout the twelve building complex a true-to-life picture of life in the 1920s and 30s," says a village brochure. In ad-dition, the Carlsons acquired, relocated, and renovated the Stan-hope Depot; it now sits in their backyard with a section of track awaiting the acquisition of a caboose. The depot contains a gift shop and a collection of farm machinery that can also be rented. Guided tours, Christmas strolls, weddings, and catered receptions are offered, and plans to develop an annual country-relic minia-tures festival are under way. A 1923 Model-T Ford provides a memorable ride from the little village to downtown Stanhope and the surrounding countryside. Three thousand people visit the place each year, and eleven couples got married in the little church. It was awarded the 1991 Best Visitor Attraction in Iowa by the gov-ernor in a special ceremony.

The Carlsons' "country business" and the Carstens' Memor-ial Farmstead, west of Shelby and a half-mile from Interstate 80, indicate a new trend in theme farms. At the Carsten farm visitors are invited to observe demonstrations of an Avery wooden cream separator, threshers, and a sawmill and are offered overnight ac-commodations at the farmhouse. A Carstens' Farm Day is held every summer. The conversion of the Iowa family farm into a theme park is the ultimate victory of the landscape theming syndrome. It empties the idea of farm of its content and meaning and separates the state of Iowa from its history and identity.

REFLECTIONS

It is both my concern with the incongruity between the marketable image and the internal reality, and my sympathy with the economic hardships and identity crises of Iowa's small-town communities that urge me to scrutinize these processes. It is easy for the outsider to pass severe judgment on the present landscape and the people who are bringing it into being. It is similarly easy to dismiss this landscape as a violent modification of the traditional small-town landscape and culture, as did Edward Relph in his book *Place and Placelessness*. Tourism, he claimed, is a homogenizing influence, destroying local and regional landscapes, which are replaced by conventional tourist architecture, synthetic landscapes, and pseudo-places. His counterpart Erik Cohen argued otherwise. In "Authenticity and Commoditization in Tourism," Cohen maintains that the emergence of a tourist market facilitates the preservation of communities and cultural traditions that would otherwise perish. "Isn't there, after all, a continuous invention of traditions that sets all viable cultures in the process of making themselves up all the time?" asks Cohen.

When we take a second look at these towns, we are bound to recognize that the contemporary theme town landscape offers little in the way of entertainment or quality of life. Fantasy-seeking tourists find more excitement in urban theme parks. Inhabitants of rural small towns and farms suffer a loss in sense of place and community. Both tourists and local communities are invited to participate merely as consumers in a whole ideological fantasy of a past.

Once independent of the consumer marketplace, rural small towns now depend on advertising and on producing entertaining environments to survive. It is my tenet that small Iowa towns must sustain the priority of a place-rooted community over a tourist-based economy—a commercial fantasyland—in order to remain viable in the long run. Environmental designers can provide a conceptual alternative to the theme town phenomenon. Developing numerous themes, instead of a singular one, can ensure a diversified, less-regulated place. Themes that are based on genuine, idiosyncratic landscapes of the community, the workaday features of the rural small town, like the corner café, train trestle, water tower, or stockyard and auction house, can help restore community identity and can promote the preservation and the historical continuity of the town's landscape. Themes that mark and celebrate buildings *in situ* can strengthen community roots. And when a new institution or attraction is planned, locating it in the downtown area can serve both residents and outsiders. Themes that highlight both past and present can meet the demands for both nostalgia and newness, and secure a non-segregated and dynamic environment. A farmers' market on Main Street and harvest celebrations on farms can sustain the ties between townspeople and farmers.

New settings for themes that connect historical sensibilities with contemporary midwestern arts can be designed. Abandoned farm structures—grain elevators, silos and dairy barns—can be recycled as play structures, galleries, or public buildings in the midst of parks that feature the "ruins" of farms. Other abandoned town buildings can be located at special grave sites that both commemorate the past and invite visitors to explore. Outdoor art made of recycled cast-iron stairs, limestone window cornices, storefront window frames, and other building details can be installed throughout town to enhance the pedestrian environment. A field of abandoned farm windmills and amusing weather vanes can be constructed on the highest spot in the community alongside the communication tower, a modern wind-powered generator, and satellite dishes. Old discarded farm machinery, so visible at town entryways, can be painted and organized into large-scale sculptures adjacent to the giant new farm machinery at the dealerships.

New themes that speak to today's ecological and social needs can be nurtured. The city of Osage, Iowa, does not claim energy conservation as its theme, but the town is well known for its community-wide energy savings, which boost the town's economy by allowing greater local investment. Similarly, Belle Plaine does not consider elder care to be a theme; however, the community has made affordable housing and services for the elderly, an expanding segment of Iowa's population, a viable strategy for economic development.

These are only a few examples of the many fresh relationships that can evolve between Iowa culture and the Iowa landscape. Instead of promoting only greater consumption, new relationships that generate conservation and social benefits promise a healthy future. And instead of embodying simulation, segregation, control, escape, and nostalgia, new relationships true to the spirit of place—inclusive, varied, democratic, and communitarian—promise congruity between image and reality.

FURTHER READING

Edward Ball. "To Theme or Not to Theme: Disneyfication without Guilt." In *The Once and Future Park,* ed. Deborah Karasov and Steve Waryan. New York: Princeton Architectural Press, 1993.

Daniel J. Boorstin. *The Image: A Guide to Pseudo-Events in America.* New York: McClelland and Stewart, 1961.

Rebecca Christian. "A Quartet with Main Street Appeal." *Iowa* 38, no. 3 (1990):10–17.

Grady Clay. *Close-Up: How to Read the American City.* Chicago: University of Chicago Press, 1980.

Erik Cohen. "Authenticity and Commoditization in Tourism." *Annals of Tourism Research* 15 (1988):71–86.

Amy Godine. "Iowa for Collectors." In *Take This Exit,* ed. Robert F. Sayre. Ames: Iowa State University Press, 1989.

Spiro Kostof. *America by Design.* New York: Oxford University Press, 1987.

Alan A. Lew. "Authenticity and Sense of Place in the Tourism Development Experience of Older Retail Districts." *Journal of Travel Research,* Spring 1989, 15–22.

Dean MacCannell. *The Tourist.* New York: Schocken Books, 1976.

Edward Relph. *Place and Placelessness.* London: Pion, 1976.

Michael Sorkin. *Variations on a Theme Park.* New York: Noonday Press, 1992.

Robert Thayer. "Beyond Landscape Guilt." *Landscape Architecture* 74, no. 6 (1984):44–55.

Wilbur Zelinsky. "Where Every Town is Above Average." *Landscape* 30, no. 1 (1988):1–10.

❧ 14 ☙

Hardware Stores:
Iowa's Tool Boxes

Robert F. Sayre

In most Iowa hardware stores, spring is the really busy season. Go look at Jim Schotter's Ridgeway Hardware in Waterloo on a warm afternoon in early April, and the evidence is right out front, in the rows and rows of lawnmowers lined up in the parking lot. Some are now fixed and ready to be picked up, others reconditioned and ready for sale. But all are ready for use, ready to start on the first pull and begin their annual campaign, back and forth, over the green lawns of suburban Waterloo. Inside are sparkling new mowers, plus bags of fertilizers, weed-killers, and grass seed in neatly stacked piles. Nearby are racks of flower and vegetable seeds, and not far off, shiny black backyard grills; from the simplest pot-shaped Weber charcoal model to very fancy gas ones, with rotating spits, and matching long-handled tongs and spatulas. Keep looking, and you will also see electric hedge trimmers, Weed Eaters, gardening gloves, loppers, and trowels; a dazzling variety of hoses, nozzles, and sprinklers; the latest in cleverly shaped rain gauges; and, of course, shovels, spades, and hoes.

Hardware stores get little attention in guidebooks, which are mostly concerned with snooty restaurants and historic sites. But if guidebooks are serious guides to the landscape, and if landscape is, in the most basic sense, land as it is seen and altered and managed

Fig. 14.1. *Jim Schotter of Ridgeway Hardware, Waterloo,* serves suburban Waterloo's needs, especially for garden equipment and small engine repair (lawnmowers and snowblowers). "The cookie-cutter hardware stores of the past can't make it," he says. "One must find a niche and serve it." (Photograph by Robert F. Sayre.)

by people, then hardware stores belong in every American guidebook, because they arguably have a more direct effect on the American landscape than any other institution we can study. They are our toolboxes and toolsheds, the places where most of us have to go first before we can go out and do anything to our houses and gardens. You want to plant a garden? You go to the hardware store for your shovel (or to buy a roto-tiller). You want to paint the house? Off to the hardware store for paint, sandpaper, scrapers, brushes, and rollers. To wax the car, fix a screen, or get a new mailbox requires the same trip. The hardware store is the essential link for American home owners between their property and their work, their land and their hands. Moreover, by presenting us with the possibilities and limitations on how we can do such things, the hardware store is the immediate agent for uniting millions of pieces of private property into the total national landscape.

Second—but just as important—good hardware stores are where we also get advice on when and how to use these tools. Most American home owners are not as wise about gardening and household maintenance as we would like to be. (The first time I bought grass seed, I had to ask the hardware store clerk when to plant it!) Even if we do know some simple things, we still need re-assurance or want to learn about recent improvements. So a good hardware store, with a knowledgeable owner and clerks, is a major community asset. You can't get this kind of advice from the young high school or college kid at a big chain store.

Third, and this is especially so in small towns and rural areas, the hardware store is where you get advice from friends and neighbors, including the old-timers who used to sit on the front porch or gather around the pot-bellied stove. ("Too early to plant corn, young man. Ground's still too cold. Seed'll just lie there and rot.") Or you go there *as* an old-timer, to reminisce and gossip. One hardware store, Lockridge's in southern Iowa, used to stay open till ten at night because the old-timers wouldn't leave. Today, others still have coffeepots and chairs in the back.

Hardware stores in Iowa are easily recognized. Usually the word itself is in the name, as in "Bob Miller's Hardware" in Des Moines or "Eddyville Hardware" in Eddyville. Most also display the name of the nationwide buying cooperative they belong to, like Ace, Hardware Hank, or TrueValue. And most are locally owned and managed (the buying co-ops are not chains but suppliers who provide a brand name of tools, paints, etc. and some advice on store operations). Thus, hardware stores are easily distinguished from lumberyards, garden shops, paint stores, and discount stores, even though there is some overlap. Come spring and you will find brightly colored bedding plants, potted annuals, tomato plants and ornamental evergreens displayed in the parking lots of nearly all these places. Come December and you know that in many of them you can now find Christmas tree lights and ornaments and a lot of little electrical appliances like toasters, carving knives, and coffee-makers. The tendency of American merchants to stock seasonal merchandise is universal. But you know that only in the hardware store will you always find hammers and saws, electrical sockets and switches, nuts and bolts. For that is what it finally comes to.

Hardware stores are, literally and figuratively, for tools—for the nuts and bolts that hold everything together.

That, however, makes them all the more amazing. One might think that such simple, elementary merchandise could easily be marketed by other stores, putting the hardware store out of business. But despite Home Depot and Menards, this hasn't happened. Hardware stores, in most Iowa towns, have survived this powerful inroad on their turf. They have had to scramble and adjust, "to find niches," as the owners say, but they have actually ended up doing better than ever. In recent years they have expanded, both by enlarging their stores and by increasing shelf space in the stores, and most merchants will tell you that they are doing more business all the time. They also appeal to a wide variety of people, having long ago shed the image that they are for men only. "We have a lot of women," says Bob Miller of Des Moines. "You'd be surprised by the number of women who like to come into a hardware store and look around." Loren Larson says that in his store in Osage the majority of his customers are women.

So there is something about hardware stores that is very dear and very essential to Iowa and the Iowa character—something, I believe, that is closely related to the vernacular landscape of Iowa and how people regard and maintain it. The variety of their merchandise, their local ownership and outlook, and their friendliness also connect them to the old-fashioned general store, so that they have a heritage that few other stores possess. But this heritage, in turn, is just one more connection to the physical and social landscape. Iowa's hardware stores may not be as numerous and highly visible as its churches, or quite as friendly and chatty as its cafés, but they are just as revealing of the landscape and culture. If you want to understand Iowa, go to the hardware store. Better yet, go to many of them and see the relationship between the store, the owner, and the place and people they serve.

HARDWARE STORE AS OLD-FASHIONED GENERAL STORE

J.C. Herbert, a retired minister in Washington, Iowa is very fond of Hammes Brothers Hardware in the little town of Harper in Keokuk County, and as he describes it, it is so similar to the old-fashioned general store that if an early settler returned, the tools and fixtures would be different, but the "ambiance . . . would seem very familiar." Herbert goes on:

It is the only retail establishment in the village. There is also a grain elevator, stockyard, and a natural gas pumping station, but only Hammes Brothers is operated as a store selling to individual customers as it has since the days when it was also a hatchery. Upstairs there are still some remnants of the days of hatching.

Mick Berg, the owner, once worked for the Extension Service helping farmers find some other source of income when farming was not enough. He grew tired of the bureaucracy, and when his cousin offered, somewhat in jest, to sell him the hardware, he jumped at it.

Mick comes in at 5 A.M. and puts on the coffee. Often grain haulers will be in early for coffee as well as farmers who can't sleep because of worry about the crops. When there are enough for a fourhanded game of cards, that begins with a lot of male camaraderie. If no one comes in for a time, Mick writes poetry. It is homespun and comes out of his life in the store.

My Whining and Dining Room

They lose their crops a thousand times,
Losing their dollars but spending their dimes
On candies and snacks, here in my store;
They want something different, or else they want more.

The world's gone to hell; the kids won't obey;
The hogs are all sick and it rained on the hay.
If prices are up, they know they won't last;
The profits last week are all in the past.

Hog prices will plummet, cattle will die;
Machinery don't last and governments lie,
But a Pepsi and Snickers will alleviate doom
In my whining and dining room.

Hammes Hardware carries only the necessities of farm life, and Mick has them displayed randomly in a walk-through room where you can see and feel the power tools and garden rakes at will. He also has a line of feed, mostly of the speciality sort since big feeders buy directly from the feed companies. Mick has skill as a butcher, and he helps you with that on the tables over at the nearby hall. If you have bagged a deer, you bring it in for dressing.

My own first contact with such a store came many years ago. I had been looking for months for one of those gizmos that are shaped like pie pans and are stuck over holes in chimneys, such as where old stove pipes used to be connected. Finally I was driving through Garnavillo, near the far northeast corner of the state, and went into Garnavillo Hardware. "Oh, you mean a chimney hole cap," said the owner's wife. She went to the back of the store, and brought back two, each with a different picture painted in the center. "We haven't much demand for them anymore, but we keep

Fig. 14.2.   *Garnavillo Hardware* in northeast Iowa occupies a handsome 1940's building. Owner Dale Wahls stocks wood stoves, home generators, and Grade 8 bolts for farm machinery. He also repairs flashlights and wristwatches and even has "chimney hole caps." The sign beneath the United States and Iowa flags says, "Our Own Hardware." (Photograph by Robert F. Sayre.)

them just in case somebody needs one." The price, as I recall, was seventy-nine cents.

When I went back recently, Dale Wahls, the owner, said he still has some. Over the years, especially during the energy crisis of the 1970s, he has done a good business selling wood stoves, and so the chimney cap was no novelty or cutesy item, as it might have been at "Ye Olde Fashioned Gift Shop" on an Interstate. He even heats the store with a wood furnace. He also makes and sells furnace ducts and pipes, and happily does minor repairs, like fixing flashlights and replacing watch batteries.

But one of the things most in demand is his line of Grade 8 bolts, made of a steel so hard "you can't cut it with a hacksaw." Grade 8 bolts have a gold tinge to them and six little marks or ticks on the head, while the softer Grade 5 bolts have only three ticks and the softest bolts, Grade 2, have no ticks. The system doesn't seem to make sense, but the loggers and farmers who come into Garnavillo know it, and buy the Grade 8 bolts to use in heavy equipment. Nuts and bolts.

Another store of this type is Fairground Hardware, just a block away from the main entrance to the Iowa State Fairgrounds in Des Moines. The building, built in 1893, originally had a grocery story on the east side, a shoe shop in the back, and a hardware store on the west side. The turntable for the trolley from downtown Des Moines was across the street. Bud Irvine, who bought the store in 1996, loves its history and he proudly shows old pictures of it and displays his own collection of old tools and old farm and kitchen equipment on a balcony over the first floor. There's also a punchboard from the 1950s (a simple old form of a lottery), and a shelf grabber (that gadget reputedly invented by Benjamin Franklin for plucking things off high shelves). Less prominent, but equally amazing, is an old set of drawers with saw buttons, parts for crescent wrenches, set screws for doorknobs, and even old skate keys. "I'm nuts on inventory," Bud says. "I'd rather put my money in inventory than the bank."

And sell these things he does. Old hand-cranked meat grinders, which he picks up at antique shows and estate sales, sell regularly. So do new coal buckets, washtubs, washboards, and cast-iron cookware. (Native Americans buy the large iron pots to make drums, he says.) At state fair time in August the demand is particularly strong.

But Bud also wants "Fairground Hardware" to be a neighborhood store. People come in for plumbing supplies—it's a neighborhood where you fix your own toilet and leaky faucet and install your own washing machine. Other, less self-reliant folks have Bud rewire lamps and sharpen lawnmower blades. Several of the clerks are local retired people, led by Elaine Lockridge, who worked in the store for twenty-three years, retired, and then came back to work when Bud bought it. "I won't put in a computer, though I have one at home, and I won't paint the walls," he says, pointing to some flaking paint. "I want a store where people can come if they are having a bad day and feel good." Frosty, Bud's little white bichon frise, sits in a chair of his own and welcomes a gentle pat on the head.

A similarly friendly, resourceful merchant is Pat Cruzen of Eddyville Hardware, on the Des Moines River, about fifty miles southeast of Des Moines. His picturesque, 1900s-era store also has a display of antique tools and implements. In the front are the vault and safe deposit boxes of the old bank, which used to occupy one corner of the store. In the back is a huge row of dark wooden drawers, seven drawers high and twenty-six drawers long, a common feature of old stores, which he is reusing rather than replacing. Farther back is a full selection of nails—all in bins. "I hate to have to sell things on cards," he says. "I don't want to sell people any more than what they need, and I try to keep prices as low as possible. This is a *needs store,* where people can get what they need. I try to be like the GP of hardware, a general practitioner who can help with whatever is needed."

Pat grew up in Eddyville and for years worked at Cargill Corporation's nearby mill and processing plant, where he earned a good salary. But in 1988 he took his family to California for a vacation, and met a contractor who offered him a job in his construction company. Pat took it. When the contractor died unexpectedly, Pat took over and ran the business until all the work the company had been doing was finished. But then, tired of California, he returned to Eddyville. He heard the store was for sale, worked in it a few months to see if he liked it, and decided to buy it. His experience in construction enables him to advise people on all kinds of tasks, and the store's income has increased each year. Two of his other sidelines are making up chainsaw chains to order, and selling load binders for the big trucks that rumble through town to the Cargill plant. Thus despite the atmosphere of an old general store and the antique surroundings, Eddyville Hardware is thriving.

I'm not writing a guide on how to succeed in the hardware

Fig. 14.3. *Pat Cruzen, Owner of Eddyville Hardware* came back to Eddyville, located on the Des Moines River after experience as a building contractor in California. "This is a *needs store*," he says. "I try to be a general practitioner who can help with whatever is needed." (Photograph by Robert F. Sayre.)

business; I'm writing on how these stores relate to the landscape. But the two subjects are connected, because the successful hardware merchants are those who, in the old salesman's phrase, "know the territory." They know their communities and the kind of farming and other work people do, what to stock for them, and how to advise them. They also, on occasion, are ready to get into profitable sidelines that arise from changes in the community.

An outstanding example of this is Yotty's Ace Hardware in Kalona, southwest of Iowa City. Kalona is in the heart of the Amish and Mennonite communities, where farming is still general farming and needs are traditional. Thus at Yotty's you can find three kinds of hanging dairy scales, rings for hog snouts and the devices to install them, and a huge variety of vegetable seeds, most sold in bulk. You can buy 66-day, 72-day, 75-day, 78-day, or 84-day sweet corn seeds. For the heavy timbers of Amish barns you can buy drills with extra long shanks. And you can look over two long shelves of kerosene lamps and lanterns and three shelves of replacement globes for them. In the gourmet department you can select a fine White Mountain ice cream maker, either electric or hand-powered.

But that is not all. Upstairs, on the second floor of Yotty's barn-like building, is their furniture department, which features a large selection of recliners. On one side of the first floor, in addition to a full line of Granite Ware porcelain-covered pots, pans, pitchers, cups, and spoons, you can find Dorothy Yotty's beautiful selection of fine china and crystal. For Kalona not only serves local farmers, it also draws busloads of visitors who are interested in the Amish and Mennonite cultures and want both the functional and durable, and also the elegant. The same shoppers are even ready to buy Santa Clauses and illuminated snow-covered Swiss chalets, winter and summer. Afterward, especially in summer, they will stop in the Yotty's adjoining ice cream store. Farther down the street is what may seem like the most incongruous of the Yotty family's enterprises, the garage where they sell and service golf carts. Bart Yotty explains that he got into golf carts in 1981, and that his son Steve now manages this business.

The history of the store is told in a little quilt, hanging over the stairs, that was sewn by a former employee. It was founded in 1880 and included a harness shop. Bart started working there in 1950, bought an interest in 1966, and took full ownership in 1979. He has twice been elected president of the Iowa Retail Hardware Association. Yet he is very unpretentious and keeps the store plain and unpretentious too. The Christmas season begins with a day in December when the store gives away peanuts and people just drop the shells on the floor. Katie Miller, Bart and Dorothy's assistant, dresses very plainly and speaks Amish German. And Bart sometimes philosophizes with his customers. Hand him your Visa card, and he will take it, but warn you not to charge too much on it. "I tell these kids they'll never enjoy their golden years if they don't get rid of their plastic years," he says.

Nose rings for Amish hogs; ice cream and crystal for the tourists; golf carts for the Kalona golf course. Bart Yotty definitely knows his territory. He himself is a part of it.

Fig. 14.4. *Dorothy and Bart Yotty* have made Yotty's Hardware in Kalona an indispensable local institution and also a tourist attraction. Dorothy stocks both Granite Ware and fine china and crystal. Bart sells furniture, seeds, and hardware. Their son Steve sells and repairs golf carts. (Photograph by Robert F. Sayre.)

THE URBAN-SUBURBAN HARDWARE STORE

As I have been saying, hardware stores are community and landscape mirrors, and this applies not only in Kalona but in the stores serving the urban and suburban residents of Iowa's larger towns. It is the nature of modern suburbs, however, to be more homogeneous in their appearance than farms and farm towns are. The suburban ranch houses of the fifties and sixties and the "townhouses" of the seventies and eighties can be found all across the country. Urban and suburban Iowans follow the national media and want the assurance of being up-to-date, both to maintain status and to maintain the value of their property. Consequently, Iowa's suburban hardware stores tend to be more uniform.

This is especially so in their broad category of products for that American obsession, as Virginia Scott Jenkins calls it—the lawn.[1] Most hardware stores in Iowa, as in the rest of the United States, are like Jim Schotter's Ridgeway Hardware in Waterloo—they sell a tremendous amount of mowers, lawn fertilizers, and weed-killers. In spring many stores even smell of lawn fertilizer, with sometimes an added bouquet of 2-cycle engine oil. Although people now realize that these chemicals are environmentally harmful, and end up in the water we drink and the rivers and lakes we fish and swim in, the pressure to have these green, water-intensive, chemically dependent, outdoor carpets still overwhelms the Iowa home owner.

But that makes lawns awfully good for the hardware business. In fact, lawns are doubly good, because they have to be both made to grow and kept from growing. They need seeds and water and fertilizer to make them grow; mowers and trimmers and edgers to cut them back. So the more successful the lawn-tender is with one set of products, the more he (and it is usually a he) must use the other. Stimulate the lawn one day; cut it back the next. The process—along with trips to the hardware store—goes on spring, summer, and fall, eight or nine months of the year. The lawn-tender also buys trees to shade the lawn and fertilizers and root-feeders to make the trees grow; then in the fall, yet another line of products—rakes, baggers, and mulchers—to get rid of the leaves.

There are signs, however, of change. All suburban hardware stores now sell a variety of composting barrels and boxes to help home owners recycle their yard and kitchen waste. They also sell books on how to build compost bins and how to get the contents to "cook" and "break down" most rapidly. And they sell increasing amounts of organic fertilizers, as the trend toward organic gardening reaches the suburbs. Still, one does not yet see seed for prairie grasses or the flappers and water tanks needed for doing prairie burns. In fact, most cities now forbid outdoor burning. Much more will have to change before lawns change fundamentally. But the contents of hardware stores will then change too, we can be sure.

What is more unique in suburban and urban hardware stores around Iowa is the kind of good advice and assistance given out on home repairs. Jim Schotter of Waterloo calls such service the salvation of all small businesses. If a customer comes in with a prob-

Fig. 14.5.   *Devon and Doug Schueth* of Schueth Ace Hardware in New Hampton stand in front of their patio grills. Overhead are a Fourth of July apron and a long-handled fork and spatula. "It is fun to come to work here," says an employee. "It is like having a second family." (Photograph by Robert F. Sayre.)

lem fixing a sink drain, Jim can recommend the best new system that is easy to put in. If another wants to screw something into a cement wall, Jim will advise the customer to start by renting a hammer drill. It will save lots of time, he adds, and save your temper. And this attitude is not limited to suburban store-owners. The Scheuth family, which operates an Ace Hardware in the small town of New Hampton, posts their telephone numbers on the door facing the parking lot, for customers to call if they come by after hours.

Bob Miller's Hardware, which is near Drake University and an older part of Des Moines, provides full service to people who are keeping up old buildings. He has parts for heavy galvanized gutters, with both three- and four-inch eave trough strainers to put in them. One of his employees, Denny Halbfass, specializes in repairing aluminum storm windows and screens. This requires an inventory of nearly a dozen different sizes and colors of spline cord, a dozen more sizes of aluminum spline, and hundreds of kinds of corner pieces and latches. You would never guess screens and storm windows were so complex—until you try to fix one. Then a person like Denny seems like an angel to the distressed. He also fixes patio doors, keeping hundreds of kinds of rollers for all the myriad varieties of them.

Bob runs the store with a staff of twelve, ten of whom are salesmen. "We have more salesmen per square foot than any other store in the state," he says modestly. Moreover, the store is incredibly well stocked. One cabinet, for instance, just contains Vice Grips, from the very small needle-noses to the rare broad-nosed ones used for holding sheet metal. There are roughly sixty sizes and grades of electrical and telephone wire. In the back of the store are ten-foot-high shelves for a huge selection of screws, bolts, nuts, and washers. People in Des Moines say, "If Miller's hasn't got it, you can't find it." And that seems to be a kind of motto, a reputation that Bob and his staff take great pleasure in. It is, as he explains, wonderful free advertising. But it also epitomizes an attitude possessed by Miller, his salesmen and repairmen, and perhaps Iowa hardware merchants generally. The truly devoted ones simply get a kick out of having the hard-to-get tool or part, and fixing the unfixable.

Dixie Eklofe, at Mike O'Hara's Hardware in Ottumwa, provides a further illustration of this principle. Dixie, who is in charge of kitchen and housewares, small appliances, and the bridal registry, has found that her customers are thrifty and much prefer fixing their coffeemakers and toasters to having to buy new ones. So she is glad to order repair parts for such things, if O'Hara's does not have them in stock. She also tries to sell better brands than are available at the discount stores—ones that last and are worth fixing. And why does she handle the bridal registry, too? Because small household appliances are on the list of things young couples in Ottumwa want, along with their glasses, china, and flatware.

Fixing things is a real theme at a store like O'Hara's Hardware. There are glue guns (both battery-powered and electric), bolt and screw extractors (for that situation where the darn screw breaks and you need to get it out), and lots of different-sized drive belts for cars, lawnmowers, and tractors. There are three aisles of plumbing parts and four aisles of automotive stuff—good indicators of what else gets repaired in Ottumwa and its surrounding towns in southeast and south-central Iowa. And there is a big selection of power drills, electric saws, electric sanders, routers, grinders, and polishers. But Ottumwa is also in an area where people love to hunt and fish. So one other item in stock is the "Char-Broil Deluxe H_2O Smoker" that "holds up to fifty pounds of food" and even has a pan above the coals for water and "your favorite marinade."

THE RURAL AND SMALL-TOWN STORE

Because hardware stores in Iowa all sell a lot of the same nationally known products, the superficial visitor or customer may still have trouble distinguishing among them. How, after all, is one well-run TrueValue really different from another?

The answer, as I've been saying, depends basically on three factors. The first is the character of the owner or owners, which shows up strongest in the old-fashioned, general-store type. Individualists like Mick Berg, Bart and Dorothy Yotty, and Bud Irvine are local institutions, and their stores reflect their personalities. The second factor is the regional culture (for there definitely are regions in Iowa, despite the outsider's assumption of its uniformity), and the third is the differences in the size of the community.

And so here are some of the signs of the final kind of store, the small-town and rural one:

- They sell gallon cans of WD-40 as does Brown's Hardware, on Court Street in Marengo, which is a busy farm community about halfway between Des Moines and Davenport, or

Lockridge's in Promise City, in Iowa's deep south. This seems like a minor point, but it is telling. The suburban home owner uses oil only for a squeaky hinge or door knob and needs only the familiar little spray can. But a farmer uses it by the gallon.

- They do a very big business in paint, like the Schueth Ace Hardware in New Hampton and Larson's Hardware Hank in Osage. Bigger towns have specialty paint stores and professional painters. In small towns and on farms people do their own painting. And so these alert small-town stores have very modern, well-appointed paint departments. They are decidedly not back-of-the-store sidelines hidden on dark shelves and dirty counters. They are found on bright and spotless shelves, and the stores have the latest computers to analyze and match the subtlest tint of any sample you bring in.

- They sell real, serious rope and chain. Not just clothesline and dog chain and the decorator chain used to hang plants. This is chain for heavy equipment. Lockridge's sells it with links that are 3/8-inch thick and that has a working load limit of 5400 pounds. Rope is sold in almost as many sizes and grades as in a marine hardware store. Some even sell bridle rope, the large diameter but soft and flexible rope used to lead horses.

- Like Brown's and Lockridge's, they have full lines of work clothes. They carry Carhart vests, jackets, and overalls; Durango boots; LaCrosse rubber boots; and StormMaster galloshes.

- They are likely to do a big rental business, in everything from air compressors to tents for wedding receptions and graduation parties.

- They are likely to sell hunting and fishing licenses.

- They carry notices of farm sales, church suppers, fishing tournaments, and Izaac Walton League picnics.

These are some of the well-nigh universal goods and services to be found in small-town and rural Iowa hardware stores. They reflect the farm work and an even stronger do-it-yourself culture. They are stores that have to provide multiple services that are provided in larger towns by specialty stores. They also function like general stores in being community meeting places. And yet they are by no means stores of the old-fashioned "general store" variety.

You don't feel you have to be in overalls. They reflect, instead, the interesting mix in rural Iowa of hard, often rough and dirty work with urban gentility. "Sure," such stores say, "haying is hot and dirty, but we still like modern kitchens and bathrooms and freshly painted houses." The generally trim and carefully tended look of rural Iowa is sustained by the scores of these small-town hardware stores, all over the state.

Yet even as they have all of these things in common, there is still a great deal of regional difference among these stores, reflecting the differences in the landscape and kinds of work done on it and also differences in the local cultures. In Larson's Hardware in Osage, I was intrigued not only by the splendidly stocked paint department, which Loren Larson's daughter runs, but by a big display of bird feeders, including hummingbird feeders, and neat plastic bins of twelve different kinds of bird food. Equally intriguing was a line of hoes, rakes, and shovels with padded handles, for "blister-less" gardening, and a spread of lawn products that could compete with the best-stocked suburban store, though the population of Osage is only about thirty-five hundred. I asked Loren Larson about all this, and he said, "Well I guess that's for the three things people like to do here in Mitchell County—feed the birds, garden, and take care of lawns!" A look around Osage (once the home of Hamlin Garland) and its surroundings proved his point. Mitchell County is flat. The farms are huge cash-grain operations. And the tractors are big double- and even triple-wheelers. But each house, whether in town or out in the country, is neat as a pin, with a big well-trimmed lawn, lush garden, and an array of bird feeders that could outfit an aviary.

A very different store, in a very different part of the state is Lockridge's, in the tiny town of Promise City (population 132, according to the latest Iowa Department of Transportation map). It's in Wayne County, just above the Missouri border, where the land is so hilly ("highly erodable land," the Department of Agriculture calls it) that the major land use is cattle grazing. Thus the shelves of Lockridge's pole-barn type of building are filled with equipment for fencing and with repair parts for the windrowers and mowers and balers used in haying. They also have sophisticated machines for customizing hydraulic hoses, which are an integral part of this kind of machinery, and for repairing the ten- or twelve-inch-wide, thirty-five- and forty-foot belts used in the balers that spin together the great, round modern hay bales. The clerks at Lockridge's—men like Don Jackson and Russ Parker—are friendly, efficient, and knowl-

Fig. 14.6.   *A Portrait of Bob Lockridge,* the founder of the store, still hangs behind the counter of Lockridge's Lumber and Hardware, Promise City, in south-central Iowa. Lockridge died in 1981. (Photograph by Robert F. Sayre.)

edgeable about all this equipment. You could call them the kind of people who really run the infrastructure of American farming.

You could, in addition, say that Lockridge's isn't really a true hardware store. It may be more like a farm-service store. It's also a darn good lumberyard, and one of the employees, Phil Swanson, specializes in doing the bids and estimates on the farm buildings, garages, decks, and additions that will be built with Lockridge lumber. But the name is still Lockridge's Lumber and Hardware, and it qualifies as a hardware store by the basic test: it sells lots of nuts and bolts. It is into these other lines because farming, and especially grazing and haying, is the major activity in Wayne County and its environs. This is beautiful country. Hunting and fishing are popular, and Rathbun Lake, one of Iowa's largest artificial lakes, is nearby in Appanoose County. But you don't imagine that people here have a great deal of time for other diversions like barbecues and feeding the birds, at least not when there are fences to be built or mended and hay to be cut and baled. The population of Wayne County, 7,067, according to the 1990 census, is nearly the lowest in the state, barely enough, some would say, to sustain itself and manage this hilly, beautiful land. And so Lockridge's Lumber and Hardware supplies the essentials—and does a very good job of it. Jill and Dale Housh, who are part owners, also run similar Lockridge stores in Unionville, Missouri about twenty-five miles south, and Centerville, Iowa fifteen miles east. The Houshes know the

Fig. 14.7. *Don Jackson at Lockridge's* repairs the forty-foot belts used in modern hay balers, saving farmers hundreds of dollars they would otherwise have to pay for new belts. (Photograph by Robert F. Sayre.)

Fig. 14.8. *Janette Parker and Courtney Housh* in the lumber and farm supply area behind Lockridge's. Courtney's parents are the current managers and part owners of the three Lockridge stores in Promise City and Centerville, Iowa, and Unionville, Missouri. (Photograph by Robert F. Sayre.)

territory, just as did Bob Lockridge, who founded the business but died in 1981. In turn, their fascinating store tells us a lot about the region and its people.

But so do all Iowa hardware stores. At all seasons of the year they sell the tools with which Iowans care for their houses, farms, shops, and land. Customers' success depends directly on the quality of the tools, the skill with which they are used, and the advice they get from the owners and clerks in these stores. So it should be no surprise that in most stores spring is indeed the busy season. That is when the people go back to their annual tasks of cleaning and painting, planting and cultivating, and making things grow.[2]

NOTES

1. See Virginia Scott Jenkins's very entertaining and informative book, *The Lawn: A History of an American Obsession* (Smithsonian Institution Press: Washington, D.C., 1994). One of the first companies "to realize the potential market provided by the vision of a nation of front lawns was the O.M. Scott and Sons hardware and seed company of Marysville, Ohio," which in the 1870s began cleaning its grass seed (p. 74).

2. I would like to thank J.C. Herbert for first suggesting this article on hardware stores, Bart Yotty and Jim Cory of the Iowa Retail Hardware Association for suggesting stores to visit, and all of the store owners and their clerks for spending time answering my questions.

❯ 15 ❮

Outstanding in the Fields: Alternative Agriculture in the Iowa Landscape

Laura B. Sayre

Farming, it is sometimes said, is a spectator sport. What you plant, when you get it in the ground, how well you stay ahead of the weeds, the condition of your equipment and the speed of your harvest—virtually all of the decisions and the skills and the luck of a farmer are in plain sight out in the fields every day of the year. This is especially true in Iowa, where the grid gives access to nearly every square mile, the hills roll gently out to the horizon, and there aren't that many trees to block the view. When you think about it, watching the annual contest between work and weather on the land is one of the major entertainments of Iowa back-roads traveling, for farmers and non-farmers alike. Even our newspapers, in the spring and fall, publish graphs to show the daily progress of planting and harvesting across the state. And we read them.

It is surely this public nature of farming which makes agriculture such a controversial, even emotional issue for many people. Agriculture affects more of the landscape than any other type of land use—in Iowa, 31.2 million of the state's 34 million acres—so it is not surprising that nearly everyone has an opinion about its methods. If we are no longer technically a state of farmers (a 1997 census recorded just 90,792 farms among a total population of 2.8 million), we are still very much a state of farm spectators, a kind of permanent fanclub for agriculture. Like other fans, we feel we have an interest in what goes on in the fields, and we should, because it affects not just the quality of the food we eat but the quality of our water, our air, our economy—our entire way of life. For farmers, for the player-spectators, watching the fields is a way of gathering news about the neighborhood, of comparing techniques, of making lists of things to do. For the rest of us it is a vicarious experience, a way of marking time, an ongoing lesson in land management. Yet if farming impacts the lives of non-farmers, the reverse is also true, though easier to forget: the shape of the rural landscape is the cumulative outcome of everyone's choices and habits, even those of city-dwellers and suburbanites.

Anyone observing the Iowa landscape over the past twenty years will have witnessed innumerable local changes—a pasture being burned, an old-fashioned corncrib back in use, the occasional field of barley—as well as long-term trends—the return of spring over fall plowing, the spread of no-till planting, the rise and fall of livestock containment facilities. As everyone knows, these are hard times for most farmers, and have been for nearly two decades. Rising commodity prices and global food insecurity in the 1970s encouraged aggressive agricultural expansion, with the federal government, banks, and the suppliers of agricultural inputs all encouraging farmers to assume heavy debt loads in order to finance ever larger and more technologically advanced operations. When exports shrank and the bottom fell out of the inflated land market in the 1980s, many farmers were forced out of business. Numbers of small-town equipment dealers, elevators, and other businesses closed in turn; and rural areas became emptier as people left for the cities in search of work. While other sectors of the economy recovered dramatically in the 1990s, agriculture has continued to suffer: commodity prices keep reaching new lows, severe weather seems to be growing more common, and criticisms of agricultural subsidies are mounting. Since 1975, the United States has lost an estimated half million farms, over thirty thousand of them in Iowa.

All of this has been visible from the road, and it is lamentable, unjust, even tragic. No one can watch farmers go under without regret. But there is a bright side to this grim picture. Periods of agricultural crisis force everyone—farmers, consumers, legislators, scientists—to rethink conventional assumptions about farming practice and to make room for experimentation. Historically, agricultural boom periods have been associated with a streamlining of the farm sector, while agricultural depressions, painful though they are, have fostered diversification. Twenty or twenty-five years ago alternative agriculture was virtually unheard of; today, it is receiving more serious attention than ever before. An almost bewildering array of government agencies, cooperatives, for-profit and non-profit groups are now working to support research on sustainable farming techniques, to forge links between producers and local markets, to encourage new farmers or facilitate intergenerational farm transfers, and to develop educational resources for growers and consumers.

This essay is intended to offer a guide to the work of some of these groups, and to suggest ways in which the average farm spectator can make informed judgements about the state of the rural landscape.

ALTERNATIVE, SUSTAINABLE, ORGANIC

"Alternative agriculture" is an umbrella term for a wide array of new kinds of farming proposed over the last twenty or thirty years: "sustainable," "regenerative," "low-input," "closed-system," "organic," "biodynamic," "biological," "local," "natural," "integrated," "community-supported"—to name just a few. Distinctions may be made among most of these, but more important is what they have in common: the conviction that an alternative agriculture can and should protect and conserve natural resources, improve the livelihoods of farmers, and provide better quality food for consumers.

The two types of alternative farming which have thus far gained the widest recognition and implementation—sustainable agriculture and organic agriculture—should, perhaps in theory, be more or less identical, but they have come to refer to two largely separate movements. Sustainable agriculture insists that the raw materials of farming—soil, water, nutrients and minerals, and power—be employed so as to maintain reserves for future generations, but doesn't make specific restrictions on how this goal is to be achieved. It is sometimes referred to as low-input agriculture because practitioners strive to minimize the use of off-farm inputs, to create diversified farm systems which recycle as many elements as possible and, ideally, to buy and sell locally. Organic agriculture, on the other hand, wholly prohibits the use of chemical fertilizers and pesticides but allows the use of natural fertilizers and minerals (which may be produced thousands of miles away) and may also target distant markets. Sustainable farming, for example, accepts the use of sewage sludge from rural towns as a fertilizer; use of sewage sludge is prohibited under organic standards because of potential contamination from heavy metals or other pollutants.

Both systems have their virtues and at least in Iowa, such divisions are relatively amicable. In the words of Rick Exner, farming systems coordinator for the Practical Farmers of Iowa, "twenty dollars [per bushel for organic] beans [in 1998] did a lot to break down barriers." Many Iowa farmers became interested in sustainable farming years before converting to organic, and many operate small organic operations within larger sustainably-farmed units. More and more organic farmers are finding local markets for their vegetables, fruits, soybeans, and pork, as well as local suppliers for their inputs. Because every farm is unique in soils, drainage, equipment, resources, and markets, a farmer's decision about how to farm will depend not just on beliefs about agricultural chemical use, for instance, but also on relationships with neighbors, the availability of labor and specialized supplies, and, of course, buyers.

The main reason advocates of alternative agriculture quibble about the definition of "sustainability" is simply because agriculture faces so many problems: overproduction and low commodity prices; farm consolidation and the loss of family farms; soil erosion; environmental pollution; the exploitation of farm laborers, especially migrant workers; the loss of biodiversity in crop and livestock populations; threats to food safety and food security—inevitably, agricultural reformers disagree about which crisis should take priority. A common complaint about organic farming, for example, is that it caters primarily to wealthy urbanites: in response, activists have developed farmers' markets in poorer neighborhoods and encouraged vegetable growers to donate surpluses to women's shelters and soup kitchens. On the other hand, keeping farm-gate prices down for the sake of disadvantaged customers may translate into lower wages for farm laborers, already among the lowest-paid workers in the United States. Some advocates of sustainable agriculture—particularly those working on agricultural issues in "underdeveloped" countries—argue that global "sustainability" for agriculture will be achieved only with the elimination of world hunger and the canceling of foreign debt. A healthy alternative agriculture will include all of these efforts and arguments. Only by considering as many options as possible will we find appropriate solutions for each case.

SOME PIONEERS IN IOWA

Iowa took its first official steps toward the promotion of alternative farming with the founding of the Leopold Center for Sustainable Agriculture (LCSA) in 1987. Based at Iowa State University in Ames and named after Aldo Leopold, the Iowa-born pioneer of natural resource conservation and land stewardship, the Leopold Center supports research and education on a wide range of topics relevant to sustainable agriculture. The LCSA sponsors regional conferences, workshops, and seminars; coordinates the efforts of interdisciplinary issue teams on subjects like agroecology, weed management, and animal management; and awards more than fifty annual grants for research and demonstration projects around the state. Recent projects included experimental control of a fungal disease in soybeans with a mycoparasite, the development of sustainable horticulture curricula for vocational agriculture programs, the restoration of farm woodlands, and a study of farm employee compensation. Other accomplishments of the LCSA are too numerous to list—the agroecology issue team, for example, designed and implemented a vegetative buffer strip demonstration on Bear Creek in Story County which has become the model for a state-wide initiative to create one hundred more such sites over five years.

But there were Iowa farmers thinking differently well before the founding of the Leopold Center. When the National Research Council published its landmark textbook, *Alternative Agriculture,* in 1989, two of the eleven case studies included were of Iowa farms. Both of these—the BreDahl Farm in Adair County and the Thompson Farm in Boone County—were profiled as mixed crop-and-livestock operations employing a combination of strategies to reduce off-farm inputs, conserve resources, and maximize net income. Ten years later, both the BreDahls and the Thompsons remain active in the promotion and practice of sustainable agriculture in Iowa. Clark and Linda BreDahl now sell organic apples, cherries, and raspberries from their farm and are in the process of converting their row crops to organic production. In addition, Clark BreDahl is chair of the research committee for the Neely-Kinyon Farm near Greenfield, home to Iowa's first long-term organic field crop trials. Funded in part by the Leopold Center, this work is under the supervision of Kathleen Delate, ISU Extension's first organic agriculture specialist, and will examine nutrient cycling, soil amendments, and alternate weed and pest management strategies. ISU also recently established the Henry A. Wallace Endowed Chair for Sustainable Agriculture, and there are rumors that an undergraduate and/or graduate degree in sustainable agriculture may soon be offered.

Dick and Sharon Thompson began conducting on-farm research trials and hosting Field Days at their farm in the early 1980s. In 1985 they formed Practical Farmers of Iowa (PFI), a non-profit group dedicated to facilitating research partnerships between farmers and agricultural scientists. Today PFI is among the most successful grass-roots sustainable agriculture groups in the country, with around thirty cooperating farmer-researchers and over five hundred members throughout the state. PFI now works closely with ISU Extension, with two Extension staff members working full-time on PFI programs, and maintains the ideals established by the Thompsons. In 1998, PFI sponsored nearly three dozen Field Days in cooperation with the Leopold Center, the University of Northern Iowa, the Iowa Natural Heritage Foundation, the Iowa Farm Bureau, Heartland Organic Marketing Co-op, and the Langwood Institute of Forest Economics. PFI on-farm research examined corn yields under different rates of nitrogen application, weed control in ridge tillage systems with and without herbicides, biological controls for major pests, native perennial legumes for feed and forage, and many other topics.

ORGANIC FARMING

Organic farming, for many years the poor cousin to sustainable farming, is now rapidly becoming the most dynamic sector of the alternative agriculture movement. Nationwide, the scale of organic farming has increased from 2,841 organic farms on 550,267 acres in 1991, to 4,060 farms on 1,127,000 acres in 1994, to an estimated 10,000 to 12,000 farms on 2 million acres in 1998. Sales of organic foods have risen by twenty percent a year for the last nine years, and sales of organic dairy products are rising even faster. Organic fruits and vegetables, organic milk and yogurt, and an ever-increasing variety of packaged organic foods are now available in most mainstream supermarkets across the country, including Hy-Vee and Econofoods; and the USDA recently approved a label for organic meats (which previously could only be labeled as "natural," "grass-fed," "antibiotic- and hormone-free," or something of the sort), paving the way for continued market expansion.

As these facts suggest, the great strength of the organic movement is its consumer support. Organic farming has tapped into mounting concerns about the safety of the food we eat, as well as about the environmental toll exacted by conventional agriculture. Organic items generally command a price premium of between twenty and fifty percent over the conventional equivalent, and sometimes even more—a great incentive to struggling farmers, and a sufficient indication of the power of consumer demand. Prices like that can also attract fraud, however, and as a result organic growers have worked since the 1970s to develop a certification process to control casual or illegitimate use of the word "organic" in product labeling. Today organic status is regulated by a collection of state and regional certifying groups, most of them grassroots in origin, under the leadership of larger bodies like the International Federation of Organic Agriculture Movements (IFOAM). Details of organic standards vary from group to group, but all define organic farming as more than just the absence of chemical fertilizers and pesticides; a farm can't be "organic by neglect." Farmers must show that active soil-building methods are in use, including crop rotations, composts, cover crops (to reduce soil erosion in the off season), and green manures (plowing under of a cover crop while still green). Organic standards also require the maintenance of buffer strips to prevent contamination from neighboring roads, lawns, or conventional farms; they request regular soil and water tests; and stipulate that all pest control products and soil amendments be checked against a list of prohibited, regulated, and permitted materials. Finally, farmers must maintain field histories and other records and provide documentation for all off-farm inputs. Standards for livestock, dairy, and processing operations are even more complicated—animals must receive organic feed, have maximum access to fresh air and pasture, and may not be fed sub-therapeutic levels of antibiotics. In some countries, organic standards even carry recommendations regarding product packaging and the treatment of farm workers.

Organic farming's dramatic growth has been achieved with minimal support from the federal government. Less than one percent of the USDA research budget is devoted to organics, and federal lawmakers largely ignored the organic movement until the 1990 Farm Bill, which included the Organic Foods Production Act, mandating the development of uniform and enforceable U.S. organic standards, but these have been slow to appear. In the meantime, some fifteen states (including Colorado, Idaho, Ken-

Fig. 15.1. *Regis Zweigart's Organic Farm* in east-central Iowa in late April. Like many organic farmers, Zweigart uses a cover crop of hardy rye to protect the soil from erosion over the winter. In the spring, the rye is disked under and incorporated, providing a "green manure" for the soil. (Photograph by Michael Evans.)

tucky, Maryland, New Hampshire, New Mexico, Texas, and Washington) have established their own standards and begun to regulate certification. In May of 1998, then-Governor Terry Branstad signed a law mandating the development of an organic certification program for the state of Iowa, and you could say it was in the nick of time. According to Maury Wills, director of the newly-formed Organic Agriculture Bureau (OAB) at the Iowa Department of Agriculture and Land Stewardship (IDALS), organic farming in Iowa exploded from around 175 certified farms operating on 62,000 acres in 1997 to nearly 700 certified farms on

Fig. 15.2. *Headland buffers* in western Iowa—organic oats on the right, conventional corn on the left. Most organic standards require a fifty-foot buffer strip between organic and conventional fields to absorb drifting chemicals during fertilizer and pesticide applications. (Photograph by Jim Riddle.)

120,000 acres in 1998. Rules establishing state organic standards and an Iowa organic certification program took effect on November 10, 1999, and are obtainable from the Organic Agriculture Bureau of IDALS.

With that rate of growth, few people are willing to guess what the numbers will be like even in the near future. Everyone agrees that much of the increase in organic acreage for 1998 came from farmers planting soybeans on land coming out of the federal Conservation Reserve Program (CRP), a set-aside scheme which put land down to native perennial grasses for five to ten years. Since organic standards require acres certified for organic production to have been free of prohibited inputs for three or more years, former CRP land was ideal, and organic soybean prices of between $14.50 and $24.50 per bushel (compared to 5 to 8 dollars per bushel for conventional soybeans) were powerfully attractive. Of course, no one knows whether prices like that will hold: some observers point to continued increased demand, both at home and abroad; others fear that global economic instability—particularly the financial crisis in Japan, a principal buyer of Iowa organic soybeans—will dampen the export market. Current conventional bean prices, however, are already below production costs, while organic beans generally have lower production costs and only moderately lower yields in the first years of transition. Yields tend to rise as soil quality improves under organic management, and the best organic yields are as high or higher than conventional yields.

Private certification agencies active in Iowa include Farm Verified Organic (FVO), based in Medina, North Dakota; the Organic Growers and Buyers Association (OGBA), based in New Brighton, Minnesota; and three chapters of the Organic Crop Improvement Association (OCIA, headquartered in Lincoln, Nebraska): Chapter 1, based in Arthur (Ida County), Chapter 2, based in Decorah, and the newly-formed Chapter 3, based in Fairfield. Representatives of these groups confirm the growth charted by the IDALS and suggest that interest in organic agriculture is fairly evenly spread around the state. Wills reports that the OAB office has been receiving lots of inquiries, and is currently putting together a directory of Iowa organic producers, processors, and handlers. Iowa's organic farms, he says, range in size from just a couple of acres to five or six hundred acres. The majority are grain farms, producing soybeans, corn, small grains, and hay in rotation; some of these also raise organic chicken, pork, beef, or lamb. The smaller farms are fruit and vegetable growers, amounting to around twelve percent of the total acreage; there are also a number of dairies, mostly in northeast Iowa. Most have converted from chemical production, but there are plenty of Iowa farmers who remember when everyone farmed without chemicals, and there are some—including many Amish and Mennonite farmers—who never started using them, or who used them only briefly before returning to traditional methods.

Iowa's organic farmers are optimistic about potential for further growth. "In ten years, all the food grown in the United states could be certified organic," declares Regis Zweigart, who farms

219 acres near Watkins, and is a vice-president of Heartland Organic Marketing Co-op in Harlan. If that sounds audacious, consider the math: if the number of organic farms in Iowa continued to double each year (1997 to 1998 showed a four-fold increase), they would exceed the number of non-organic farms currently in the state by the year 2006. "More and more farmers are deciding that there's no future in chemical agriculture, that there's no way they can survive that way," notes Larry Miles of OCIA Chapter 1. Ironically, the drive toward genetically-modified (GM) crops in conventional agriculture has further strengthened the organic movement. When the European Union announced in the spring of 1999 that it would refuse all shipments of grain that could not be certified as GM-free, a wave of anxiety spread across the Midwest. Grain buyers in Iowa and other states sent word to growers that the farmer would have to be responsible for making sure seed stocks were clean. Because GM crops are already prohibited in organic standards, organic farmers are in the best position to meet this requirement. In the United States, consumer backlash against GM foods is pushing more people toward organics because here, buying organic is virtually the only way to avoid eating GM foods.

Nevertheless, the GM issue is a major concern for organic farmers. Contamination from GM crops can come about in two ways: through cross-pollination, and through the accidental mixture of grain in hoppers, trucks, augers, and bins. Just a handful of GM beans in a bushel of organic beans used as seed could result in an entire field becoming worthless on the organic market. This state of affairs leaves no room for accidents—a load of grain dropped into the wrong bin has the potential to ruin relations between near neighbors in the countryside. In England in 1998 an organic grower sued a neighboring farmer for contaminating his sweet corn with GM pollen. "They're creating an agriculture that's too complicated for people to live with," says Tom Frantzen, who farms near New Hampton. "It's going to tear this community apart."

LOCAL AGRICULTURE: CSAS, FARMERS' MARKETS, AND DIRECT MARKETING

Another type of "alternative agriculture" gathering momentum in Iowa is local or community-based agriculture, which strives to create direct links between producers and consumers in a given area. Advocates of local agriculture focus on a sobering paradox:

Fig. 15.3. *Reiff Grain and Feed,* north of Fairfield, one of many local grain elevators that has begun buying and selling organically grown grain. (Photograph by Michael Evans.)

although Iowa boasts some of the best growing conditions in the world, more than eighty percent of the food consumed here is produced somewhere else (and, of course, most of the food produced here is consumed elsewhere). If appropriate marketing relationships and facilities were developed, they argue, Iowa could support a greater variety of farm products, Iowans could enjoy fresher, healthier food, and more of the consumer's food dollar could go to farmers rather than to middlemen.

One such marketing arrangement, first pioneered in the United States in 1986, is known as CSA, or community-supported agriculture. In a CSA individuals pay a lump sum at the beginning of the year for a season-long "share" of a farm's produce. Once a week from May to October, these farm "members" receive an assortment of whatever is ready for harvest at that moment; from lettuce, peas, broccoli, and radishes in the spring, through tomatoes, peppers, eggplant, and watermelons in the summer; to carrots, squash, onions, and leafy greens in the fall. Also known as "subscription farming" or "box-scheme" production, this gives the farmers cash up-front for operating expenses (like buying seed and other supplies) and helps them determine appropriate production levels. The consumer often saves money (since most share prices are cheaper by the pound than equivalent items at a shop or market) and gets the satisfaction of knowing exactly where his or her food came from and how it was produced. CSA members also learn—or relearn—which vegetables are in season when; and many report that they eat more healthfully in the attempt to use up what they've already paid for. "It's an education for many people," says Jodi Biershenck, who runs Blue Ridge Garden CSA near Newhall.

CSAs tend to do best around cities and larger towns where residents want high-quality fresh fruits and vegetables, but frequently don't have the space, time, or expertise to grow them themselves. This fact has made the CSA concept slower to catch on in Iowa than in states with large urban populations like California, Massachusetts, and New York. But here and in other midwestern states the trend has now taken hold. Today there are over thirty CSA farms in Iowa, up from just three in 1995. In northern Iowa CSAs can now be found in Belmond, Cedar Falls, Geneva, Kanawha, and Postville; in western Iowa in Aurelia; in central Iowa in Ames, Boone, Des Moines, Geneva, Johnston, McCallsburg, Mitchellville, Nevada, State Center, Story City, Waukee, West Des Moines, Winterset, and Woodward; in eastern Iowa, in Belle Plaine, Bellevue, Blairstown, Fairfield, Garrison, Greeley, Iowa City, Kalona, Mt. Vernon, Newhall, Olin, Solon, Vinton, and Wellman; and in southern Iowa in Centerville and Mt. Sterling. Most CSAs include a wide range of vegetables, fruits, flowers, and herbs, and some provide options for other items like eggs, bread, or honey. While some are certified organic, others use organic methods but rely on the personal relationship between grower and consumer to provide a kind of informal "certification." Toward that end, most CSAs sponsor newsletters, member work-days, or pot-luck suppers to keep members in touch with what's going on at the farm.

Several Iowa CSAs involve more than one farm. The Magic Beanstalk CSA in Ames, begun in 1995, now has 125 share members and five producers, including Heenah Mayah, the ISU student farm. Each week the Magic Beanstalk growers bring their produce to a central distribution point in Ames and are joined there by vendors of other items like wool, soap, beeswax candles, and baked goods, creating a kind of market atmosphere. Jeff Hall, one of the original organizers of Magic Beanstalk, says that working together to supply a CSA allows farmers to focus on crops particularly well-suited to their soils, or which fit into the work schedule of a larger operation. Susan Zacharakis-Jutz grows spring crops for Local Harvest CSA, based in Wellman, but her farm also produces organic field crops, naturally-raised pork and lamb, and goats' milk. The CSA model can offer a way of gaining additional income for a family farm without requiring additional acreage. Gary Guthrie, who with his wife and son runs Growing Harmony Farm near Nevada, says that the CSA is part of a coordinated family transfer of his parents' farm to the next generation: his parents still live on the farm and receive income from renting most of the ground to a neighbor, while he operates the CSA garden on just a few acres.

But it's not necessary to join a CSA to enjoy fresh, locally-grown Iowa produce: you can also just head over to the farmers' market, or drive out to a local pick-your-own or farm stand. In 1999, there were 118 regular farmers' markets in seventy-three Iowa counties, most running once or twice a week from late-May or early-June to late-September or mid-October. A complete farmers' market directory, including locations, hours, and contact numbers is available from the Iowa Department of Agriculture and Land Stewardship and can be downloaded from the IDALS website (see the "Resources" section at the end of this chapter). The IDALS also maintains a directory of 244 fruit and vegetable growers in seventy-two counties who sell directly from their farms, with notable concentrations around urban areas in Story, Polk, Warren, Black Hawk, Linn, Muscatine, and Pottawattamie counties. Just looking at the lists of items for sale is mouth-watering: apples, raspberries, plums, gooseberries, rhubarb; leeks, pumpkins, cucumbers, sweet peppers, and much, much more.

Other forms of community agriculture include on-farm direct marketing, in which items are sold directly from the farm to the consumer, and links between producers and local institutions like hospitals and schools. Direct marketing is frequently used for the sale of pork, beef, and lamb. In southwest Iowa, six diversified farms have joined together for a direct marketing effort they call Audubon County Family Farms. Food Services at the University of

Northern Iowa now does some local buying of produce and other items, and the Iowa Network for Community Agriculture (INCA), a non-profit group formed in 1996, has received a grant from the Leopold Center to support more institutional buying of locally-grown food. Jan Libbey, coordinator for INCA and owner with Tim Landgraf of One Step at a Time Gardens near Kanawha, is enthusiastic about the range of possibilities. Their group recently met with Patty Judge, Iowa's Secretary of Agriculture, regarding the creation of a state task force on community agriculture.

Finally, many Iowa-grown products are as easy to find as your local grocery store or health food shop. Everybody's in Fairfield, Big Creek Market in Mount Vernon, Foods Naturally in Kalona, Days Gone By in Osage, New Pioneer Coop in Iowa City—the number of these, particularly in small towns, seems to be on the rise as well. Many make a conscious effort to stock locally-produced items whenever possible. As you shop, remember: your buying habits can directly affect the rural landscape.

RECOGNIZING ALTERNATIVE FARMING FROM THE ROAD

Even though sustainable, organic, and community-based farming are spreading quickly in Iowa, they still have a long way to go. Most farms in Iowa are conventional farms—one might say by definition—so it takes a keen eye to recognize signs of alternative agriculture as you drive through the countryside. At first glance, sustainable or organic farms may in fact not look very different from conventional farms, especially because farmers often choose to convert to new methods in stages over a number of years. Many of Iowa's organic farms are so-called "mixed" or "parallel" operations, in which part of the farm is certified organic and part is not, or the crop acres are certified but the animals are not. Farmers experimenting with alternative cropping techniques such as ridge-till, also are likely to begin with just one or a few fields, so it can be difficult to draw clear lines between a "sustainable" and a "conventional" farmer. Orchards and vegetable plots are usually easy to recognize, but they may be down back roads, and some CSA fields are not much larger than a traditional Iowa farm garden. Finally, it is important when observing farms and farmsteads not to confuse farming philosophies with farming styles: there are neat, orderly farms and overgrown, disorderly ones, but this will not necessarily tell you anything about the condition of a farmer's

Fig. 15.4. *Big Creek Market, Mt. Vernon.* Small-town grocery stores like this one have begun carrying organic and locally grown items. (Photograph by Michael Evans.)

soil, or the health of his or her livestock, or the quality of runoff heading into the nearby creek.

Of course, some farmers put up signs which may tell you something about the nature of the operation. PFI supplies its co-operating farmer-researchers with a sign, and the Iowa OAB intends to develop a sign for organic growers certified by the state. Some private organic certifiers like OCIA provide "Do Not Spray" signs so that farmers can prevent road maintenance crews from applying herbicide to ditches adjacent to organic fields. Farmers that rely on direct marketing may be more likely to set up roadside displays, but at this stage most farms offering CSA shares or selling meat directly to individuals have more interested customers than they can supply, and largely rely on advertising by word-of-mouth.

Often more conspicuous than a sign at the farmgate is the machinery parked in the yard or at work in the fields. The equipment in use on a farm will often tell you a great deal about a farmer's practices. Some hard-core advocates of sustainability have gone back to farming with horses (in parts of Iowa there are concentrations of Amish and Mennonite farmers who have always farmed with horses), but most practitioners of alternative farming aren't going to give up their tractors anytime soon. Instead, the differences will lie in the implements. Because weed control must be achieved mechanically rather than chemically, sustainable farming requires a greater number and variety of tillage tools: rotary hoes, ridge-till planters, bed-formers; and an array of different types of cultivators, hillers, and sweeps. Some organic growers create what

Fig. 15.5. *Weed-free organic oats* surround Al Steffan, who farms near Marion. Contrary to popular belief, organic farming can indeed be "clean" farming. (Photograph by Jim Riddle.)

is called a stale seed bed where weeds are allowed to germinate before a final soil disturbance just before planting, which thus often takes place two to three weeks later than on conventional farms. You may also see a flame-weeder, an attachment with a propane tank and a number of horizontal torches, used to kill weeds in the rows after planting but before the crop has emerged; broad-cast seeders, used for sowing a cover crop before the primary crop has been harvested; or silage-choppers and mulch-layers for handling organic matter.

Before planting and cultivating, of course, comes fertility management, and here too there are tools and techniques distinctive to sustainable farming. Virtually every organic farm will have at least one manure spreader—that essential piece of equipment which on conventional farms has been replaced by the anhydrous tank and the spray rig. Along with the spreader, you are likely to see large piles or windrows of compost being carefully managed with bucket-loaders or specialized turners. If you do see spraying equipment, however, don't immediately assume that a farm is using chemical fertilizers or pesticides; even organic farms often rely on sprayers to distribute the types of fertilizers and pesticides permitted under organic regulations, including fish emulsion, dried molasses, ascorbic acid, rotenone, copper, sulfur, garlic or hot pepper oils, and soaps.

Another important sign of sustainable farming is the use of rotations. Unless you drive past a farm year after year, this can be difficult to ascertain, but you can usually get an idea by observing the size of the fields and the number of different crops being grown in one season. Breaking pest life cycles, controlling disease, and maintaining soil fertility and good soil structure without chemicals, requires longer and more elaborate crop rotations than the two-year corn-beans routine that has become dominant in Iowa. Most organic standards require at least a three-year rotation (for instance, corn-soybeans-oats), and many farmers prefer five (say, corn-beans-oats-hay-pasture). This means that in any given year, only one-third to one-fifth of a farm's arable acreage will be in any one crop. It also means that you're more likely to see other plant species and varieties—buckwheat, millet, barley, rye, popcorn, sunflowers, alfalfa, red and white clovers, hairy vetch, canola, flax, turnips—as farmers experiment with different techniques and search for the best crop to perform a specific function in their rotation.

One standard five-year rotation in this part of the country—

Fig. 15.6. *Jeff Zacharakis-Jutz* prepares to spread manure prior to planting on his farm near Solon. The manure spreader is making a come-back against the anhydrous tank on organic and sustainable farms. Mixed with straw or other bedding material, composted manure replenishes organic matter and improves soil structure as well as boosting fertility. (Photograph by Michael Evans.)

corn-beans-oats-hay-pasture—of course requires animals, and that's no accident. Most alternative farms in Iowa resemble the mixed crop-and-livestock operations that were the norm here fifty years ago, more than they resemble the large-scale cash-grain enterprises which became standard in the 1960s and '70s. It's an age-old arrangement: the animals eat the grain, hay, and grass produced on the farm, and bed on the straw, which together provide the manure and organic material to return fertility and tilth to the soil. Tom Frantzen, who has been farming near Alta Vista since 1974 and transitioning toward organic since 1995, stresses the

Fig. 15.7. *Pigs Enjoying Fresh Grass,* Washington Co. Pasture-based systems for livestock reduce stress, produce leaner meat, and minimize waste problems. (Photograph by Michael Evans.)

importance of breaking land in and out of pasture as a part of the rotation. "Terrible damage was done in this country by continuous grazing at low stock-density," he laments. "I don't know how to make a good soil structure without sod, and without massive disruption—moldboard plowing—one year out of five."

Other organic farmers, like Francis Thicke of Radiance Dairy near Fairfield, practice rotational grazing, in which animals are pastured in small paddocks for short periods of time and moved on to fresh pasture at regular intervals. Systems like this are readily recognizable because of the portable electric fences that divide the paddocks, and you may also notice the healthy, productive appearance of the pasture itself. Because the animals are forced to graze the paddocks clean one by one instead of browsing over the whole area for an entire season, the grass can fully recover in between grazings, pasture weeds are discouraged, and the overall species diversity of the pasture is enhanced. Thicke, who with his brothers converted his family's Minnesota dairy farm to organic production in 1975, agrees that crop-and-livestock systems are essential to sustainable farming. In Thicke's view, dairy farms "are a natural place for organics" because of the inherent balance between animals and land. "I think any dairy farmer could be organic," Thicke says, although he cautions that marketing is another question.

Needless to say, keeping livestock on sustainable and organic

Fig. 15.8. *Hog Hoop-House* on the Tom Frantzen farm, near Alta Vista. First developed in Sweden, these structures are gaining popularity on Iowa farms. Ventilation is natural, and the bedding of straw or corn stalks is composted and spread on fields. (Photograph by Michael Evans.)

farms doesn't mean large-scale confinement facilities. The types of animal buildings in use are one of the best indications of the type of farm. Sustainable farmers are more likely to keep cows, pigs, and even chickens on grass for much of their diet, allowing them the fresh air and exercise they need to stay healthy. For pigs, hoop houses are gaining popularity: over a thousand of these were erected in Iowa between 1996 and 1998. In a hoop-house the animals are bedded on a deep layer of straw, which absorbs odors, minimizes injuries, and allows the pigs to root around and build nests.

Other good signs of sustainable farming are conservation measures like terracing, contour-plowing, and grassed waterways

Fig. 15.9. *Farming on the Contour,* Winneshiek Co., early May. Last season's corn was grown in wide strips alternating with a grass mixture. The grass has been cut for hay, and the corn stubble has been left over the winter. On rolling ground, cropping systems like this help control sheet erosion and may boost corn yields by letting more sunlight into the middle of the fields. (Photograph by Michael Evans.)

to control soil erosion; buffer strips to protect riparian areas; and shelterbelts and windbreaks to provide habitat for wildlife and to minimize wind erosion. Information on installing these features is available from any Natural Resource Conservation Service (NRCS) office. The Iowa Organic Standards currently in preparation are designed to be "cross-compliant" with NRCS requirements, so that any farm certified organic will also automatically qualify for federal programs tied to conservation measures. Conversely, every Iowan should recognize the signs of poor conservation of agricultural resources: gullies in the corners of fields from sheet and rill erosion; snow in the ditches black with wind-blown topsoil; or excessive flooding after heavy rains.

Good conservation measures mean more wildlife habitat and in turn more wildlife. This, in my opinion, is the most dramatic difference between conventional and alternative farms, although to appreciate it fully you have to get out and walk around a farm, not just drive by. Agricultural pesticides are estimated to kill sixty-seven million birds and at least ten million fish in the United States each year (in addition to poisoning 300 thousand farmworkers), and on an organic farm you begin to feel the force of those numbers. Most conventional farms can certainly boast some songbirds, raccoons, opossums, maybe coyotes, but on organic farms you will be amazed at the diversity and numbers of birds and butterflies, the wild turkeys and herons, the fresh smell of life in the soil. The difference can lie in small practices: once on an inspection in Wisconsin I noticed that a farmer had covered his combine, which was parked in the barn, with a tarp. Swallows were nesting in the rafters and the droppings were falling on the machinery, so he wanted to keep the bin clean. In his conventional farming days, he said, he would have solved the problem by putting poison on the rafters. "Fifteen years ago, we used to try to kill everything except what we wanted to have stay alive," he reflected. "Now we try to let as many things live as possible."

Other indications of the current success of alternative agriculture in Iowa are found not in the fields, but in the towns. The number of small-town groceries and natural-food stores carrying Iowa-grown products has already been mentioned. But in today's world there are often a lot of steps between the field and the table, or the supermarket shelf. Some people might say this is among the problems alternative agriculture should be solving, but until we are all ready to give up the convenience of canned soup, packaged breakfast cereals, corn chips, even store-bought butter and bread, there will surely be a place in the economy for sustainably-produced—but nevertheless processed, packaged, and distributed—foods. Moreover, many of these essential activities take place, or could take place, in the small towns whose fortunes have always been linked to the prosperity of the farms they serve. Farmers and farm neighborhoods have always been interdependent, and in organic agriculture especially, this becomes more rather than less true. The viability of an organic livestock operation, for example, depends on the local availability of organic grain and the proximity of a small-scale butcher as well as on a market for its meat. (Dick

Fig. 15.10. *Integrity Mills, Cresco,* buys organic corn from around the Midwest and mills it to different specifications for processors of corn flakes, flours, and polenta. Companies like this demonstrate how the success of alternative agriculture can bring jobs back to rural Iowa towns. (Photograph by Michael Evans.)

Blackburn, who runs a cow-calf operation near Keosauqua and advises on organic farming for the local NRCS office, reports that his area could really use a homeopathic veterinarian.)

Similarly, small-town processors can provide the link between area farmers and wider markets. With its strong commodity base and central location, Iowa is an obvious choice for food processors supplying buyers across the country and even around the world. Natural Products in Grinnell, Iowa Soy Specialties in Vinton, Iowa Oat Processors in Chelsea, and Integrity Mills in Cresco all specialize in organic or sustainably-produced grain processing for a wide range of products. Heartland Organic Marketing Co-op in Harlan, Frontier Herbs in Norway, and Soil Technologies Corporation in Fairfield are other examples of small-town companies which have gained a national reputation serving Iowa's alternative agriculture movement.

Ultimately, finding unique farms, like finding other unique places, requires a little spontaneous exploration. Get off the main road and follow that hand-painted sign that says "Fresh Eggs," or "U Pick Asparagus," or "Cider For Sale." Stop at the small-town grocery or farmers' market for some bread and sweet corn. Pick up a local paper, or ask around. It just might change the way you look at the country.

RESOURCES AND PLACES TO VISIT

Iowa Department of Agriculture and Land Stewardship
Henry A. Wallace Building
Des Moines, IA 50319
515-281-5321
//www.state.ia.us/agriculture/index.html

Iowa Network for Community Agriculture
Jan Libbey, Education and Outreach Coordinator
1465 120th Street
Kanawha, IA 50447

Leopold Center for Sustainable Agriculture
209 Curtiss Hall
ISU, Ames, IA 50011
515-294-3711
//www.ag.iastate.edu/centers/leopold/

Prairie Talk
P.O. Box 733
Solon, IA 52333
//www.leepfrog.com/prairietalk
Prairie Talk is an educational resource group that sponsors a lending library of books and videos on sustainable farming. The collection is housed at the Solon Public Library and is available via interlibrary loan. Write for a list of materials.

Practical Farmers of Iowa
2035 190th St.
Boone, IA 50036-7423
or
PFI Coordinators at ISU Agronomy Extension
Room 2104, Agronomy Hall
Iowa State University
Ames, IA 50011-1010
515-294-1923
//www.agron.iastate.edu/pfi/

Seed Savers Exchange
3076 North Winn Road
Decorah, IA 52101
319-382-5990
The Seed Savers Exchange has gained worldwide recognition for its work in the collection and conservation of genetic resources for garden plants. Established in 1975 by Kent and Diane Whealy, Seed Savers currently maintains eighteen thousand heirloom vegetable varieties, as well as flowers, herbs, fruit trees, and grapes at Heritage Farm near Decorah. The farm is open to visitors Memorial Day through October, 9 AM to 5 PM.

Alternative Farming Systems Information Center
National Agricultural Library, Room 304
1301 Baltimore Ave.
Beltsville, MD 20705-2351
301-504-6559
//www.nal.usda.gov/afsic

Center for Rural Affairs
101 S. Tallman St.
P.O. Box 406
Walthill, NE 68067
402-846-5428
//www.cfra.org/index.html

Land Stewardship Project
2200 4th St.
White Bear Lake, MN 55110
651-653-0618
//www.misa.umn.edu/lsphp.html

Organic Consumers Association
860 Highway 61
Little Marais, MN 55614
218-226-4792
//www.organicconsumers.org/

Organic Farmers Marketing Association
C/TC
8364 S SR 39
Clayton, IN 46118
//web.iquest.net/ofma/homepage.htm

Organic Trade Association
50 Miles St.
P.O. Box 1078
Greenfield, MA 01302
413-774-7511
//www.ota.com

Sustainable Farming Connection
//metalab.unc.edu/pub/academic/agriculture/farming-connection/
An excellent website maintained by the former editors of *New Farm* magazine.

Contributors

Douglas Bauer is a native of Prairie City, which became the subject of his first book, *Prairie City, Iowa,* a non-fiction account of reunion and reacquaintance with his hometown. He's also the author of the novels, *Dexterity, The Very Air,* and *The Book of Famous Iowans,* and of a book of essays, forthcoming, entitled *The Stuff of Fiction: Observations and Advice on Elements of Craft.* He lives in Boston and in Strafford, Vermont.

John Deason is a photographer from Muscatine, Iowa. He teaches photography in the local high school and works out of his studio, printing black-and-white prints from large format negatives. He shoots with 8″ by 10″ and 4″ by 5″ view cameras, and panoramic cameras of various sizes.

He received his Master of Fine Arts degree from the University of Iowa in 1998. Besides his "lost towns" project, he has documented people and traces of mankind along the Fifth Principal Meridian in eastern Iowa. He is currently cataloguing all of the animal and plant varieties in a 385-acre savanna along the Cedar River in Muscatine County.

He lives with his wife Carolyn in an old house on a bluff overlooking the Mississippi River. He is in the process of building a new timber-frame studio near his home, where he intends to make limited edition books of poetry and essays illustrated with photogravures made from his negatives.

James J. Dinsmore grew up in southern Minnesota and has lived in Ames since 1975, where he is a professor of animal ecology at Iowa State University. His book *A Country So Full of Game: The Story of Wildlife in Iowa* (University of Iowa Press, 1994) has been widely praised.

Patricia Eckhardt is an architectural historian with special interests in nineteenth-century American architecture and historic preservation. After receiving her Ph.D. from the University of Iowa in 1990, she began Eckhardt Research, a historic preservation consulting service which she continues today.

Mira Engler is an associate professor of landscape architecture at Iowa State University. Discovery of the particular cultural landscape and expression of a sense of place are central aims of both her teaching and practice. Engler's work with small towns in Iowa seeking town themes to promote community development taught her much about Iowa culture and the value of the land and instigated this inquiry. In transforming research into writing, she was greatly encouraged by the help of Mark Chidister.

Hanno Hardt is the John F. Murray Professor of Journalism and Mass Communication and a professor of communication studies at the University of Iowa, and Professor of Communication at the University of Ljubljana, Slovenia. He is also a documentary photographer and is currently working on a volume of his photographs, *A Time in Iowa.*

Carl Kurtz is the author of *Iowa's Wild Places* (Iowa State University Press, 1996). His photographs and articles have appeared in over fifty different national and regional publications. He and his wife Linda live on their 172-acre family farm near St. Anthony in Marshall County.

Nina Metzner has been a writing performance assessment specialist at National Computer Systems in Iowa City, Iowa for the past five years. She recently left that position to begin her own consulting firm helping teachers with techniques for teaching and assessing writing on the classroom level. Prior to working for NCS, she taught English, writing, and journalism classes at the middle school, high school, and university levels. She has a Master of Fine Arts in creative nonfiction from the University of Iowa.

Jean Cutler Prior is a research geologist at the Geological Survey Bureau, a branch of the Iowa Department of Natural Resources in Iowa City. She is the author of *Landforms of Iowa* (University of Iowa Press, 1991) and the editor of *Iowa Geology,* published annually by the Geological Survey Bureau. She is also a past member of the State Preserves Advisory Board and a contributor to the Iowa Public Television series, "Land Between Two Rivers."

Laura B. Sayre is a native Iowan and has spent six years working on organic farms in Kansas and New Jersey. She currently serves as an organic inspector for the Northeast Organic Farming Association and is finishing a Ph.D. at Princeton University.

Robert F. Sayre recently retired from the English department at the University of Iowa, in order to have more time for travel and writing. He has also edited *Take This Exit* (Iowa State University Press, 1989) and *Recovering the Prairie* (University of Wisconsin Press, 1999).

Jon Spayde grew up in Fairfield, Iowa and in Iowa City. A graduate of Harvard and Stanford, where he studied Japanese, he currently lives in Minneapolis, where he works for the *Utne Reader.*

Richard H. Thomas is a professor of history and chaplain emeritus of Cornell College, Mt. Vernon, Iowa. He has worked in professional assignments for city, county, state, and federal agencies. He continues to teach and is the unofficial city historian for Mt. Vernon, where he has made his home for thirty-three years. For years he has used historic structures as teaching tools to engage students in the study of American history. His academic training includes degrees from Macalester College, Garrett-Evangelical Theological Seminary, and Rutgers: The State University. He thanks the Iowa State Historical Society for permitting him to use portions of this essay which have twice appeared in their publications.

Index

Headstones, symbols on,
124–25, 127–33
Heartland Organic Marketing
Co-op, 304, 309, 323
Hedges, 50
Heenah Mayah, 312
Heer, Fridoline, 144, 152, 162,
163, 166, 168
Heer, Martin, 164
Herbert, J. C., 280–81
Heritage Farm, 324
Hesalroad, Anna Louisa, 133,
134
Hesalroad, Henry Wilson, 133
Hesalroad, M., 133
Hesalroad, Margaret Ann, 133
Hesalroad, Mary Catherine, 133,
134
Hesalroad, Minnie Sophia, 133,
134
Hesalroad, William, 133
Hesalroad Cemetery, 133–134
Heubinger's Good Roads Atlas,
105
High Lake, 213
Highway 14, 125
Hill, Roger, 251
History lessons from cemeteries,
133–35
History of Palo Alto County,
219
History of Wright County, The,
219
Hites, Roger, 135
Hog Hoop-House, 319
Holbrook, 115, 116
Holstad, Dave, 226
Holy Angels Catholic Church,
158–59
Holy Trinity Catholic Church,
162–64, 168
Homestyle Café, 37, 40
Hometowner, 37
Honey Creek Lake, 216
Hoover, Herbert, National
Historic Site, 268

Hotel Manning, 69
Hotels, porches on, 56–57
Hottes Lake, 213
Housh, Courtney, 296
Housh, Dale, 295–96
Housh, Jill, 295–96
Hubinger Landing, 200
Humboldt County, 216, 218,
221, 225
Hy-Vee, 304

Iggers, Jeremy, 35
Illinois Graveyard School, 18
*Illustrated Historical Atlas of the
State of Iowa* (Andreas),
211
Impassable Marsh, 216
Indianola, 83, 153–54
Integrity Mills, 322, 323
International Federation of
Organic Agriculture Move-
ments (IFOAM), 305
Iowa, University of, 19, 20,
102–3
Iowa, University of Northern,
20, 304, 312–13
Iowa City, 11, 13, 62, 83, 104,
127, 137, 268, 285, 311,
313
Iowa Department of Agriculture
and Land Stewardship,
306–7, 323
Iowa Falls, 43
Iowa Farm Bureau, 304
Iowa Geological Survey, 211
Iowa Lake, 213, 214, 216, 267
Iowa Lakes and Lake Beds,
211–12
Iowa Natural Heritage Founda-
tion, 236, 304
Iowa Network for Community
Agriculture (INCA), 313,
323
Iowa Organic Standards, 321
Iowa Prairie Network, 20–21